GNVQ Intermediate

Media: Communication and Production

**Guy Starkey, Tristram Shepard,
Neil Nixon, Simon Phillips, Jill Poppy
and Amanda White**

Stanley Thornes (Publishers) Ltd

First published in 1998 by:
Stanley Thornes (Publishers) Ltd
Ellenborough House
Wellington Street
Cheltenham
GL50 1YW
UK

A catalogue record for this book is available from the British Library.

98 99 00 01 02 / 10 9 8 7 6 5 4 3 2 1

ISBN 0 7487 3064 8

Typeset by Paul Manning
Printed and bound in Great Britain by Scotprint Ltd, Musselburgh, Scotland

Contents

Acknowledgements

The authors and publishers are grateful to the following individuals and organisations for permission to reproduce copyright material:

BARB, page 9
Channel 4 Television and Channel 5 Broadcasting Ltd, page 9
Ark Soundwaves Ltd, *UFO Reality*, page 15
Kent Messenger Group, extract from 'Kent's X Files', page 15
Kent County Council Social Services (*Denton News*) and Challenge TV, page 20
Radio Times, radio listings, pages 25 and 113
Retail Data Entertainment Services, page 62
National Viewers' and Listeners' Association, page 24
Independent Television Commission (ITC), page 28
Nothing Borough Parks Team, page 80
Martin Wingfield, *Reds Review*, page 81
Ladybird Books, page 83
Talk Radio, page 107
Commercial Breaks/Diet Coke, page 115
Performing Rights Society (PRS), Phonographic Performance Limited (PPL) and the Mechanical Copyright Protection Society (MCPS), page 125
RAJAR, demographic information, page 201, and audience figures, page 219
Cheltenham and Gloucester College of Higher Education, use of *Junction* magazine in collage of magazine covers, page 239

Tristram Shepard would like to acknowledge the help of Hazel King in the preparation of material for Chapter 7 of this book.

Picture credits

Kobal Collection, photograph of George Formby, page 3
Planet Dog records, photograph of Eat Static, page 3
David Newman, photograph of *The Times* and *The Sun*, page 6, and magazine collage, page 239
Louise Hunt, photograph of Mittal Karia, page 23
Rank Xerox, photograph of DocuTech machine, page 52
Heavenly Records, photographs of St Etienne, pages 96–7
The Parallel Group, photographs of County Sound Radio, pages 103 and 211
Capital Radio, photograph of Chris Tarrant, page 106
The Kilroy Television Company, page 149
BBC Picture Publicity, photograph of Archers cast, page 111, and Radiophonic Workshop, page 201
Sony Corporation, photograph of Sony MiniDisc recorder, page 139
Alice Broadcast Solutions, photo of mixing desk, page 214
The *London Evening Standard*, photo of newsroom, page 241

Introduction

What is a GNVQ?

GNVQ stands for **General National Vocational Qualification** and it can be studied instead of – or alongside – A Levels or GCSEs. There are two different levels of GNVQ for Media: Communication and Production:

- **Intermediate** – equivalent to four GCSEs at grades A–C, normally studied full time over one year
- **Advanced** – equivalent to two A Levels, normally studied full time over two years

How is your GNVQ structured?
GNVQ courses are made up of the following:

- **Mandatory vocational units** – you must study these
- **Optional vocational units** – you may choose optional units to suit your interests
- **Mandatory key skills units** – these are usually taught and tested at the same time as the vocational units, because they involve everyday workplace skills

On the following page you will find a summary of the course requirements for Unit 1: Investigating local and national media. This explains the terms used and shows how the Units are structured.

What is the Intermediate GNVQ in Media: Communication and Production?
The course consists of eight different vocational units:

- **Four mandatory vocational units**:
    - Unit 1: Investigating local and national media
    - Unit 2: Planning and producing print products
    - Unit 3: Planning and producing audio products
    - Unit 4: Planning and producing moving image products

- **Four optional vocational units**
  Those offered by Edexcel/BTEC and covered by this book are:
    - Unit 5: Video production
    - Unit 6: Plan and produce sound products
    - Unit 7: Producing a graphical product
    - Unit 8: Photography
  and it also has:

- **Three mandatory key skills units**
    - Communication
    - Information Technology
    - Application of Number

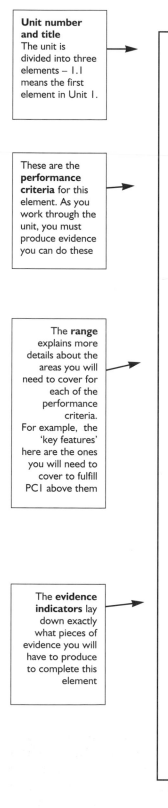

Unit number and title
The unit is divided into three elements – 1.1 means the first element in Unit 1.

These are the **performance criteria** for this element. As you work through the unit, you must produce evidence you can do these

The **range** explains more details about the areas you will need to cover for each of the performance criteria. For example, the 'key features' here are the ones you will need to cover to fulfill PC1 above them

The **evidence indicators** lay down exactly what pieces of evidence you will have to produce to complete this element

UNIT 1: Investigating local and national media
Element 1.1: Investigate local and national media provision

PERFORMANCE CRITERIA
A student must:
1 describe **key features** of UK **media** provision
2 explain **differences** between local and national **media** provision
3 identify **sources of revenue** and **types of expenditure** for local and national **media** producers
4 describe the roles and **responsibilities** of **regulatory bodies** in the media
5 identify **issues of representation** in media products
6 identify **issues of access** to **media** production and **dissemination**

RANGE
Key features: audience trends, access, public ownership, private ownership, production, distribution
Media: print (newspapers, periodicals, books), audiovisual (radio, television, film)
Differences in: content, style, audience
Sources of revenue: consumers (subscription, cover price, licence fee), advertisers, public funding
Types of expenditure: generation of material, production, dissemination
Responsibilities: over content, over conduct, over ownership; self-regulation
Regulatory bodies: Press Complaints Commission, Independent Television Commission, Radio Authority, British Board of Film Classification, Advertising Standards Authority, Department of National Heritage, Monopolies and Mergers Commission
Issues of representation: social groups, social issues
Issues of access: by individuals, by interest groups
Dissemination: broadcast, distribution

EVIDENCE INDICATORS
Examples of two types of media provision in the UK, one of which must be local, the other national. These should be supported by a report identifying and explaining the relationship and differences between the local and national provision, giving consideration to:
• key features of each type of provision
• differences in content, style and audience
• sources of revenue and types of expenditure.
The report should include a summary of issues relating to representation, access and dissemination.
A summary of the roles and responsibilities of regulatory bodies relevant to media products with a description of their roles.

At Intermediate level you will study each of the four mandatory vocational units plus two optional vocational units. You must also complete all three mandatory key skill units.

What are the units about?

- *Unit 1: Investigating local and national media*
  - The different media industries
  - How the media are consumed
  - Trends and employment in the media industries

- *Unit 2: Planning and producing print products*
  - The nature of print products
  - Planning print products
  - Producing print products

- *Unit 3: Planning and producing audio products*
  - The nature of audio products
  - Planning audio products
  - Producing audio products

- *Unit 4: Planning and producing moving image products*
  - The nature of moving image products
  - Planning moving image products
  - Producing moving image products

- *Unit 5: Video production*
  - Planning for video production
  - Producing and editing videos
  - Reviewing and evaluating video production

- *Unit 6: Plan and produce sound products*
  - Planning sound products to a given brief
  - Recording and editing sound products
  - Evaluating sound products

- *Unit 7: Producing a graphical product*
  - Preparing a graphical product to an agreed brief
  - Producing a graphical product
  - Appraising a graphical product

- *Unit 8: Photography*
  - Planning for a photographic assignment
  - Creating photographs for a given brief
  - Reviewing a photographic assignment

How will my GNVQ work be assessed?

By people within your college or school

This is called **internal assessment**. Your teachers will assess the evidence you produce and, where possible, grade it. One of them will be the **Internal Verifier (IV)** whose job it is to check that the other teachers are marking to the correct standard. This means you will need to keep all the evidence you produce, and be able to produce it when it is required for inspection. The collection of work will be your **portfolio**.

By people from outside your college or school
This is called **external assessment**. As well as producing evidence for each unit and each key skill, you will sit tests for each of the four mandatory units (1–4). Also, an **External Verifier (EV)** will visit your college or school to ensure the Internal Verifier is assessing the work to the correct national standard.

Grading criteria

The national minimum standard for the evidence in your portfolio is a **pass**. To earn the GNVQ you must achieve a pass in the correct number of units and each of the key skills. You must also pass all four written tests.

You may be awarded the overall grade of **merit** or **distinction** if you show that you have worked to higher standards in the following areas (which are called **themes**):
- planning
- information-seeking and information-handling
- evaluation
- quality of outcomes

You should ask your tutor what you must do to produce work of a merit or distinction standard. The verifiers will assess the best third of the evidence for each of the four themes.

Creating your portfolio

You now know how important your portfolio of evidence is. You should store it in a box-file which will keep it secure. The box-file should be clearly labelled with your name, course and tutor group. The evidence itself should be clearly labelled with the unit number. Some pieces of work – for example, a page layout for a magazine or newspaper – may not fit easily into the box-file. In that case you should put a sheet of A4 in the file which refers the verifier to the item outside the box. Again, loose items should be clearly labelled.

Types of evidence

The evidence may be any of the following:
- audio or videotapes you have produced
- slides and photographic prints
- page layouts
- notes from meetings
- written reports
- OHTs for an overhead projector
- forms
- questionnaires
- videotapes of presentations you have made in class

In your portfolio you need only what is asked for by the evidence indicators – and the activities and assignments in this book are designed to help you to produce exactly what is needed. Sometimes one piece of work will help you produce evidence for a number of performance criteria. This information is provided in the book.

You will need to discuss the contents of your portfolio with your tutor at regular meetings throughout the course. These tutorials will help you to understand what is expected of you, and your tutor will be able to follow your progress carefully.

Key Skills: Summary of units at Level 2

This summary shows how the activities and assignments provide opportunities to gather evidence of the key skills. When planning a piece of work, think carefully about the key skills for which you can provide evidence. For example, use information technology as often as possible when producing written work, charts and diagrams.

Key skills	Activities	Assignments
Communication		
2.1 Take part in discussion	1.2, 1.5, 1.9, 2.1, 2.2, 2.5, 2.6, 2.7, 2.8, 2.9, 2.10, 2.11, 2.13, 2.14, 3.3, 3.6, 3.7, 3.8, 3.10, 3.13, 3.15, 3.17, 3.18, 3.25, 4.2, 4.3, 5.1, 5.2, 5.5, 5.7, 6.2, 6.3, 6.4, 6.5, 6.6, 6.7, 6.8, 6.10, 7.5, 7.12, 8.1, 8.7, 8.9, 8.12	1, 2, 3, 4, 5, 6, 7.1, 7.2, 8.1, 8.3
2.2 Produce written material	1.1, 1.2, 1.3, 1.4, 1.5, 1.6, 1.7, 1.8, 1.9, 1.10, 1.11, 2.1, 2.3, 2.5, 2.6, 2.7, 2.8, 2.9, 2.10, 2.11, 2.12, 2.13, 2.14, 3.1, 3.2, 3.3, 3.4, 3.5, 3.7, 3.8, 3.9, 3.10, 3.11, 3.12, 3.13, 3.15, 3.16, 3.17, 3.18, 3.19, 3.20, 3.22, 3.23, 3.24, 3.25, 4.8, 4.9, 4.10, 4.11, 4.12, 4.13, 4.17, 4.19, 5.1, 5.3, 5.5, 5.8, 5.13, 6.1, 6.2, 6.3, 6.4, 6.5, 6.6, 6.7, 6.8, 6.9, 6.10, 7.1, 7.5, 7.6, 7.7, 7.9, 7.12, 8.2, 8.9	1, 2, 3, 4, 5, 6, 7.1, 7.2, 7.3, 8.1, 8.2, 8.3
2.3 Use images	2.2, 2.3, 2.5, 2.9, 2.10, 2.11, 2.12, 2.13, 2.14, 4.3, 4.4, 4.6, 4.15, 5.9, 7.6, 7.9, 7.10, 8.1, 8.3, 8.4, 8.5, 8.6, 8.7, 8.8, 8.11, 8.13	2, 4, 5, 7.2, 8.1, 8.2, 8.3,
2.4 Read and respond to written material	1.1, 1.2, 1.3, 1.4, 1.5, 1.6, 1.7, 1.8, 1.9, 1.10, 1.11, 2.1, 2.2, 2.3, 2.6, 2.7, 2.10, 2.11, 2.12, 2.13, 2.14, 4.17, 5.1, 6.1, 6.3, 6.4, 6.5, 6.6, 6.7, 6.8, 6.9, 6.10, 6.11, 7.4, 7.10, 7.11, 7.13, 8.9	1, 2, 3, 4, 5, 6, 7.3, 8.1

Key skills	Activities	Assignments
Information Technology		
2.1 Prepare information	1.5, 2.6, 2.9, 2.10, 2.11, 2.12, 2.13, 3.16, 3.18, 3.24, 4.1, 4.5, 5.2, 5.8, 6.6, 7.9, 7.10, 7.11	1, 2, 3, 4, 6, 5, 7.1, 7.3, 8.3
2.2 Process information	1.5, 2.6, 2.9, 2.10, 2.11, 2.12, 2.13, 3.16, 3.18, 3.24, 4.1, 4.3, 4.5, 4.7, 5.2, 5.10, 5.12, 6.6, 7.2	1, 2, 3, 4, 5, 6, 7.3, 8.3
2.3 Present information	1.5, 2.6, 2.9, 2.10, 2.11, 2.12, 2.13, 3.16, 3.18, 3.24, 4.18, 5.1, 5.3, 5.12, 6.6, 7.2, 7.3, 7.8, 7.9	1, 2, 3, 4, 5, 6, 7.3, 8.3
2.4 Evaluate the use of information technology	2.11, 2.12, 2.13, 2.14, 4.14, 5.13,	2, 4, 5, 7.3
Application of Number		
2.1 Collect and record data	1.3, 1.6, 1.7, 2.5, 2.14, 3.22, 3.24, 4.1, 4.18, 5.2, 6.10, 7.8, 8.8	1, 2, 4, 5, 6, 7.1, 7.3, 8.3
2.2 Tackle problems	1.3, 1.6, 1.7, 2.5, 2.14, 3.22, 3.24, 4.14, 5.8, 5.9, 6.1, 6.10, 8.2, 8.8	1, 2, 4, 5, 6, 7.1, 7.3, 8.1, 8.2, 8.3
2.3 Interpret and present data	4.2, 4.16, 4.19, 5.2, 5.10, 5.12, 6.1, 6.10, 7.2	1, 2, 4, 5, 6, 7.1, 7.3, 8.3

1 Investigating local and national media

Element 1.1	Investigate local and national media provision
Element 1.2	Explore consumption of local and national media
Element 1.3	Investigate developments and opportunities in the media industries

What is covered in this chapter

- Key features of UK media provision, local and national
- Sources of income and expenditure for UK media
- Representation and access to the media
- Regulatory bodies

- Audience research and trends in media use
- Models of audience behaviour and consumer profiles
- Media influence
- Changes and development in the media industry
- Employment and training opportunities

Your 'Investigating Media' file will need to contain the following:
- Your written answers to the activities in this chapter
- Evidence of action plans and research used to carry out the activities in that element, including original research you have designed and completed
- Your written answers to the review questions in this chapter

Your teacher may wish you to make a presentation of your work, playing suitable extracts from programmes and showing key points on an OHT. It may be possible to re-use this material in later projects.

Introduction

The chapter you are about to read is based on the first unit of your GNVQ course. It will deal in detail with all the topics listed above. It is broken into sections called **elements**.

During this chapter you may find it useful to refer to the Glossary on page 295. Throughout the book you will see that certain key words appear in **bold** type. These words will be explained as you come to them, and the Glossary will also provide you with a rapid way of revising their meaning later on.

Element 1.1 Investigate local and national media provision

Media Studies is the study of an industry. The media industry provides us with entertainment, information and a means of communication. In Western countries like the UK the influence of the media is very strong and most people could not imagine life without their favourite television programmes and pop stars.

Because the media is an industry, it depends on the existence of a **market.** The word **market** means the place where suppliers and consumers come together for the purpose of buying and selling goods and services. Like any market, the media market is controlled by laws and regulations. Other controls come from the decisions of the people who own the media, and from people who make decisions about which media products to buy, watch or listen to.

It is possible to divide the media into three broad groups or **categories.** This helps us to identify and compare features of media products. It also allows us to identify common elements in different media products. The categories are:

Category	Examples
Print	Newspapers, magazines, books, comics, leaflets, fanzines
Audio-visual	Radio, television, film, recorded music, retail video
Electronic/interactive products	Computer games, CD-ROM, Internet

Each of these types of product is covered in detail in later chapters of this book. This opening chapter looks at some of the general issues which concern all types of media in the UK.

Provision means what is available and how it is made available. The word is often used outside the media. For example, people in the army talk about 'provisions' for a military operation. They mean everything they will need – from food to tents and sleeping bags.

Influences on media provision

There are a number of different features of the media market which have an effect on media provision in this country. The media have particular ways of making their products available. Media products can be distributed to shops, broadcast via transmitters or sold through the mail. Each of these methods of making work available will be examined later.

Audience trends

Although audiences rarely behave according to any set rules, it is true to say that certain media products tend to appeal to people who have similar opinions and do similar things.

People in the media talk about **audience trends** to describe these patterns and similarities in audience tastes. These trends naturally have an effect on the type of products available, their content, cost, etc.

A good example of an audience trend is the growth in publications dealing with the paranormal (see Case Study focusing on the magazine *UFO Reality* on page 15). Newsagents also sell magazines like *Fortean Times*, *UFO*, *Sightings* and *Encounters*.

Case Study: Audience Trends

Study the two pictures. One shows George Formby, a popular singer from the 1930s and 40s. The other features Eat Static, a current electronic band who produce 'Techno' dance music. The popularity of each act is shaped by **audience trends** at the time. The table below helps to explain this.

	George Formby	**Eat Static**
Audience	Family-based, range of ages	Largely young, mainly 16-23
Promotion	Concerts, record sales and films	Record sales, live DJs, radio, video, live performance, music press
Image	Cheeky singer, playing jokey songs about everyday life. Based on personality of Formby	Based on youth culture, ideas of UFOs/paranormal behind most tracks, linked to dance/rave scene. Personalities of band members not important

In George Formby's day, audiences often went to the theatre in family groups. Formby's songs dealt with subjects like work and romance. He dressed in the style of a working man, and often portrayed ordinary working men in his films. This met the demand from his audience. 'Youth culture' as we know it today did not exist.

Today much media production, particularly in the music industry, is aimed specifically at a young audience. The appeal of a live dance act like Eat Static is based on providing their audience with an escape route from worries about money, work, studying for exams, etc. Like the TV show 'The X-Files', Eat Static's music feeds on popular interest in the paranormal. The personalities of the musicians matter a lot less than the hypnotic rhythms and pulsing lights of a large-scale dance event.

You can see from the table that Eat Static have many more ways of promoting their music than George Formby. Most of these options have been developed in response to audience demand. As young people have gained more access to jobs, money and free time, they have developed interests of their own which set them apart from older people. The type of dance music played by Eat Static is one example of this. Other examples of 'youth culture' are the magazines, television shows, live DJs and other events which may feature the music of Eat Static and bands like them.

The trend towards publishing magazines on this subject has occurred for a number of reasons:

- A growing interest in this subject amongst the young
- Falling costs of magazine production, making it possible to gain profits from a few thousand magazine sales
- Links between the paranormal and other fashionable developments like dance music

Because a market exists, and because advertising can be drawn from other areas such as the music industry, publishers have put a range of magazines on the market. These have raised the level of interest and a definite trend has occurred. Twenty years ago hardly any magazines were devoted to this subject.

Access

The term **access** means the chances that people have to get involved in the media. Many people want to make their own points and promote their own ideas. Because the media can be a powerful means of putting over a message, there are many people who want media access.

In the past it was often very expensive to produce media products. This meant that ownership and control of the media tended to rest with the wealthy and powerful. Nowadays the technology to make media products is getting cheaper all the time, and media **hardware**, i.e. equipment such as camcorders and computers, is within the reach of large sections of the population.

In some cases the media are keen to offer access to the public. Some parts of the media, such as the BBC, set aside air time for members of the public to put over their own views.

This access may be offered because the public will contribute interesting material. Phone-in shows on radio are a good example, and a station like Talk Radio UK depends on members of the public with opinions and stories which they are willing to share on radio. Some television programmes also use material gathered by the public because this allows the television companies to save on the costs of hiring film crews, scriptwriters, etc. Channel 4 has

Some TV channels are required under their charter to provide community access

broadcast a programme called 'Take Over TV', in which members of the public are paid a small fee for video clips of all kinds, some serious and some humorous. Many people with ambitions to work in the media work hard to make clips in the hope that they will be noticed on the show.

The rules by which some media companies operate mean that they have to offer access. Under its charter (see below), the BBC has to give the general public some 'slots' in which to present their own programmes and opinions. For example, 'Points of View' allows the public to air their opinions on BBC programmes. Other programmes such as 'Video Diaries' give members of the public the opportunity to make short films in which they can present ideas and information and share personal experiences.

Ownership

Some media outlets are publicly owned. The BBC (British Broadcasting Corporation) is a good example. The BBC has been a 'public service' organisation since 1927 when a Royal Charter outlined its powers and mission. This charter has been changed several times but the main aim of the corporation has always been to provide 'public services'. In practice this means that the BBC should inform, educate and entertain everyone. Because it exists to serve the public and is paid for by the public through the TV licence, the BBC can devote time and effort to producing more educational and informative material than other television or radio organisations.

Private ownership

Most media producers in Britain are owned by individuals or companies. These companies are responsible mainly to the people who own them, and their first aim is to make a profit. They make their income from selling work and selling advertising space. Because of their need to make money, they are obliged to produce material which is popular enough to attract a large audience.

The media producers

There are a great many differences between the kinds of media producers who put work onto the market, although they all need to make a profit. Some examples are discussed below.

National newspaper companies

Most national newspapers belong to big organisations who produce a range of material. A good example is the Mirror Group which owns *The Sunday Mirror* and *Daily Mirror*. This company also owns Scotland's *Daily Record* which contains the same kind of news and features as *The Daily Mirror*.

The Mirror Group has interests in other areas of the media and pools its resources to make these other interests profitable. One example is the cable channel L!ve TV which presents regional programmes for a small audience. The channel runs on £5 million per year – a very low budget for a 24-hour television channel. L!ve TV saves money by drawing on the newsgathering resources of the Mirror Group newspapers. The channel has also been helped by the fact that the parent company has contacts and offices in major British cities and has promoted the cable channel in its newspapers.

All Britain's national daily newspapers are based in London and are owned by large companies who have other interests besides newspaper publishing. The main national daily newspapers are listed below along with their owners:

Although sharply different in style and format, The Times and the Sun are both currently owned by Rupert Murdoch's News International

Newspaper	Owner
The Sun, The Times	News International
The Mirror, The Daily Record, The Independent	Mirror Group Newspapers
The Star, The Express	United Newspapers
The Daily Mail	Associated Newspapers
The Daily Telegraph	Telegraph Newspapers
The Guardian	Guardian Newspapers

We can see from this list that some newspapers have 'sister' publications – for example, the *Star* and the *Express*. 'Sister' publications are created when a proprietor owns more than one title. Most of the papers listed above have connections with other publications. The *Guardian* has links with the Sunday newspaper *The Observer*. The *Guardian* also has links with the book publishers Fourth Estate who produce titles based on material which appears in the paper. Fourth Estate publish an annual *Media Guide* which is a Guardian book listing information about the British media.

Many other papers also publish material electronically – including Web sites on the Internet. The aim is usually to make money by presenting the material linked to the paper in a wide range of settings. For example, the *Guardian*'s *Media Guide* uses information gathered by the paper for its regular Monday 'Media' supplement. The annual guide allows the paper to make an extra profit from the investment it makes in this media section.

Privately owned television companies are organised into networks and form similar connections. As we have seen from the example of the Mirror Group, some of these companies have links with other areas of the media. Rupert Murdoch, who owns a massive global media empire including the News International print group, also owns BSkyB television and other channels around the world.

Books and magazines

Britain has a rapidly growing industry devoted to books and magazines. The costs of producing print material are falling at the moment – this topic is covered in Chapter 2. Some examples here are used to show the kind of material available from private print companies.

Some companies have massive operations and publish a large range of titles. For example, from its base in South East London, IPC magazines publishes dozens of periodicals including *Mizz* magazine and the music paper *NME*, both aimed at the young.

A big magazine company, like a big television company, can benefit from economies of scale. For example, it can employ specialist staff to deal solely with advertising sales. It can offer advertisers the opportunity to reach a wide variety of different markets and audiences. A company like IPC also has enough money to own and control its own printing and distribution, which again has cost advantages.

Sometimes it is useful for a title to have connections with a big company for the purposes of distribution. The *Independent* newspaper, which is listed above as a part of the Mirror Group, is a case in point. As well as owning a 46% stake in the paper, the Mirror Group handles distribution, printing and much of the day-to-day management. The other 54% of the paper is owned by a combination of overseas concerns, including a Spanish publisher. It is in the interests of the other owners that production and distribution of the paper are managed by one of Britain's biggest newspaper printing organisations.

Smaller companies exist to provide material for specialist markets. An example of such a company is Ark Soundways which publishes *UFO Reality* magazine (see page 15). This company has none of the advantages of a big organisation like IPC. However, it does have a very good understanding of its own small market. Ark Soundways also release a range of videos about UFOs and the paranormal. Their work in this area has given them a specialised knowledge of the dedicated market that will buy their magazine.

Book publishers follow similar patterns to the magazine and periodical publishers already discussed in this chapter. Some book publishers have links with massive companies with interests inside and outside the media. Some are large companies themselves, with offices and staff around the world. Others are small organisations serving a specialised market.

One large company with an interest in books is **The Virgin Group**. The company also has interests in record production, music and video retailing, television, radio, transport – including aircraft and trains – and soft drinks.

Virgin books often deal in areas that have links to other areas of the company's work. For example, Virgin is well known for producing quality books about rock music. These books cover acts signed to the Virgin record label and are sold in Virgin stores.

The BBC

The BBC operates via a network of television and radio channels and stations. Nationally, it has two television channels, BBC1 and BBC2. It also produces work for cable and satellite and is presently looking to add to its television output. Recently the BBC has launched a 24-hour national television news network available via cable or satellite.

The BBC owns and runs five national radio networks. These are Radios 1, 2, 3 and 4, and Radio 5 Live. Each has its own audience and distinctive style of programmes. The BBC also owns local radio stations around the country. These local stations sometimes produce radio and television programmes for the national networks. National networks also use material broadcast from local studios. In 1997 the Radio 1 Breakfast Show began broadcasting from a local studio in Manchester because Mark Radcliffe and his sidekick 'The Boy Lard' lived in the area and had been using the studio for their earlier work.

The BBC and the regions

The size of the BBC means that radio and television productions can draw on staff and contacts all round the country. The BBC news network has reporters and production staff throughout the world producing material for a wide range of BBC departments. Because it has a public service responsibility, the BBC has to produce material that meets the needs of people in all parts of the country. Programmes often concentrate on a particular region or locality and present this information to viewers nationwide.

One successful example is the police drama 'Hamish Macbeth' which deals with a policeman in a remote part of Scotland. Some of the problems he faces would not occur in a big inner city. The drama presents images of Scotland and the Scots people. It also presents strong storylines that appeal to people throughout the country. The BBC is well placed to make 'Hamish Macbeth' because it has a production staff permanently based in Scotland.

A small film company might have found this programme hard to make because it would have had to spend money gathering information about locations, actors, etc. in Scotland. The BBC in Scotland gathers much of this kind of information as part of its normal duties and is therefore able to operate with lower research costs.

Independent national TV networks

ITV companies in this country bid for the right to broadcast in their local area. If successful, they are awarded a franchise which gives them the right to broadcast for a limited period – usually several years. Each regional independent company is part of the ITV network. Some programming for the network – such as ITN news – is produced centrally and fed to all the regions. Other programmes are produced by particular regions and sold to other companies within the network. 'Coronation Street' is ITV's most popular programme and is broadcast by all regions. It is produced in Manchester by the local franchise- holder, Granada Television.

Channel 4 and Channel 5 are national networks which are privately owned. Channel 4 broadcasts via the ITV network, but Channel 5 has no affiliation to ITV and transmits a terrestrial service which is also available on cable and via satellite. Both channels broadcast a combination of material originated in-house and bought in from outside. Some of the bought-in material is produced by the regional ITV stations. Channel 4 and Channel 5 and ITV are subject to controls from the **Independent Television Commission** (see page 28).

Cable and satellite TV

At the time of writing, over 2 million people in the UK subscribe to privately owned cable and satellite channels. Many of the companies involved in this area of the market have links to other private British media operations, for example newspaper publishers. Some others have links to foreign companies.

The British cable channel Challenge TV (see page 20) has links to a parent company in the USA.

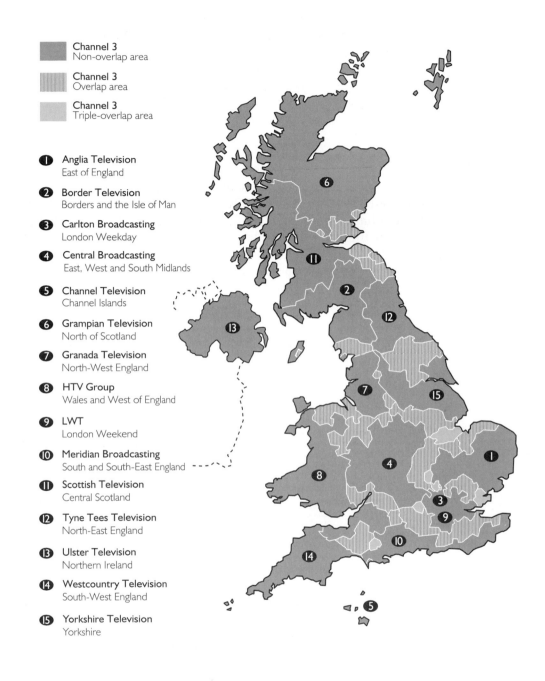

	Channel 3 Non-overlap area
	Channel 3 Overlap area
	Channel 3 Triple-overlap area

❶ **Anglia Television**
East of England

❷ **Border Television**
Borders and the Isle of Man

❸ **Carlton Broadcasting**
London Weekday

❹ **Central Broadcasting**
East, West and South Midlands

❺ **Channel Television**
Channel Islands

❻ **Grampian Television**
North of Scotland

❼ **Granada Television**
North-West England

❽ **HTV Group**
Wales and West of England

❾ **LWT**
London Weekend

❿ **Meridian Broadcasting**
South and South-East England

⓫ **Scottish Television**
Central Scotland

⓬ **Tyne Tees Television**
North-East England

⓭ **Ulster Television**
Northern Ireland

⓮ **Westcountry Television**
South-West England

⓯ **Yorkshire Television**
Yorkshire

The ITV regional network

Commercial radio

There are now over 180 commercial radio stations covering all parts of the country. These include national stations such as Classic FM and Talk Radio UK, regional stations like Century in the North East and local stations like 95.8 Capital FM in London, Piccadilly Radio in Manchester and Clyde 1 in Glasgow. All of these gather their income from advertising.

Independent national, regional and local radio stations in the UK

Key to map of radio stations

Scotland
1 SIBC
2 Isles FM
3 Lochbroom FM
4 Moray Firth Radio
5 NECR
6 Waves Radio
7 NorthSound One
8 NorthSound Two
9 Nevis Radio
10 Heartland FM
11 Radio Tay AM
12 Tay FM
13 Oban FM
14 Central FM
15 Clyde 1 FM
16 Clyde 2
17 96.3 QFM
18 Scot FM – Regional service for central Scotland – R1
19 Forth AM
20 Forth FM
21 West Sound AM
22 West Sound FM
23 Radio Borders
24 South West Sound

Northern Ireland
25 Q102.9 FM
26 Townland Radio
27 City Beat 96.7
28 Cool FM
29 Downtown Radio
30 Radio 1521

Wales
31 Coast FM
32 Radio Maldwyn
33 Radio Ceredigion
34 Sound Wave
35 Swansea Sound
36 Touch Radio
37 Red Dragon FM
38 Valleys Radio

England
39 CFM
40 CFM
41 GNR
42 Metro FM
43 Century Radio – Regional service for North East – R2
44 Sun FM
45 TFM
46 Alpha 103.2
47 Yorkshire Coast Radio
48 The Bay
49 Yorkshire Dales Radio
50 97.2 Stray FM
51 Minster FM

52 96.9 Viking FM
53 Sunrise Radio
54 96.3 Aire FM
55 Kiss 105 – Regional service for Yorkshire – R6
56 Magic 828
57 The Pulse
58 Huddersfield FM Ltd
59 Classic Gold 1278/1530
60 Radio Wave
61 Dune FM
62 Red Rose 999
63 Rock FM
64 Radio City 96.7
65 MFM 97.1
66 Crash FM
67 Magic 1548 AM
68 102.4 Wish FM
69 Asian Sound Radio
70 1458 Lite AM
71 Jazz FM 100.4 – Regional service for North West – R3
72 Key 103
73 Kiss 102
74 Piccadilly Radio 1152 AM
75 Magic
76 Hallam FM
77 Magic
78 Lincs FM
79 KCBC 1584 AM
80 Signal 105
81 MFM 103.4
82 Marcher Gold
83 Signal One
84 Signal Two
85 Ram FM
86 GEM AM
87 Trent FM
88 KLFM 96.7
89 Beacon Radio
90 WABC Classic Gold
91 Radio 106 – Regional service for East midlands – R7
92 Leicester Sound
93 Sabres Sound
94 102.7 Hereward FM
95 Classic Gold 1332 AM
96 Amber Radio (Norfolk)
97 Broadland 102
98 The Beach
99 107.7 FM The Wolf
100 96.4 FM BRMB
101 100.7 Heart FM – Regional service for West Midlands – R4
102 1152 XTRA AM

103 Choice FM Birmingham
104 Radio XL 1296 AM
105 Sunshine 855
106 Classic Gold 1359
107 Kix 96
108 Mercia FM
109 Classic Gold 954/1530
110 Wyvern FM
111 FM 102 – The Bear
112 Northants 96
113 Classic Gold 1557
114 B97
115 Classic Gold 792/828
116 Q103 FM
117 Cambridge Community Radio 107.9 FM
118 Vibe FM
119 Amber Radio (Suffolk)
120 SGR-FM
121 Cheltenham Radio
122 Severn Sound FM
123 Classic Gold 774
124 FOX FM
125 Oxygen 107.9
126 Mix 96
127 Chiltern FM
128 FM 103 Horizon
129 96.6 FM Classic Hits
130 Ten 17
131 Mellow 1557
132 SGR Colchester
133 GWR FM
134 Brunel Classic Gold
135 Galaxy 101 – Regional service for Severn Estuary – R5
136 GWR FM
137 2-Ten FM
138 Classic Gold 1431/1485
139 Eleven Seventy
140 Star FM
141 Thames FM
142 Essex FM
143 The Breeze
144 Medway FM
145 Invicta FM
146 Invicta SuperGold
147 Thanet Local Radio
148 106 CTFM Radio
149 Neptune Radio
150 Channel Travel Radio
151 KFM
152 Arrow FM
153 Sovereign Radio
154 Fame 1521
155 Mercury FM
156 96.4 The Eagle
157 County Sound Radio 1476 AM

158 Wye Valley Radio
159 Delta Radio 97.1 FM
160 South Coast Radio
161 Southern FM
162 Surf 107
163 Spirit FM
164 Ocean FM
165 Power FM
166 South Coast Radio
167 Isle of Wight Radio
168 Spire FM
169 2CR FM
170 Classic Gold 828
171 97.4 Gold Radio
172 Wessex FM
173 Orchard FM
174 Gemini AM
175 Gemini FM
176 Lantern FM
177 Plymouth Sound AM
178 Plymouth Sound FM
179 Pirate FM102
180 Island FM
181 Channel 103 FM
182 Asia FM Ltd
183 95.8 Capital FM
184 963 Liberty Radio
185 1548 AM Capital Gold
186 Choice FM London
187 Heart 106.2
188 Jazz FM 102.2
189 Kiss 100 FM
190 LBC 1152
191 London Greek Radio
192 London Turkish Radio LTR
193 Melody FM
194 Millennium Radio
195 News Direct 97.3 FM
196 Premier Radio
197 RTL Country 1035 AM
198 Spectrum Radio Ltd
199 Sunrise Radio
200 Virgin Radio London
201 Xfm

Film and TV production companies

Some companies involved in the broadcast media also make films for the cinema. A few specialise in film production, but most produce a range of work including television and making commercials. Much film production work in the UK is aimed at a worldwide audience. Many famous Hollywood films include sequences filmed on British sound stages, with British workers forming most of the film crew. There are a few totally 'British' films, i.e. made with cast and crew exclusively from this country, but almost all of these films recover at least some of their money from abroad. *Trainspotting* is a well known British film which was successful in the UK and was also shown abroad.

Production and distribution

The range statements for your GNVQ require you to know something about production and distribution for the print and audiovisual media. Detailed examples from these media are presented throughout this book. Most fit the patterns of production and distribution outlined below.

1 Production

This word is used to describe everything involved in the business of making a media product. A media product usually starts life as an idea. It is turned into a media product through a series of stages which may include scripting, planning, recording, editing, etc. You will be involved in production work for different areas of the media from Chapter 2 of this book onwards.

Cost is an important factor when deciding which ideas will go on to become media products. Media products are often expensive to make. This is why companies often decide to 'play safe' and stick to making products that have a proven record of success. The success of other products is often taken as an indication that similar products will generate good money.

Consumers can be suspicious of new products too. People who buy and use media products often have set ideas about what they want. Any idea or product that falls outside of these can face a struggle before it becomes successful. There are already a lot of people and a lot of products within the media industry. To beat the competition, new products and performers need to offer something distinctive that will gain audience interest.

2 Distribution

This word is used to describe moving media products from their place of production or manufacture to reach their audience.

Some distribution involves physically moving things – like newspapers from the printworks to the newsagent's shop. In other cases, products are 'broadcast' directly to the audience. Broadcasting involves using equipment to transmit information to audiences. Audiences have their own equipment – for example, radios and television sets – which receive these broadcast products.

Producing and distributing print products

Print products are generally produced using computers in offices. They are then printed either in-house in the case of a large company like IPC, or by a smaller print company which is paid to produce an agreed number of copies. The ability to send information **digitally** via cable or computer disk has revolutionised the printing industry in recent years. It is now increasingly common for material – like newspapers – to be sent in digital form to a number of printing centres. The *Sun* newspaper, for example, is now printed in Spain and sold by newsagents in Spain, Portugal and France to British tourists.

Most print products are still distributed in large quantities by lorry or train and stored in warehouses from which they can be moved to shops. But some material is now distributed electronically into people's homes, where it can be read by computer or printed out on paper. At the time of writing, this is a very small part of print distribution, but the growth of computer technology is likely to make it increasingly common in the future.

Producing and distributing audiovisual products
Audiovisual products may be manufactured in the form of video or sound recordings and sold in shops. When this happens, the process of distribution is similar to print, but the production process involves facilities like film and television studios. Other material is broadcast by television and radio transmitters, relayed by satellite or transmitted by cable into people's homes.

It is also now possible to download audiovisual material via computer. Most material in this country is still broadcast by TV and radio transmitter but, as with print products, the expanding use of computers and other new technology is gradually changing the way we receive such material.

Local and national provision

As we have seen, media products can serve both local and national audiences. In some cases 'local areas' may cover thousands of square miles. The television company that covers the North of Scotland, for example, has a massive area with a relatively small number of viewers. This is because the region has few large towns, many mountains and relies on industries like farming and tourism. By contrast, a city like Manchester can easily support its own local television station.

Some issues covered by the media are best dealt with on a national level. Television programmes, films and books sometimes take one particular subject – like unemployment – and explore it in depth. The idea of such work is to bring the issue to the attention of a national audience. Sometimes social problems are dealt with in fiction – through a film, TV drama or a character in a soap opera.

Local coverage has its advantages. Locally based journalists can get to know an area very well. Certain subjects can be covered in great depth by local media and largely ignored by the national media. Sport is a good example. If there is a small football club near you, or if your area has a good team in a little known sport like cycling, you will probably see this difference.

But the same is also true in reverse. If there is a controversial industry like a nuclear power station in an area, the local media will often find it hard to criticise because they need advertising and depend on having good relations with the industry. A national newspaper may not have these problems. It can therefore afford to cover a story that would give the local media some trouble.

The differences between the local and national media are largely due to funding. Most local areas do not have enough interest to support specialist magazines, television shows, etc. Similarly, in order to justify making a very expensive media product such as a feature film or a large-scale rock concert, the promoters need to be sure of attracting an international audience. Stars like

Michael Jackson, Tom Cruise and Oprah Winfrey command huge fees because the work they produce is understood and appreciated by people all around the world.

Activity 1.1

1 Begin a study of two UK media industries. Choose ONE national newspaper or television channel and ONE local radio station or local newspaper. The two examples MUST be from different industries – e.g. they cannot both be newspapers.
2 Identify the key features of each one in terms of: ownership; production and distribution; access and audience trends. Explain the differences between them under each heading.

Content, style and audience

Whether a product is aimed at a local or national audience has an important bearing on the content and style of the material it handles.

Most people are familiar with local television and radio, and many also read local newspapers. These examples of local media often do a similar job to the national media. But there are important differences in the size and profile of the audience. In the case of a national product the audience may run into millions. A newspaper like the *Sun* can sell over four million copies in one day. A local paper may sell tens of thousands of copies. Local papers have to spread their coverage wide enough to satisfy a range of people in an area. A national publication can often aim at one type of reader or 'target audience' because there are groups of these people all around the country.

This difference in audience has implications for style and content as well. The *Sun*'s content is sharp and simple in comparison to newspapers like *The Times*. Its visual style is bright and visually appealing. The purpose of this content and style is to appeal to the four million people who buy the paper. Inevitably this leads to some simplifying of ideas and information.

Case Study: national and local audiences

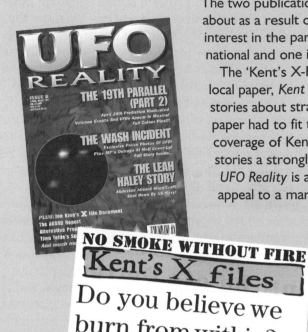

The two publications featured here both came about as a result of the current growth in interest in the paranormal. One example is national and one is local.

The 'Kent's X-Files' story comes from a local paper, *Kent Life*. This paper ran a series of stories about strange events in Kent. The local paper had to fit these stories into its regular coverage of Kent life. It also had to give the stories a strongly local angle.

UFO Reality is a national magazine. It aims to appeal to a market of people who share an interest in paranormal phenomena.

There are some important differences in the coverage these publications provide. There are also differences in their audiences and the way they make money.

	UFO Reality	**Kent Life**
Audience	National, a few people in each region, all share similar interest	Some not interested in paranormal. Most interested in Kent life
Age	Young, mostly between 18 and 30	Varied, mainly 35+ but readers of all ages
Income	Most with medium to high income	Varied; unemployed to very well paid
Subject matter	Centred on UFOs and other strange phenomena	All local news, sport and general interest with local angle
Advertising	Well known national products drinks, video tapes etc, a few small ads	Many local events, some consumer products, local businesses, small ads
Style	Bright and colourful magazine layout, well illustrated, much use of graphics	Traditional newspaper, plenty of text, a few columns on each page
Cover price*	£3	50p

* Correct at time of going to press

Other print products aimed at a smaller number of people take a different approach. This book is aimed at a potential audience of a few thousand students a year. Its purpose is to provide enough information to allow readers to pass their GNVQ course. Because of this, it has to make the information easy to understand – hence the use of illustrated examples. However, it also makes certain demands on the reader – for example, by presenting quite detailed and complicated information. This is because the few thousand students who read this book *expect* to have to work through their course and are motivated to learn a lot about each element within it.

The same considerations of style and content apply to broadcast products. Popular radio shows like the Radio 1 Breakfast Show use hit records, sharp and witty observations and a lot of jingles to provide a cheerful background to the nation's breakfast. Like the *Sun* newspaper, the content is easily understood and the ideas often catchy and simple.

Audiovisual products which are aimed a smaller audience can afford to spend time exploring much more complicated ideas. An entire phone-in radio show or TV documentary might be devoted to a problem like crime. In a case like this, the style and content will be closer to this book, using detailed examples and facts which build into arguments.

You should be aware from this short section that style and content are linked to other factors like the numbers in an audience, the purpose(s) for which the audience will use a media product and the budget available to produce the work. From Chapter 2 on, you will be involved in producing your own media products, and you will have to consider style and content as part of this work.

Activity 1.2

1 Identify and explain the differences between the TWO media products you chose in Activity 1.1. You should analyse content, style and audience.
2 Use examples taken from the media products you are studying to illustrate your results. Make a presentation to your class to explain your findings.

Media revenue and expenditure

The guidelines for your course state that you should be able to *'identify sources of revenue and key areas of expenditure'* for both local and national media producers. When companies produce work, they need to be sure that it can cover its costs and earn enough to make a profit. The actual figures involved vary a great deal depending on audience numbers, the length of time a product is on sale, the possibility of repeating or reprinting work, etc. Some examples are provided here to give you some idea of the comparisons.

Example 1: *What does it cost to broadcast an hour of television?*
The answer is that an hour's television on BBC costs an average of £50,000, whereas an hour on L!ve TV costs £2,000.

We can see from these figures that high-quality national television is expensive. The BBC gets its funding via the licence fee and recoups money from sales of its programmes. One important source of revenue for the Corporation is the sale of programmes such as major historical dramas to foreign TV channels. Popular programmes such as 'Middlemarch' or 'Pride and Prejudice' can bring in several million pounds each. L!ve TV does not produce work which sells so easily abroad and their low costs means that advertisers can pay hundreds of pounds for a few showings of an advert. A typical package might cost as little as £500 for less than ten runs of one advert. This is equivalent to 15 minutes' budget for the station.

Example 2: *What can you print for £1?*

This depends entirely on the size, number of copies printed and complexity of the job. A local printer would probably charge you around 6–8p per double-sided sheet for a black and white magazine with illustrations. This means that a 26-page school or college magazine would cost around £1 per copy. Your 'print run' – i.e. the number of copies – would probably be around 200.

A magazine like *Sessions,* which deals with indie and related music, also costs just over £1 per copy to produce. However, this buys colour printing, glossy paper and around 50 pages. The costs are cheaper per copy than the school or college magazine because many more copies are printed.

The figures for huge-selling products like tabloid papers are cheaper still. As we have seen, one reason for this is that the publishers own and control their own printing. Papers like the *Sun* sometimes reduce their cover price to 10 pence, but in practice, it would easily be possible to print between 15 and 20 copies for £1.

Example 3: *How much advertising can you buy for £1,000 ?*

This is hard to say exactly, because publishers and broadcasters often offer deals to regular advertisers which cut the cost of individual adverts but tic advertisers to publication over a long period. However, if a band decided to spend £1,000 on an advert for a new album they could generally buy:

- One page in a music magazine with sales of around 40,000 copies. For example, *Sessions* magazine offers a page for exactly £1,000
- Half a page in a larger-selling publication like *Q* or *Vox*
- Around two minutes' airtime on a commercial radio station with an audience of dance music fans. Currently London's Kiss FM is offering 30-second commercial slots for £245.00. One-minute commercials work out cheaper by the second. Kiss's rate for one-minute advert is £345.00.

A figure of £1,000 would *not* buy advertising on most national ITV channels because advertising space is usually sold in blocks, with an advertiser spending a minimum of a few thousand pounds to place the same commercial ten times or more. The best chance of television advertising within the £1,000 budget would be to place adverts on cable or satellite within a local region. This would allow some targeting of specialist music programmes and audience. At the time of writing, the cable network supplying MTV (Music Television) to a large part of the south east of England is offering blocks of advertising for £475. If the band bought two of these blocks they would get the following:

- 160 showings of a 30-second commercial over a 4-week period. This would be spread over six channels including MTV. The adverts would be limited to one region – usually around the size of one English or Welsh county
- The adverts would also appear on channels like UK Gold which shows popular television programmes from the past. These channels attract an audience with little interest in dance music

Showing the advert nationally or internationally on MTV would mean spending well over £1,000.

All the figures cover just the *insertion* of an advert. In the case of radio, television or print, the band and their record company would also have to pay an agency to make an advert.

Sources of media revenue

Revenue is a word used to describe all the money available to an industry. Sometimes there is confusion between the terms **revenue** and **income**. In practice the two meanings are very similar. The major difference is that income is money that comes in to the media. Revenue is all of the money available to the media. This means that the media can provide some revenue for itself. Income has to come from somewhere else.

As with any industry, the media industry's main sources of revenue are the sales of its products and services. A **product** is anything that can be manufactured and sold by the media, and a **service** is anything that the media can offer which might help someone to do something. An example of a product is a video tape. An example of a service is the travel pages on Teletext.

The media industry earns income by selling a wide range of goods, including videos, newspapers, comics, etc. Commercial television companies use their products to attract an audience and then offer a service to advertisers. They show adverts in return for money. Television companies also sell programmes. Many British television shows are seen around the world.

In some cases, the sales of individual products are linked together. For example, it is possible to subscribe to magazines and comics for a year or even longer. A **subscription** is an agreement to go on buying something – e.g. a magazine – for a given period of time. This is useful to the publishers because it guarantees them an audience and gives them an idea of the level of income they can expect from it. Many media companies try to tie their work in with subscription, pay-per-view and other deals.

Pay-per-view screening of sports events is becoming more and more common

The BBC licence fee

The BBC is a special case in terms of funding. When people buy television licences they pay a **licence fee**. This funds the BBC. The BBC also has a worldwide radio network which has, historically, been paid for by the government. In the future, both arrangements may change.

Through the BBC, the government has a convenient means of putting important messages across to the general public. **Public service broadcasts** such as adverts aimed at drink drivers are an example of this. Those who control the BBC's funding, i.e. the government, have a choice over how the money is spent. Clearly, it could be spent on things other than media products. For example, anti-drink-driving campaigns also involve work outside the media, such as the police visiting schools and colleges.

Most of the companies and organisations within the media are driven by the need to make a profit. They therefore plan to spend less money than they make. They do not always succeed. One reason is that most media products require expenditure before they start to earn money. **Expenditure** is a general term which is used to describe any area in which the media spends money.

Three main areas of expenditure in the media are discussed below. It is normal for money to be spent in all of these areas before a media product begins to generate any income in return.

Areas of media expenditure

The three main areas of expenditure are discussed in the Case Study on pages 20–1:

- **Generation of material** This is the money spent on planning, thinking up ideas and researching into the competition and likely audience for the product. All this helps to produce – or 'generate' – work which can be sold.
- **Production** This is the money that goes into actually making things. It may include actors' wages, paper for printing, time in a recording studio, etc.
- **Dissemination** This is the money that goes into physically getting the products to the audience. In practice it has a lot in common with 'distribution', except that dissemination can also mean informal exchanges of products and ideas. You might disseminate information about a fanzine simply by talking about it and passing it around a classroom. However, this talking is not a means of distribution because the interested people still have to find the fanzine and buy it for themselves.

In addition, money is also spent on **promotion**. Promotion involves making people aware of your work. It may include advertising, giving away low-cost or free copies, or providing material for review. Some of the best known types of promotion include advertising and adding bonus items to products – such as free books or discs stuck to the cover of magazines – to boost sales. Promotion money can also be spent on the salaries of people involved in promoting work. Leaflets or brochures produced to promote a media product – such as advertising flyers – are often called 'promotional material.'

Promotion does not appear on the GNVQ range statements because it is a hard activity to define. It is also possible for promotional activity to take place without any money being spent at all. This might happen, for example, if a book were featured in a TV discussion programme or if a match-day programme was sold outside a football ground. When producers know that an audience will seek out the work anyway they can afford to ignore promotion.

Falling costs

As the cost of making media products falls, many organisations and individuals are turning to media production. Some good examples of this are promotional videos made by hospitals and schools. Other examples are TV shows such as 'You've Been Framed' which use video clips sent in by members of the public.

Case Study: comparing media expenditure

Denton News is a newsletter produced for a housing estate in the South of England. Challenge TV is a satellite and cable broadcasting company which sends programmes all over Europe. *Denton News* is produced with public money, with the aim of bringing positive changes to an area that has seen some problems. Challenge TV's schedules are intended to attract a family audience by offering entertainment which is free of swearing or violence. The channel makes its money from advertisers and by selling programmes.

The table shows how the two media compare in terms of their expenditure.

	Denton News	**Challenge TV**
Generation of material	Social workers and people in the community worked together on the idea for this newsletter. People in the community gave their time for free. The social workers – and some charity representatives involved – were on a salary. This salary was paid to cover their responsibilities to work within the community and deal with problems. The generation of the idea for *Denton News* was an attempt to deal directly with a local problem.	Managers and staff are paid to arrange the schedule. There was much research into the likely success of the channel itself before the decision was taken to buy the studios and start broadcasts. This work included research into the likely competition. There were also meetings and business deals to purchase the headquarters buildings and buy in programmes from outside sources.

Case Study (Contd.)

	Denton News	**Challenge TV**
Production	All writing was done for free, much of it by local school-children. Local college students completed the layout and word processing as part of an assignment.	Have their own production staff on contracts to make programmes. The channel owns its own studios and equipment.
Distribution	Dropped through letterboxes in the local area. Some copies are made available in council offices, etc.	Uses satellite and cable broadcast and receiving equipment. The channel has large bills for ownership and renting of such equipment.
Promotion	The minimal budget for the publication does not include any money for advertising or promotional material. The main means of promotion is through the time and effort of those involved. Because the distribution covers a very small area it is possible for the producers of the newsletter to speak directly to many of the intended audience. The newsletter is delivered within a housing estate and so the purpose of 'promotional' work is to encourage people to read it and get involved. The inclusion of work from schoolchildren and well known residents in the area also helps to promote *Denton News* by encouraging friends, family and neighbours to read the publication.	Is part of a larger broadcasting network. Promotion for this organisation is handled on two levels. Challenge TV organises its own promotion which includes making and paying for adverts which appear in the press, on television, etc. Other promotional work at this level includes staging live events, producing material to be handed out, etc. The parent company and other companies with common interests also promote the station. For example, companies involved in selling and installing cable and satellite equipment produce brochures showing potential customers the range of programmes which are available on these services. The output of Challenge TV may be featured in this material.

Another effect of the decline in the cost of media products is the increasing amount of choice for media audiences. There are more magazines, television channels, videos and records available now than at any time in the past. Experts suggest the amount of choice will continue rising well into the future. This has already made it difficult to control the output of the media. Some products available at the moment break the law. They are hard to control because few people actually get to see them.

A good example is the Internet, the worldwide network of computer users. Because the Internet crosses national and international boundaries, controlling access to the information and images stored on it is a practical impossibility. The Internet cannot be said to be based in any one country, so which laws apply? The laws in the country where the information is held? Or the country in which the information is accessed or downloaded? Most people using the network can do so without identifying themselves, and this makes it even harder to track them down.

Activity 1.3

1 What are the main sources of revenue for each of the two media products you are studying? Identify and explain the differences between them.
2 What are the main types of expenditure for each of the two media products? Explain the differences and similarities between them.

Representation, access and dissemination

Representation means the way in which the media portray or represent people, events, ideas and issues. The media are constantly making choices about *who* is portrayed and who is ignored, and about *how* people or events are portrayed. This gives them great power to influence the way their audiences think and behave. We will look at some examples later in this section.

Two factors which can influence representation are who has **access** to the media and how a particular product is **disseminated**, or distributed to its audience.

Representation

The audience or market for media products is made up of a huge range of individuals, each with different opinions, attitudes and values. We have already seen that public opinion has to be considered when producing media work. Your earlier work comparing local and national media – like newspapers and television – will already have given you some idea about the way your area might be seen by other people. People who study the media use the term **representation** to describe the images produced by the media. A 'representation' can be an image – or a series of images – of any person, place or thing. It can also be a representation of something larger, such as a group of people, a race or ethnic group or an entire country.

Stereotyped representations

A common complaint about the media concerns the way people and places are 'represented' in programmes and in the press. Many people working in the media like to use familiar images and ideas because this means that audiences are more likely to understand the products. If audiences understand products quickly, they are more likely to buy them. Over-familiar or 'well-worn' representations of people, places or things are often referred to as **stereotypes**. A stereotype is a representation that is instantly understood but which is also simplistic and potentially misleading. Stereotypes often have their basis in truth but miss out important information.

You may well recognize some stereotypes yourself. For example, traffic wardens are often represented in the media as being miserable and mean-spirited. In fact, most people only notice traffic wardens when they have been given a parking ticket. Since people do not like getting parking tickets, they often direct their anger towards traffic wardens and see them in a stereotypical way. In the past, traffic warden characters have often been used as stereotypes in comedies and dramas.

Many other people and groups are sensitive about the way they are represented in the media. This is understandable in the case of groups who tend to get a 'bad press'.

For example, the media often present a very bad image of people who break the law. This may be perfectly reasonable in the majority of cases. But there are situations in which people who break the law do so out of a deeply held belief or conviction. For example, protesters against road building sometimes occupy land illegally and even damage equipment belonging to road builders. They argue that they are fighting for the environment. The arguments about representations are often complicated. It is usually impossible to satisfy everyone.

Case Study: a typical student?

Mittal Karia

This photograph is typical of many which appear in magazines aimed at young people. It shows Mittal Karia, a Media Studies student living in the South of England.

Mittal is somebody with whom many readers of these magazines will easily identify. She could be said to 'represent' a number of groups within society. These could include:

- Students
- Young Asian people
- Young women
- Happy, healthy people
- Casually dressed people

Testing reactions

If you showed the same picture to different groups of people you would probably find that reactions varied. Most researchers find that responses to questions about representation change with the people asked. So, you may find that people over 60 are more likely to think Mittal is a typical student. Students themselves may disagree. Students' ideas of what is 'typical' are often linked to the subjects they study.

There may be people in your school/college who have their own ideas about typical Media Studies students. You could think about this idea for yourself. Do *you* have typical representations in your own mind of students doing particular subjects?

Editorial decisions

All media images are the result of decisions made by people in the media. These are **editorial decisions**. Editorial decisions involve deciding what is included and what is left out of a product.

Newspapers, television news, books and many other products which include material gathered from a range of sources usually **credit** – i.e. mention by name – an editor who has made the final decisions about the material they contain. When you work on your own productions as part of your GNVQ course you will have to choose people to work as editors.

Pressure groups

The greatest number of complaints about representation come from people who have suffered for one reason or another as a result of belonging to a particular group, usually a minority. There are laws to prevent discrimination on the grounds of race, sex or disability. These laws cover the work of the media. Some people feel that the laws do not go far enough. Others have particular opinions about the work of the media and want to have their opinions noticed by others.

When many people with similar opinions get together, they can exert influence over the media by forming what is known as a **pressure group**. This group will sometimes try to persuade the media to change the content, style or nature of its products. When groups become well established they often get access to the media and can wield some influence. In many cases, their entire purpose is to have regular access so that their opinions are noticed and taken into account.

The material below is published by The National Viewers' and Listeners' Association. This group campaigns to rid programmes of material which it considers to be offensive, such as gratuitous swearing, violence and sex scenes.

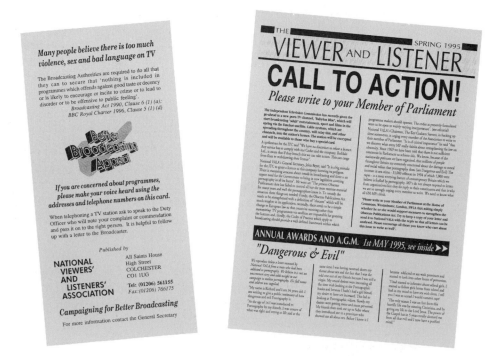

Publicity material for the National Viewers' and Listeners' Association

The Association was founded in the 1960s and has since become very well known. It is an example of a pressure group which influences the media. Pressure groups are not usually interested in making media products or distributing media products themselves. But they are interested in influencing people with decision-making power in the media, such as editors. In some cases, pressure groups get access to the government. They do this because they want to make a difference to government decisions. The government are important in the media because they set out the roles of groups like the Radio Authority and ITC (see page 28).

Access

We have already seen that people with money and influence are likely to dominate the media. This situation is changing in one way because the technology needed to make some products – especially printed material – is now becoming so cheap that most people can manage to produce something. This theme is explored more fully in Chapter 2 when we look at making a print product.

Another change is that people now have much greater access to media companies. This is largely due to the influence of bodies such as the ITC. Often television companies are required under the terms of their licence to allow local groups to have some say and involvement in programme-making.

On the right you will see an extract from a programme listing for BBC Radio Cambridgeshire in September 1996. You can see from these listings that local community groups play a significant part in providing programme input. On Sunday mornings at 8.00 am, 'Something To Think About: Talking Points and Christian Life' requires local community involvement, and the same is true of the programme on disabilities at 4.45 the same day. The station also invites listeners to contribute directly to the regular morning phone-in at 8.35 am on weekdays.

As a local station, Radio Cambridgeshire has to meet the needs of local people. This involves providing access in all of the ways outlined here. But it is also possible for well organised groups to arrange their own access. For example, local groups can send in press releases and news items for inclusion in the regular weekday review between 5.00 and 7.00 pm. Also, school or college open days are featured on programmes such as the 'BBC Cambridgeshire Review'.

In some cases groups and individuals take the process further and find their own way of distributing or disseminating their work. The music press often carries small ads for other printed products. An example is shown below.

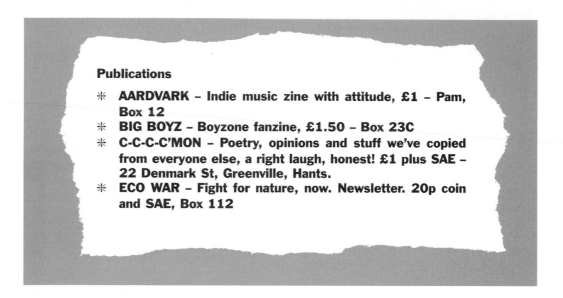

Publications

* **AARDVARK** – Indie music zine with attitude, £1 – Pam, Box 12
* **BIG BOYZ** – Boyzone fanzine, £1.50 – Box 23C
* **C-C-C-C'MON** – Poetry, opinions and stuff we've copied from everyone else, a right laugh, honest! £1 plus SAE – 22 Denmark St, Greenville, Hants.
* **ECO WAR** – Fight for nature, now. Newsletter. 20p coin and SAE, Box 112

Small ads for publications in the music press

None of these magazines really exists, but many like them are printed and sold by mail order. Using mail order is one way of distributing home-produced or self-published work cheaply. More organised methods include setting up a small company. Some people start up shops and sell their own material along with other work. You may find magazines, books, tapes and videos in local shops which have been placed there by agreement with the shop owners, usually on a 'sale or return' basis. Similarly many bands sell their first recordings in local shops after paying for the records, tapes or CDs to be produced with their own money.

It might seem from these examples that it is possible for almost anyone to get access to the media. Whilst this is true, the products with the largest audiences are often those which cost the most to make. This is often because these very expensive products – TV programmes like 'London's Burning' and 'Baywatch' – try to appeal to as wide an audience as possible. Work like the magazines featured in the small adverts above will only appeal to people who share certain opinions. A magazine like *Eco War* would only be read by an audience with strong views about the environment. When people push their own opinions very strongly they run the risk of limiting their audience.

Dissemination

Another issue linked to access is the chance that people have to produce and disseminate media work. **Dissemination** means getting the products out to people. This one word covers all the ways of allowing products to reach people, including broadcasting, selling and delivering. Within the media industries there are a variety of issues which have to be addressed if material is to be disseminated effectively.

The table below shows the main means of dissemination for a selected range of media products:

Product	Means of dissemination
Print – including newspapers, books and periodicals	Loaded electronically onto machines, printed – sometimes in a number of locations, moved by van and lorry to shops, posted to homes, made available electronically, e.g. via the Internet
Audiovisual – including radio and television	Broadcast by mast and received in homes, carried by satellite and or film, cable, made available on videotape, carried by van or lorry to cinema and shown to audiences.

Activity 1.4

1 For each of your chosen media products, identify any issues of representation in them. How are they dealt with?
2 Now identify any issues of access in each media product. Compare them.
3 Describe how each product is transmitted or distributed. Explain the differences between them.

Regulatory bodies and their roles

In Britain there are several bodies which are responsible for controlling the media. These are known as **regulatory bodies**. Regulation means 'rule.' These regulatory bodies check that people in the media abide by certain laws and rules. Some of the laws and rules are imposed from outside the industry – for example, by the government. Others are imposed from inside. In the case of industries which impose their own laws and rules, the regulatory bodies are made up of people appointed by the industry. When an industry organises itself in this way, it is said to be 'self-regulating'.

The regulatory bodies are responsible for seeing that the industries operate within set rules and guidelines. People within the industry are also expected to act responsibly and think about rules and guidelines as they produce work.

An example of legal responsibility is the placing of certificates on videos and films. Once a film or video has been awarded a certificate, cinemas and video shops must ensure that it is only shown to people within a certain age limit. An example of a voluntary responsibility is the placing of a warning sticker on the cover of a book which contains swearing or images of violence. There is no certification system for books and no regulatory body set up to monitor standards in this part of the print industry.

The table on page 30 lists the main regulatory bodies and includes information on their work and responsibilities. It shows that the responsibilities of those controlling the media vary a great deal. There are also differences in the way these bodies get their money. Sometimes they are funded by the media they control. The Advertising Standards Authority and Press Complaints Commission are two examples. Their entry in the grid shows that they are funded from a 'levy.' This means that the industries involved place a tax on themselves. So the advertising industry is taxed to pay for the Advertising Standards Authority.

Sometimes the media are controlled by bodies who act across a number of areas. The Department of National Heritage and the Monopolies and Mergers Commission are two examples. These bodies are government departments. Their work involves keeping a check on particular issues across the country. The Monopolies and Mergers Commission makes sure that industry is organised in a fair way. It acts to prevent individual or companies taking too large a share of any one area of the industry. However, its area of jurisdiction covers not only the media but the full spectrum of commerce and industry in the UK.

Other bodies such as the ITC and Radio Authority have been specifically set up to deal with problems of control and regulation within the media. The aim was to put together a team of people with the right background and skills to make informed decisions. For example, one area regulated by the ITC through its published guidelines is advertising. In controlling and regulating television advertising, the ITC has set up its own panel of experts drawn from education, the advertising industry and elsewhere.

INDEPENDENT TELEVISION COMMISSION

The Independent Television Commission, established under the Broadcasting Act 1990:

- **licenses** commercial television services in the UK except for BBC services and S4C, whether delivered terrestrially or by cable or satellite; local delivery services; public teletext and certain other data services

- **regulates** these services through its published licences, codes and guidelines and has a range of penalties for failure to comply with them

- has a duty to ensure that a **wide range of television services** is available throughout the UK and that, taken as a whole, they are of a high quality and appeal to a variety of tastes and interests

- has a duty to ensure **fair and effective** competition in the provision of these services.

The Chairman, Deputy Chairman and Members of the Commission are appointed by the Secretary of State for National Heritage.
The Commission is supported by permanent staff, under the Chief Executive and by a range of advisory committees.

Mission statement of the Independent Television Commission (ITC)

The imaginary advert shown below is typical of the kind of material that creates work for the regulatory bodies above. The advert may offend some people – especially anyone who has suffered the effects of radiation. Other people may simply think the advert is in poor taste because it compares the taste of a drink with a powerful weapon of war.

The advertisers might defend their advert by saying that no intelligent person would think there was a direct link between the product and a real atomic explosion. They might argue that the image represents power and helps to sell the drink by associating it with a striking image. In a case like this, the regulatory bodies will consider both sides of the argument and eventually try and arrive at an informed verdict. You can put the Atomic Cola advert to the test yourself in Activity 1.5 on page 32.

Protecting consumer interests
You will be aware by now that there are a range of opinions about the media and the work the media produce. One problem faced by all regulatory bodies is that of trying to please many different people. Laws are made to protect the public, but for some, the laws just get in the way. Powerful media barons such as Rupert Murdoch often complain about the laws on ownership. When people own several newspapers they can make huge profits. The Monopolies and Mergers Commission works to make sure that no person or company gets too big a share of the market. This can frustrate people who want to own more newspapers. As we have seen, some industries such as advertising are self-regulating. Many people in these industries think that media 'insiders' will have a better understanding of their problems. But members of public often take a different view, claiming that industries who control themselves cannot be trusted to act against the interests of their own members when problems arise.

The degree of control exercised by regulatory bodies varies from industry to industry. For example, many books contain swearwords and images of sex and violence which would earn a 15 or 18 rating if they appeared in a film or video. But books are not controlled with an age rating in the same way as videos and films. In some cases, books appear with a warning sticker on the cover which explains that the contents 'may offend'.

Media regulatory bodies

Organisation	Role	Established	How financed	Powers	Role outside media
Press Complaints Commission	Monitors standards of 'taste and decency' within the press	1991	From within the industry via a levy	Can recommend, but does not make laws	Advises and informs
Independent Television Commission	Grants franchises and monitors performance of independent television companies	1991	Government funding	Can exercise rules given by government	Advises and informs
Radio Authority	Grants licenses and monitors performance of independent radio stations	1991	Government funding	Can exercise rules given by government	Advises and informs
British Board of Film Classification	Assigns certificates – PG, 18, etc – to films	1913	From film industry	Can exercise rules given by government	Advises and informs
Advertising Standards Authority	Monitors adverts to check they are within law	1962	From levy on advertising space	Recognised by government as best way of monitoring advertising standards, industry is mainly self–regulated	Advises and informs
Department of National Heritage	Monitors range of arts and social projects and makes policy decisions	1992	Public – a government department	Setting policies and making decisions on funding, etc.	Actively involved in the arts, historic buildings and many other areas
Monopolies and Mergers Commission	Monitors industry to ensure that competition remains fair	1948	Publicly funded	Can overturn or approve business deals to ensure fair competition	Operations cover the whole of industry

Regulating electronic media

Some print products like fanzines and material on the Internet (see below) present a real problem for regulatory bodies because it is hard to decide on their legal status. The Internet is accessible all round the world and it is often hard to track down people loading or downloading material. Some material may break the law in one country yet be perfectly legal in another. Regulatory bodies make an effort to keep up with developments in the media, but developments happen so quickly that it is very hard for them to keep pace.

As we have seen in this chapter, the media are always changing under the influence of audiences, legal/regulatory requirements or the advance of technology. The diagram on page 32 provides a simple illustration of the problems and pressures faced by the media.

Case Study: fiction on the Internet

'Elvis had loved James Dean since the first time he sat in the stalls and watched the classic East of Eden. *Dean's death in 1955 had left Elvis devastated. When Elvis died in 1977 the first person he wanted to meet on the other side was Jimmy. As the pair faced each other, Elvis gazed into Jimmy' eyes. "I've waited for this moment for so long," he said...*

Slash fiction is the name given to a particular kind of story which has recently begun to appear on the Internet. The name comes from the writers' practice of inserting a slash – / – between the names of characters in the stories.

Slash fiction typically features romantic encounters between famous media characters. So, for example, one notorious story dealt with a gay affair between the cartoon characters Betty Rubble and Wilma Flintstone!

Slash fiction has found an audience on the Internet. Some simply find it funny while others see it as important and claim that it tells us about the way we see popular characters. Television and film stars are often presented to us as romantic and attractive. Slash fiction deals with these qualities. In a recent survey, one collector of slash fiction actually lost count of the number of romantic stories featuring major stars like Marilyn Monroe and James Dean.

Slash fiction and the 'media triangle'

Because slash fiction is created by devoted fans letting their imaginations run riot, we can see that the work is being pulled towards the 'audience' point of the media control triangle (opposite). The Internet has made this possible. We can see from this that the 'technology' point of the control triangle is also involved in creating slash fiction.

The authors can publish their work on the Internet without much fear of prosecution – and there is a demand for it. However, the use of real people and copyrighted characters such as Betty Rubble and Wilma Flintstone means that slash fiction often breaks the law. The people who made the cartoons and own copyright in the characters would probably sue if slash fiction appeared in a major newspaper. Because the material exists in an area that is hard to regulate, the legal control has effectively been pulled away by audience demand and technology.

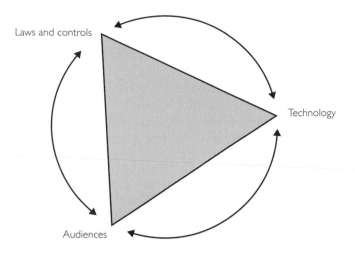

The regulating bodies all fit on the 'Laws and controls' point of the triangle. You can see from the triangle that control is pulled away from these bodies by audience demand and technology.

Activity 1.5

1 Write a fact sheet describing the roles and responsibilities of the different media regulators.
2 Present your work to the rest of the class.

Review questions

1 Explain why specialised audiences are more likely to buy 'national' media products.
2 Briefly explain one major source of revenue for local media products.
3 List two media regulatory bodies who enforce a 'voluntary' code.
4 What advantage is there in an industry regulating itself?
5 Why do the media tend to use the same kinds of representation over and over again?
6 Name a 'pressure group' and describe what it does.

Element 1.2 Explore consumption of local and national media

Audience research

Many media products are aimed at a whole range of audiences. One important part of linking audiences and products is **research**. Most large media companies carry out regular research to check on the viewing, listening and buying habits of the public.

All good research needs a clear **objective**. The word 'objective' has two meanings. It can refer to the purpose or aim of a piece of work. It can also mean 'fair' and 'not taking a particular side in an argument'. Common **objectives** of media research are outlined below.

1 **Commercial research** usually asks about the income of an audience, how they spend it, what decisions they make in spending the money, how much and how little they are prepared to spend and any factors that might affect their income. The aim is to predict likely revenue from a media product. Commercial research often tries to profile or describe the characteristics of audiences. The eventual aim may be to target these people with advertising.

2 **Social research** often tries to explain the choices of an audience. It looks at the effect of media products on audiences and the reasons for audience interest. This research often deals with issues such as the link between violence in the media and violence in real life.

Look at the following situations. Which do you think are commercial research and which are social research?

- A film company is trying to build up an idea of the income of film-goers. Their final aim is to sell T–shirts and other souvenirs to these people at a competitive price
- Children in school playgrounds are copying a fight scene from a soft drink advert. A local university is trying to explain this through research
- The producers of a Channel 4 comedy show want a bigger audience and more advertising money. They research into viewers for popular comedies on ITV and BBC1. They want to identify reasons for the popularity of ITV and BBC1 shows and use this information to make their own show more popular
- A teenage boy has been depressed and abusive since seeing a blockbuster war movie. Researchers spend a week with him trying to find any link to the film.

If you look back at some of the examples earlier in this chapter you can see how different types of research might be used. A cable and satellite channel, for example, will be very interested in building up a detailed audience profile. They need to know as much as possible about the age, income and buying habits of their viewers. This information can then be presented to possible advertisers. Advertisers are more likely to spend money with the channel if they can guarantee that their adverts will reach the right market. This research would therefore be commercial.

A newsletter such as *Denton News* (see page 20) is much more interested in the opinions of people in a particular area. The people behind this newsletter are social workers and their aim is to improve social conditions locally. They are likely to conduct research, possibly by talking to residents about their opinions of the stories and features in *Denton News*. Decisions on changes to *Denton News* will be made after the publishers have gathered information on the way that people feel about the publication. This is therefore social research.

Trends in consumption

Audience research can be used to explain trends in media consumption. 'Consumption' means to consume or use something. A 'trend' is a direction in which something might go, or a pattern that can be observed (see page 2). It is vital for media producers to understand trends in consumption because it allows them to get the right products onto the market.

Advertisements need to keep pace with changing social trends

The boom in media products based on UFOs and the paranormal which we looked at earlier was almost certainly partly based on audience research. However, some magazines and publishers were aware of this growing trend before it became obvious. They gained their knowledge from other sources. They had seen increasingly large crowds at UFO conventions, material on the Internet, fanzines being produced and a growth in the number of groups researching the paranormal. This growth of interest is an example of a recent trend in media consumption.

Many trends change slowly and in some cases the changes are not particularly obvious. 'Coronation Street' is the longest-running television soap opera in the world. Over the years there have been many changes of cast, but the essential concept of concentrating on the everyday lives of 'ordinary' people has stayed more or less the same. In Britain 'Coronation Street' can be said to have started a trend because its success inspired other soap operas.

The demand from audiences often changes the type of work produced. The magazine *One-Eyed Jack* was launched in 1997. The intention was to reach people with an interest in 'street culture' by covering football, motorbikes, music and other material likely to appeal to a young audience. The magazine was produced by a publishing company in Scotland which already published books on youth gangs and music. Their work in reprinting books about skinheads and other material about music and gangs allowed them to see that there was an audience for this material. By producing the magazine they hoped to meet the needs of the audience and also promote their existing books.

The impact of electronic media

Interactive media products are those which react to some kind of response from the reader or user. Recent examples are multimedia encyclopaedias which allow users to ask questions, undertake searches, view pictures and video clips and activate short animations. The choice of which questions to ask and which areas to explore is made entirely by the user. Like a software program or a computer game, the interactive product responds to the user's commands.

The ability of computers to store and process information has had a big effect on print and information-based media and has led to many exciting developments. Computers have also made the process of magazine production and book publishing much cheaper. This has allowed quality work to be aimed at small audiences. The magazine *UFO Reality* featured earlier was selling around 20,000 copies in 1996. Twenty years ago, a sale of 20,000 would have meant cheap paper and low production quality for a magazine. Despite its limited circulation, *UFO Reality* is printed in colour on good-quality glossy paper.

With computer technology driving down production costs there has been a rise in special interest media. This is because the chances of making a profit from a product aimed at a small interest group – like people with an interest in UFOs – has been increasing for years. Media such as video and audio recording are also getting cheaper because computers have signifcantly reduced the costs of expensive tasks such as editing. This has meant that special interest groups now often have a number of different products to choose from.

This also applies to broadcast media such as radio and television where the number of channels available is increasing rapidly. Challenge TV featured earlier in this chapter is a good example. Their distribution is via high-quality fibre optic cables which are now being laid all over the country. Thirty years ago, cable television depended on copper cables which carried much less information. The extent of the cable network and the amount of information it can carry will continue to expand the number of cable channels and services into the future. This expansion of media has had an effect on both local and national material. There are more local magazines, videos and books available now than at any time in the past. The prediction is that this figure will keep rising.

Activity 1.6

1 Choose ONE media product to study in depth. A local radio station or a local newspaper may be willing to help you. Explain the organisation's objectives in doing audience research – the objectives should be both commercial and social.
2 Study some recent audience research data, making sure that it shows a clear trend in consumption. (If there is no trend, choose another media product for this part.) Identify reasons for the trend(s) and write a brief report to explain it/them.

Consumer profiles

This chapter has already shown that people make choices about media use. The arguments and media debates about representation are also arguments about choice. Media research tries to gather and understand opinions and choices. As we have seen, this research can be used to help sell a product or help the producers understand more about the audience for their product. When researchers gather information about a particular group within an audience they are said to be generating a **profile** of that group.

The most common reason for generating a profile is to allow the producers to form a clear picture of their audience. The results form what is known as a **consumer profile**. Most consumer profiles include the following information about the target audience:

- Age
- Income
- Occupation
- Sex
- Ethnic background
- Opinions held
- Geographical location

Consider the following examples:

Name:	Ben Grover	Nick Hurwood
Age	18	21
Weekly income	£50–70	£100
Home	Dartford, Kent	Newark on Trent, Staffs.
Occupation	Student, club DJ Freelance radio and TV presenter	Student, photographic quality control – Barman – Mobile disco
Ethnic background	White Caucasian	White Caucasian
Hobbies	Clubbing, socialising	Pubs, socialising, Rock music, paranormal study and investigation

In these examples there are some similarities between the two people featured. They are from the same ethnic group and share some similar interests and work. To some people, Ben and Nick would be classed in the same group – for example 'Young males with some disposable income'. In other areas their interests and ideas are very different. Nick's interest in the paranormal would identify him as a potential reader of *UFO Reality*. Here, he would be linked with people much older and of widely different background, occupation and income.

One problem with consumer profiles is that they tend to put audiences into 'pigeonholes'. In other words, they assume that people of a similar age, background etc, will automatically share the same media interests. In fact we all know from our own experience that people of a similar age often have very different ideas about some subjects. One way to get around this problem is by making a more detailed in-depth study. But even broad categories such as age, sex and place of residence can help build up a useful picture of the audience for a particular media product.

For example, one of the commonest complaints about TV broadcasting is that too many programmes are set in the South of England and that other parts of the country are ignored. However, the South of England is the most densely populated part of the country. Because there are so many people in this area it is not surprising that more magazines, videos and other media products are purchased there than anywhere else. People involved in the media are keen to get the largest possible audience and if more people live in the South than anywhere else, it makes sense to aim products at this sector of the population.

Television companies are frequently accused of regional bias

It is therefore possible to make a rough guess that if a product – say, a videotape – dealt with a topic related to the South of England, it might make a profit. This kind of categorisation is very basic, but it might still be enough to help a product to become successful. The aim of most research and profiling is therefore to get an accurate picture of the target audience in order to meet audience demand. Some people question how good the media are at giving their audiences what they want. There is a temptation for the media to play safe. They know that certain formulas have worked well in the past and the danger is that by changing them they would drive audiences away.

When the media do similar things time and time again, we say they are following a **convention**.

Methods of collecting and interpreting audience data

When people carry out research into the media they can use different approaches or methods. A research method is a way of carrying out work. Different methods are used because each method gets certain types of result. The people carrying out research use the best methods to get the answers they want. It is possible to split the types of research into two groups:

1 Qualitative research

Qualitative information is about what people think or feel about something. It is expressed in words, feelings and impressions, rather than numbers.

For example, think of the way people feel about the different writing styles, story lengths and layout of their favourite paper. All these things contribute to the pleasure of reading. In some cases the differences can come down to individual words or items of presentation. Tabloids like the *Sun* often present their stories through a combination of pictures, short, punchy sentences and a catchy headline. This allows readers to construct instant pictures in their own minds. The value of short, punchy sentences is that they are easily understood and lend themselves to being passed around and read aloud if needed. One of the most famous *Sun* headlines of all time appeared in 1986:

The story concerned the antics of a well-known comedian. The headline attracted so much attention that the front page was featured on T-shirts for years afterwards. That day's issue sold exceptionally well. The headline is still famous years after it first appeared.

Suppose for a moment that we commissioned a qualitative survey of readers' reactions to the Freddie Starr headline. The results might be as follows:

- **Feelings** – People were shocked, stunned and amazed.There was a general feeling of disbelief which made people want to read the story and find out the truth. (In fact, no hamster had been eaten and the story was just a joke)
- **Preferences** – Many people like entertaining and amazing stories. They like to gossip, and the odd things that people do provide material for these discussions. Celebrities like Freddie Starr often provide material which can be discussed in this way
- **Opinions** – The actions suggested in the headline provoked people to form an opinion. Some people were revolted; others found it funny.

The paper was trying to provide a story that would grab attention and raise the profile of the paper. The fact that the story became so famous indicates that the audience found a range of appealing qualities within the headline. Qualitative research explores these links between media audiences and the features – or qualities – they value in products. Methods include discussion groups, case studies looking at the lives of individual members of an audience and observations of audience behaviour.

2   Quantitative research

Quantitative research is based on statistics and on aspects of the media which can be counted or quantified. It seeks to compare figures and is often used to provide information on the most popular or best-selling products.

Charts and tables which record levels of sales for media products are quantitative. Critical work which ranks media work as 'better' or 'worse' on grounds of content is qualitative.

Consider the following example.

In a 1997 survey, the market research organisation MORI investigated the features that young people liked best about newspapers. They compared the answers of the young people with the answers of a group of older people. For the purposes of the survey, 'young people' were considered to be those between the ages of 15 and 24. Older people were over 24. In terms of their favourite items in papers, young people reported the following main topics of interest. The percentages for young's peoples interest are followed by those of the older group.

	Young people	**Older**
TV and radio listings	48%	41%
Sports reporting	42%	30%
Film reviews	41%	25%
Music reviews	40%	20%
Job adverts	40%	24%

These were the only five topics on which over 40% of young people agreed. The quantitative information – shown here as percentages – tells us that leisure in the form of sport, music, films and television is the most important area of interest for young people. It also shows that young people use papers as a source of job information.

In some cases the figures for older readers are very different.

Explaining these differences would involve some understanding of the way that the different audiences measure quality in a newspaper.

Some conclusions which people may draw from this quantitative data include the following:

- Young people are more likely to read TV and radio listings in newspapers than over 24s
- Young people are more likely to read job adverts in newspapers than the over 24s

There is some statistical evidence to back up these conclusions. Newspaper publishers could use this information to help in planning the contents of their papers. However, the conclusions also show the limits of quantitative research. Quantitative information records statistics but does not explain them. Good research requires the researchers to have a clear idea of what they *want* to find out. It needs good planning and definite ideas about the audience being researched, the reasons for the research and the strengths and weaknesses of the results

Designing a questionnaire

One popular method of gathering market information is through a questionnaire. Questionnaires are often used during the early stages of developing a product. This is vital if the product is to develop in a way which will meet the needs of its target audience.

A questionnaire is simply a structured sequence of questions designed to draw out facts and opinions from the people questioned. The people questioned can be either targeted (e.g. females in their twenties with children) or randomly selected. It all depends on the purpose of the questionnaire and what information is being sought. The questionnaire can either be completed by the person being questioned, or used as the basis for an interview, in which case the interviewer asks the questions and writes in the respondent's answers

Questionnaires can be devised and carried out by the company producing the product, or carried out on a contract basis by a market research agency.

There are four main purposes of a questionnaire:

1 To provide a standard form on which facts, comments and attitudes can be written down
2 To provide a structure to the survey
3 To draw out accurate information from an audience
4 To allow the results to be counted and analysed easily

The first point is obvious – using a standard form clearly makes it easier to process the results or data afterwards.

The second and third points relate to the questions being asked. The questions must be written down in a logical way so that one leads logically to the next. Not only does this help the person answering the questions, but it provides a structure for the survey to follow. More will be said about the questions later.

The fourth purpose of a questionnaire is particularly important if large numbers of people are involved. A coding system is often used for the answers, which can then be analysed very quickly by computer. Spreadsheets and market research software are available for this task. However, it does require the audience to follow instructions carefully when filling in their answers. For example, if the computer can only read black ink, using an HB pencil instead may mean their responses are wasted.

Designing your own questionnaire

Designing a questionnaire is not as easy as it sounds. It is important to be clear in your own mind what you want to find out. A rough draft must be written first and tested on other people as it is easy to miss out questions, put them in the wrong order or make them too complicated. Usually a questionnaire will have three edits before reaching its final form.

When designing a questionnaire it is worth bearing in mind the following points:

1 What are you trying to find out? What is the purpose of the questionnaire?
2 How will you carry out the questionnaire? How many people will you ask? Who will you ask? Where will you ask them? Who will fill in the answers?
3 How will you introduce the questionnaire? For example, it may be necessary to explain why the survey is being carried out and to reassure the audience that information will be confidential.
4 What 'official' information is needed? The respondent's name? Address? Age? Date? This is known as 'boiler plate' information.
5 Will you use closed or open-ended questions, or a combination (see below)?
6 Do your questions flow easily? Are they in a logical sequence?
7 When thinking of the questions, consider what possible answers you might expect to get. This will help you to keep the order logical.
8 Consider the visual appearance or layout of the page(s). Is it clear and easy to read? How much white space is there? Is the typeface big enough to read? Is there enough space for answers to open-ended questions? Try and stick to a standard format in your design. For example, number questions 1, 2, 3, etc., rather than mixing 1, 2, 3 with A, B, C, etc.
9 How will you analyse the results? By hand? By computer? How will you present the results?
10 If someone else is to carry out this questionnaire for you, you will need to give them instructions.

Writing the questions

A questionnaire needs to be written with the target audience in mind. Questions for teenagers will be phrased differently from those aimed at older people. When writing the questions, make sure you avoid:

● Biased questions, e.g. "Would you agree that fox-hunting is a disgusting sport?"
● Long, complicated questions – or the reader will give up!

- Jargon or technical words which people may not understand
- Uncommon or complicated words which people may not understand
- Ambiguous words like 'usually' and 'frequently' – how often is 'frequently'?
- Hypothetical questions, e.g. "If you were very rich, would you buy this every week...?"
- Questions that overlap, e.g. "Please tick your age group: 18–25, 25–30..." – where do you tick if you are 25?

Closed and open questions

The type of questions used in questionnaires fall into two categories: closed and open-ended.

Closed questions are particularly useful when carrying out very large surveys as they involve people choosing from a series of answers. This way, the results are much easier to calculate because the answers are simply counted up.

An example of a closed question might be:

```
Q.3  Look at page 10 of the magazine which describes 'events being held
     in college this term.' How useful did you find it?

     ❏   Extremely useful
     ❏   Very useful
     ❏   Not particularly useful
     ❏   No use at all
```

An open-ended question is the opposite of this. It allows the audience to provide their own answer to a question rather than choosing from those given. An example might be:

```
Q.3  Look at page 10 of the magazine which describes 'events being held
     in college this term.' How useful did you find it?

     _____

     _____
```

Clearly answers to open-ended questions involve a lot more time and thought.

A questionnaire can contain a combination of closed and open-ended questions. Closed questions limit the response a person can give, so sometimes it is worth following them up with an open-ended question to help the respondent explain or expand on an answer. They can also be optional, so people do not feel they have to write something.

It is also possible to add 'other' as a tick-box response, then provide a space for an answer to be filled in. For example:

```
Q.3  If you read a newspaper where would you buy it?

     ❏   Supermarket
     ❏   Delivered to home
     ❏   Newsagent
     ❏   Other (please provide details)

     _____
```

Activity 1.7

1 Begin to build up a consumer profile for the media products you are studying. Use questionnaires and interviews to find out the profile of the target audiences. Cover socio-economic group, age, ethnic background and gender. Your research should have both commercial and social objectives.

2 Keep a log of your progress – from planning the questionnaires and interviews to actually using them and sorting out the replies. Write a brief report on which methods were most successful in producing data. Explain your commercial and social objectives. Keep samples of your questionnaires and research data with the report.

Models of audience behaviour

The different research work carried out in the media has led people to form a number of different opinions about audience behaviour. Some researchers have tried to express these ideas in the form of 'models'. A model is a design or a device that tries to imitate something larger and more complicated. People often use models to help them understand or predict the way things or people behave. Among various models of audience behaviour, two contrasting types are:

- **The 'hypodermic' model** This model sees the audience for the media as being passive, i.e. quiet or inactive. It is so-called because the media are seen as 'injecting' material into audiences that influences their behaviour in the same way as a drug.
- **The 'uses and gratifications' model** This suggests that audiences are active and exercise choice in the way they react to the media. It argues that particular features of media products meet particular needs in the audience.

These models exist because experts who study the media each claim they can see evidence to support their view. Some of this evidence is listed below:

1 Evidence supporting 'hypodermic' model:

- Mass panic which followed radio broadcast of 'War of the Worlds' (see page 197)
- Acts of violence seemingly influenced by violent films
- Major advertising campaigns leading to increased sales of a product

2 Evidence supporting 'uses and gratifications' model:

- Person buying DIY magazine and using it selectively to help in home improvements
- Person compiling fanzine from stolen items clipped from other magazines
- Person making tape of favourite records off the radio

As you can see, data from questionnaires could support either one of these theories. For example, if your findings showed that a good advertising campaign has pushed people into buying a drink like Pepsi Cola, you will have evidence to support the 'hypodermic' model. Alternatively, you may find people who have their own needs in terms of buying a product. For example, serious runners may value the comfort of a particular training shoe. Most students who carry out research like this do not reach a definite conclusion either way. However, they do often gain a better understanding of the way that evidence can be gathered to support both models of behaviour.

Activity 1.8

1 Choose THREE different media products, including the one studied so far. Do some research to enable you to compare the models of audience behaviour for the three products.
2 Write down your findings as a separate report. Where possible, remember to include relevant extracts from each product in your file.

Media influence

Whatever the differences between the two models of behaviour explored above, both clearly suggest that the media can play an important role in influencing the way that people behave. Many people have a practical interest in this topic – often because they want to harness the power of the media for their own ends. Your GNVQ course also demands that YOU develop some understanding about the influence of the media.

The table below lists some of the individuals and organisations with an interest in exploring the power and influence of the media. It is not a comprehensive list because the subject is a complex one and new research and changing events keep adding to our understanding all the time.

Groups interested in the influence of the media

Group	Example	Why interested
People in the media	Producers, proprietors	Want to reach the largest possible audience and make the most impact possible.
Media pressure groups	National Viewers and Listeners Association	Have their own views, want evidence to support these views and want influence on media content and production.
Organised groups in society	Church groups, political parties	Influence of the media may overlap with some of their work and interests. May give them useful information for own work.
General public		Represent audience for media products. Discussions on influence of the media are really discussions about the way this group behave.
Media Studies students		Need good understanding of influence of the media. Require information for future study and careers.

The debate about the influence of the media is wide-ranging. Issues which are often discussed in newspapers and on television include:

- **Media violence** – Do TV and film 'reflect' violence in real life or incite it?
- **Images of women** – Are 'Page Three'-style pin-ups simply fun, or do they encourage men to regard women as sex objects?
- **Southern bias** – Does the concentration of media activity in the South of England lead to too much coverage of London and the area around it?

Activity 1.9

1 Suggest TWO current debates on the influence of the media, for discussion in class. Your teacher will select two from those suggested, and organise discussions.

2 First, research the topics chosen for debate, then take part yourself – letting others have their say as well! Make notes during the discussion, and afterwards write a report for your file. Your report should cover the class discussion, as well as your research findings.

Review questions

1 In audience research what is an objective?
2 What are the weaknesses of quantitative research?
3 Arguments about the effect of the media are often called media d_____.
4 Why is the hypodermic model of audience behaviour so-called?
5 List four areas of information usually found in a consumer profile.
6 Why are consumer profiles so important to people making media products?

Element 1.3 Investigate developments and opportunities in the media industries

Changes and developments in the media industries

Each area of the media offers jobs to people with the right skills, qualifications and ideas. In the media industry there are particular patterns in the way people are employed. Most industries have such patterns. For example, the hotel and catering industry tends to offer more jobs during the summer holidays. The way an industry takes on people and offers jobs is known as an **employment pattern**. As well as changing seasonally, these employment patterns also change over longer periods – for example, as a result of factors such as computerisation.

Employment trends in the media industry

Many people keep a check on the figures for employment within the media. Some trade unions are interested in the numbers of people employed in the media and their job roles and responsibilities. There are also organisations such as the Office for National Statistics which keep an overall check on employment patterns throughout the country.

In a moment we will be looking at some figures for employment in the media prepared by the Office of National Statistics. But first, it is important to be aware of some general points. Statistical information can be useful, and your media research work for the GNVQ course asks you to complete some work based on numbers. But statistics on their own can sometimes be misleading. There may be reasons behind statistics that are not obvious.

	Newspaper printing and publishing	Film production, distribution and exhibition	
1981	96,700	21,000	
1993	75,600	29,800	Source: *Labour Market Trends*

Employment in UK media industries, November 1981 and September 1993

As you can see, the total number of people in newspaper publishing and printing in 1993 was 75,600. However, of those 75,600, we also know that only 11,800 were actually involved in printing. This suggests that computers took many jobs away. In fact, the number of publications classed as newspapers in this country rose during the same period. This suggests that many more newspapers are being run by a smaller number of staff.

The figures also show that the film and video industry grew from 1981 to 1993. This growth was supported by many people who bought video recorders and VHS tapes. The 1993 figure can be broken down further as follows:

1993	Film production, distribution and exhibition
Film and video production	11,200
Film and video distribution	7,800
Film projection	10,800

The 1981 figure was not divided in this way. This second figure shows that the people gathering statistics had to make changes to the jobs they list in these figures. This is because new kinds of jobs were created. In 1981 the video industry in this country was almost non-existent. Today there are many people who work completely in video production – for example, making pop videos.

These statistics are typical of the kind of information that is available on work in the media. They provide useful information, but it is dangerous to read too much into it. The explanations given above are understood to be true but they may not give the whole story.

For example, trade with Europe became easier between 1981 and 1993. It is possible that jobs were created in this country to make video and television work for people overseas. British satellite and cable programmes – such as the output of MTV – are seen around the world. To be certain about this point we would need statistics for media employment across Europe. At the moment these statistics are not available in exactly the same form as the British information.

Statistical information can only tell us so much. Despite this, there are some other important points about employment in the media industries which can be noted:

1 Part-time employment/short-term contracts

In 1981 no statistics were available for people involved in 'Artistic and literary creation.' By 1993, there were 22,400 people in this category, almost all of them – writers, designers, etc. – employed on short-term or self-employed contracts.

The media now employ many people on this basis, and the development of computers has allowed many small companies – some of them based around the work of one person – to start up. This is a growing trend in media work.

2 Gender patterns in media employment

The number of men working in the media has fallen since 1981 and the number of women has risen. There are still more men than women employed in the media but the gap is closing.

There are many reasons for this. One major reason is the decline in 'skilled trades' like printing which traditionally employed men. The new creative jobs tend to employ people of both sexes. Since the 1970s there have been legal moves to promote equal opportunities and prevent discrimination on grounds of sex. The effect of the laws on sexual equality took time to appear in statistics, because industries which mainly employed men tended to keep them. It was therefore some time before new employees – taken on after the changes in the law – made up a significant part of the workforce.

Media employment by gender

| | 1981 | | 1993 | |
	Men	Women	Men	Women
Full time	265,100	111,600	177,600	129,400
Part time	19,200	44,400	50,800	41,800
Total	284,300	156,000	228,400	171,200

Careers in the media

We have seen so far in this chapter that the media is a fast-changing industry. This means changes both in the type of careers on offer and the way that people are employed. Despite these changes, many of the well-known careers like journalism are still available and rely on the same essential skills as ever.

The statistics we have looked at give some clear pointers. The numbers employed in most creative media areas are either holding steady or rising. There are job opportunities for both sexes. Some areas of the media are still expanding – so much so that the people who compile the statistics are starting to count areas like video production as separate areas of employment.

But these figures about current employment miss some important changes and developments in the recent past. We will briefly examine two important changes.

- **Bi-media and multi-skilling** News reporters for big organisations like the BBC are often required to use 'bi-media' skills. This means, in effect, that they submit a single report which is used on both radio and television. Sound recordists and other such staff now have to be 'multi-skilled'. This means that they have to know the equipment and working practices used in more than one area of their industry. Multi-skilled staff and the use of multi-media equipment (including PCs) will continue to change the working practices of the media well into the future.
- **Increase in the numbers of self-employed** These are people who work for themselves and sell their work to bigger companies. Such work is called

Case Study: careers in the media

Myra Wilson

Job Background

Just set up own media agency
Left school with few qualifications, several jobs incl. co-managing shoe shop. Returned to college to complete Media diploma. Made some freelance contacts at this stage and decided to set up agency when course finished.

Impact of new technology

Small-scale agencies touting for business in a range of media are fairly new. Myra's success depends on skills gained at college and contacts to be made in work. Big expansion of small-scale media makes such an agency a possibility. Twenty years ago such opportunities didn't exist for college leavers.

Justin Williams

Job Background

Local newspaper reporter
A levels, University degree, journalistic training

Current career

Plans to stay within journalism and work his way up through the ranks. Career structure makes this a possibility with future jobs as sub-editor and editor being the obvious moves

Impact of new technology

Has allowed many parts of the job to be completed more quickly. Computer technology lets Justin file copy directly into paper, databases hold information for future use. In the past other people did similar jobs with less help from technology. Multimedia technology is likely to offer more chances to file good stories for a range of different media in the future.

'freelance' work. We will see later in this section that there has been a great increase in this small-scale and independent area of the media. We have already seen that areas like magazine production have expanded with the introduction of new technology.

- Another important change is that many more people than before are working on **short-term contracts**. Two examples of people working in the media on short-term contracts are shown on page 47. Each is interested in writing professionally, but each is taking a different route into this career.

The importance of 'transferable skills'

The changes in media employment mean that there is more demand than ever for people to have 'transferable skills'. These are skills that will be useful in a range of jobs and situations. Myra Wilson's working life (see Case Study) will depend entirely on how well she uses and develops the kind of transferable skills she developed on her media course. Your GNVQ course is aiming to give you the same kind of skills.

Examples of useful transferable skills are:
- Coming up with new ideas for products
- Negotiating with people over money, contracts, etc.
- Computer skills
- Knowledge of how to compile and use a database
- Motivating other people
- Audience research skills

Developments in technology and products

As well as changing the nature of jobs in the media, new and more powerful technology has changed the products themselves. There have been several important changes. These concern:
- The kind of products available
- The amount of products available

Multimedia products

The success of future media ventures will depend greatly on the use of multi-media technology. The career of Myra Wilson (see Case Study, page 47) is evidence of this. She calls her operation a 'media agency'. An 'agency' is an organisation that provides a service. The best known examples of agencies in the media are press agencies which gather stories and then sell them to outlets like newspapers and television stations. Myra's agency is typical of a new type of operation that has developed along with computer technology. It aims to sell original ideas to small companies. For example, it may sell a programme idea to L!ve TV which is part of the Mirror Group. Other ideas might be sold to radio, newspapers and magazines.

Myra's career will depend on her being able to develop ideas and make contacts. Her ability to use multimedia technology will allow her to present these ideas in different forms. So, for example, the soundtrack of a video could be edited by computer into a radio feature. The technology will allow Myra to develop presentable ideas quickly and change them to meet deadlines. She will be able to add material from computer discs and this will allow her to work with other people when required.

The falling costs of production and the growing number of media outlets with a specialised audience are already encouraging people with ideas and enthusiasm to get involved in the media and take whatever chances they can to build up a portfolio of work. This phenomenon is so new that there is no one term to describe all the small-scale organisations involved, although 'media agency' is one which is used.

In a moment we will briefly consider some examples of these, but first there is an important point which supports all of these examples. We should remember that media products are all made up of *information*. This can be stored in a number of ways:

- **Visually** – for example, as an image on film
- **Digitally** – for example, as computer information which can be decoded
- **Magnetically** – for example, video and audio recordings on tape

Computers now allow the storage of massive amounts of information in a small space. Most changes brought about in recent years are linked to the storage of information. There are developments taking place at the moment which will allow most media work to be computer-generated.

Multimedia products like computer games with video clips and music are the direct result of new technology. The development of new products has led to some confusion over classifying types of products and types of job. Myra Wilson and her media agency provide an example of this. At various times in her work, Myra may be a writer for audiovisual products or print products. If she gained a contract producing entries for a CD-ROM encyclopaedia she might find herself producing text, video clips and sound effects – all for one entry. The final product would be hard to classify. In the past, encyclopedias were definitely 'print' products. These days, digitally created encyclopedias include text material but they also contain audiovisual work.

Multimedia technology is transforming the way information is processed and stored

Cheaper production in most media has led to the availability of a wider range of products. Your research into publications should have shown this to be true. One obvious way to prove it is to list all the products available about your local area. The list will almost certainly include videos, books, magazines, local television programmes and a wide range of other material. There has been a rapid growth in the amount of media material about local areas in the last few years. Interestingly, this growth has usually taken place without a very big corresponding increase in the size of the local population.

Digital design and editing

As we explained above, the ease with which information can now be processed and stored has led to a dramatic increase in the number of information-based products. At the same time, the power of computers in areas like design and editing has allowed products aimed at specialist markets – like *UFO Reality* magazine – to offer very high standards of production.

Look at the material from the book *Rock's Follies* on page 51. This book was given away free with *Maxim* magazine. The contents of the book provide a good example of the way that developments in technology have changed media products. This book contained information on famous mistakes and unusual incidents in the history of rock music, but although the content was intriguing, none of it was new. Because the information in it was stored on existing databases it could be quickly accessed and converted into book format, using digital design and editing processes. Production was quick and efficient, and costs were kept to a minimum, so the book could be given away free to readers.

An increasing number of media products, books, videos, etc. are being compiled in this way. Even when they are sold cheaply, their low production costs mean that it is possible to make a profit. If you visit a large newsagent you will find many magazines which give away free media products like CDs, books and computer discs. Twenty years ago such free gifts were rare because the cost of producing them was very high.

Future employment patterns in the media

It is hard to forecast future employment in the media. The best we can do is to use known facts to make an educated guess. However most experts believe that future employment will follow these patterns:

- The media will want people with skills that will allow them to work in a number of areas
- People with multimedia skills will be easier to employ than those with skills limited to one area
- There will be a continued expansion of short-term and freelance work. There will be more people – like Myra Wilson – setting up small-scale firms
- The expansion of work is likely to be concentrated in the areas of production and dissemination

Despite the expansion in the media, there are some jobs which are under threat. People who are skilled in production are fast disappearing, particularly in the printing industry. In the past, newspapers and magazines were printed by large numbers of people laying out pages with metal blocks of type. The introduction of computer technology has largely done away with such jobs. Now a few people using computers and print machines can handle the print run for a large magazine.

Case Study: incentive publishing

Rock's Follies was first published in 1996 as a give-away book mounted on the cover of *Maxim* magazine. The aims was to provide an attractive 'extra' item for readers.

Most of the material in the book had been collected by music journalists over many years and stored on electronic databases. Use of digital design and editing processes meant that the information could quickly and easily be converted into book form. The product could therefore be offered free to readers in order to encourage sales.

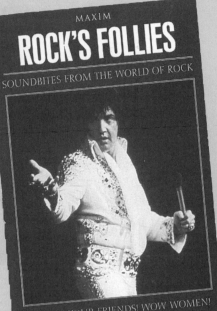

Cover and sample page of the 'give-away' fact book Rock's Follies

MAXIM
ROCK'S FOLLIES
SOUNDBITES FROM THE WORLD OF ROCK

IMPRESS YOUR FRIENDS! WOW WOMEN!
A STUPENDOUS COLLECTION OF ROCK 'N' ROLL INFOMANIA

FOR PEOPLE WHO LIKE LISTS

ROCK'S FOLLIES
PERFORMERS AT LIVE AID

Bob Geldof and his Band Aid organisation staged the Live Aid concerts, and their international broadcast, as a benefit for relief of famine in Ethiopia. The events, together with the Band Aid record, 'Do They Know It's Christmas?' and related efforts, raised more than $10 million for hunger relief. Unfortunately, the sub-Saharan region of Africa fell back into famine in less than a decade.

LONDON, WEMBLEY STADIUM
1. Status Quo
2. Style Council
3. Ultravox
4. Boomtown Rats and Adam Ant
5. Spandau Ballet
6. Elvis Costello
7. Nik Kershaw
8. Sade
9. Sting, Phil Collins and Julian Lennon. (Collins then jumped on Concorde and raced to Philadelphia, appearing at both shows)
10. Howard Jones
11. Bryan Ferry
12. U2
13. Dire Straits
14. Queen
15. David Bowie
16. The Who
17. Elton John and Wham!
18. Wembley Finale: Freddie Mercury and Brian May (Queen), Paul McCartney, Tour Ensemble

PHILADELPHIA, KENNEDY STADIUM
1. Tom Petty and the Heartbreakers
2. Kenny Loggins

3. The Cars
4. Neil Young
5. Power Station
6. Phil Collins, Robert Plant, John Paul Jones and Jimmy Page (a version of Led Zeppelin)
7. Duran Duran
8. Madonna
9. Rod Stewart
10. Patti Labelle
11. Hall and Oates
12. The Temptations
13. Mick Jagger
14. The Beach Boys
15. Tina Turner
16. Judas Priest
17. Simple Minds
18. Pretenders
19. Santana and Pat Metheny
20. The Thompson Twins and Nile Rodgers
21. Teddy Pendergrass
22. Billy Ocean
23. Paul Young
24. Joan Baez
25. Run D.M.C.
26. Bob Dylan
27. U.S. Ensemble Finale including Keith Richards

MAXIM 44 ROCK'S FOLLIES

The Rank Xerox DocuTech copying machine

The machine in the photograph above is the Rank Xerox DocuTech. This will print small numbers of copies of large items like books. Technology like this allows companies to make a profit from very small numbers of sales. This machine, and others currently in development, are totally changing the **economics** and **working practices** of the print industry. The word 'economics' means financial organisation and the way that money is moved around. The word is usually used to refer to some kind of system which has been developed to allow for the moving of money and products.

'Working practices' are the way that people are organised in an industry and the skills that they use in their work.

This situation means that in the future most people in the media will have a series of short-term and freelance jobs. Those who have good skills and can come up with good ideas will find that their jobs become more challenging and better paid as their careers develop. There are qualifications and standard career routes into the media which are explained below – these are likely to remain. At the same time, the trends we can see now suggest that in order to be successful, most people will need to push themselves to get jobs. Good interview skills and a record of work that shows you can take responsibility will be helpful. People who believe in themselves and manage to convince others of their skills are likely to be the most successful.

The media products of tomorrow

In the future the products of the media, like the jobs available, are likely to combine some familiar features and some new ones. These new features will result from changes in technology. Areas like computer games and holograms which are improving very quickly at the moment are likely to be important in the future.

There will be more products available, including new ones based on current information technology and multimedia technology. There will be more inter-active products, and areas like television and radio will offer a greater degree of interactivity. Some TV programmes have already offered viewers alternative endings, but such choices will get more common and more complicated.

There is also likely to be a greater amount of material available in the future, much of it old material cheaply recycled. You will probably have seen classic novels selling in bookstores and even in supermarkets for £1 or even less. In the future, large amounts of existing material from all areas of the media will be available cheaply. Improvements in production technology will lead to better sound and visual quality in all media and, probably, much better value for money for audiences because of increased competition.

Will traditional media survive?

Despite all these developments, it is likely that film, television, books and periodicals will continue in their present form for a long time to come. The changes brought about by technology and new working practices will raise the quality of these products. Books will be illustrated to higher and higher standards, and the quality of graphics on most television programmes will continue to improve.

The continued long-term existence of 'traditional' media products is very likely for two reasons:

● Audiences are familiar with them and have a liking for them
● The networks to make, distribute and sell the products are well established
Our lives are already organised around television and radio programmes and in some cases these products have proved to be very important. 'Drive-time' radio provides an easy way for people to get up-to-date news, travel information and other features. This product has been organised to reach an established audience. The audience – mainly people heading to and from work – is likely to stay. Improving technology and changing working practices will change drive-time radio. Computers will edit news items and improved information networks will allow instant access to live reports from around the world. These things are already a feature of radio, but the falling cost of production will allow local stations along with small cable and satellite operations to buy into large newsgathering services.

Areas like books and newspapers are already dominated by huge retail operations such as WH Smith. People are likely to want to continue going to shops and the presence of large retailers in the high street will ensure that a range of work remains on sale.

The presence of more information and ideas along with a better quality of production is likely to improve audiovisual and print products in the future. The presence of many multi-skilled people in the workforce will also allow a faster turn-round of ideas and an increase in innovative approaches to work. At the same time, the media will build on the tried and tested success of products like television programmes and newspapers.

Activity 1.10

1 Choose TWO media industries – one print industry and one audiovisual. For each industry, identify any recent changes and developments in technology. Write a report on their potential impact on employment patterns.
2 Now do the same for changes and developments in products.
3 What are the implications of changes in media technology generally? Write a brief report, covering all the media industries.

Training opportunities

Once you have completed your GNVQ intermediate course, there are a range of training opportunities open to you. These are briefly explained below. However, you should remember that successful media careers depend as much on drive and ambition as they do on qualifications. Qualifications reward your skills and knowledge and indicate your level of ability to employers. Once you have gained a qualification you have improved your chances of work. From this point on, you are in an improved position to help yourself.

Remember that GNVQ Media courses and also the BTEC National Diploma are available at Advanced level. Some colleges and sixth forms offer these further education courses in combination with A levels. These courses combine a high level of skills training with work on media theory. The courses are usually good enough to get successful students into employment, but this depends very much on the student's ability to make contacts and interview well. Students who perform well on these courses can also earn university places. Other courses at this level are offered by some colleges. These include specialist training in journalism, photography, popular music and other media-related areas. Some media organisations also offer further education courses of their own, usually based at a particular college. A careers teacher or careers office can help you in finding the exact details of any course.

Activity 1.11

Make a personal list of the following 10 skills areas. Put the skill you think is your strongest at number 1 and work down the list until you have decided for yourself which are your strongest and weakest skills.

- Working with other people in a practical situation ☐

- Managing other people ☐

- Managing your own time and effort ☐

- Motivating yourself when things are hard ☐

- Coming up with original ideas ☐

- Learning new skills ☐

- Feeling confident working on your own ☐

- Persuading other people to share your point of view ☐

- Managing money ☐

- Seeing ways of making money ☐

Note: The knowledge and skills covered by a skills audit are important in getting employment in the media. A successful professional in the media will have all these skills. He or she would also use the information in job interviews.

Most diploma courses in higher education provide a very high level of skills training with a lot of demanding practical activity. There are courses available in areas like journalism, photojournalism, film and video and sound recording. These courses are all outlined in a book called the *UCAS Handbook*. This lists all higher education courses in the university and college sector. You will need an A level qualification to get onto these courses.

In the case of students who have worked in the media for some time, the entry qualifications may be overlooked if the applicant can show that their work experience has prepared them for the diploma course.

Degree courses

There are a range of media degrees and related courses listed in the *UCAS Handbook*. Entry qualifications are slightly higher than those for diploma level courses. You will need good grades in a A level course to qualify. As with diploma courses, it is possible that special arrangements will be made for older applicants with relevant work experience.

Modern apprenticeships

The recently introduced modern apprenticeship scheme offers students the chance to work their way towards a qualification and make a positive career start. There are opportunities in the media available through this scheme, although media modern apprenticeships have been slow starting. One of the problems is that schemes require an employee to be able to look ahead to three years in a particular employment. To many employers, this is unrealistic, especially in the fastest-changing areas of the industry.

Careers teachers and officers will be able to advise you about the situation in your local area. In general, modern apprenticeships involve students finding a work placement and then using their work and the skills they are gaining to help them qualify for NVQ units.

NVQs

NVQs are skills-based qualifications centred on the workplace. Some modern apprenticeships are based in schools and colleges but most take place outside.

Media industry training schemes

Some national bodies in the media are involved with particular training schemes for their own areas. These include the National Council for the Training of Journalists (NCTJ) and the National Council for the Training of Broadcast Journalists (NCTBJ). Most of this training is available to people who are already working. Careers officers and the bodies themselves can provide more advice. The places offered by this route are usually very hard to gain.

These courses, or others like them, could help you to start a successful career. The media remains a very competitive business and you will need more than qualifications to be really successful. You will also need a good portfolio of work, the ability to present yourself well at interview and some self-knowledge that will help you to set and reach targets for your own career.

Your GNVQ course can help you to achieve all of these. It is important that you use every chance to develop skills and knowledge. You should also think for yourself throughout the course and practise using your skills and ideas outside your course if you can. The next activity asks you to think about some points that will be important in helping you plan your own way through your present course. This is also the kind of information you will need to organise before you go for interviews for other courses and for jobs.

Activity 1.12

1 List the different types of training opportunity available in the media industries.
2 Describe each type of training opportunity, giving examples.

Review questions

1 Why might Media Studies students be interested in the influence of the media on society?
2 Name one group of skilled employees who have lost jobs through the introduction of new technology in the media.
3 The fastest-growing area of the media is called m____m____
4 A collection of your own media work is often called a p_____.
5 Write down one way in which completing a skills audit might be helpful in your career.
6 Who are the NCTJ?
7 Why is it easier for a magazine to give away a book today than it was 20 years ago?
8 Using digital editing techniques, publishers can produce non-fiction or reference books from information stored on a d_____ b_____.

Assignment 1
Investigating local and national media

This assignment provides evidence for:

Elements: 1.1 Investigate local and national media provision
1.2 Explore consumption of local and national media
1.3 Investigate developments and opportunities in the media industries

and the following key skills:

Communication:	2.2, 2.3, 2.4
Information Technology:	2.1, 2.2, 2.3, 2.4
Application of Numbers:	2.1, 2.2, 2.3

1 Put together an 'investigating media' file, containing all your written work from the activities in Elements 1.1, 1.2, and 1.3, each under the appropriate element heading
2 Include any presentation material you used or videotapes of presentations.
3 Decide whether any of the work could be used as research material for print, audio or video products which you will be working on in later chapters. What could be turned into a magazine article, a short video, or radio feature?
4 Make a careful cross-check to make sure all the work produced is in the file, and submit the file to your teacher, with your name and group clearly marked.

2 Planning and producing print products

Element 2.1	Investigate print products
Element 2.2	Develop a proposal for print products
Element 2.3	Produce print products

What is covered in this chapter

- Types and purposes of print products
- Codes and conventions
- Narrative structures
- Target audiences
- Representation
- Researching and planning a product
- Producing a print product
- Evaluating print products

Your 'print' file will need to contain the following:
- Two print products, one produced on your own and one produced working with others
- Material produced while carrying out the activities in this chapter
- Evidence of action plans and research used to carry out the activities, including original research you have designed and completed

Introduction

We all know something about print products. They include newspapers, magazines, comics and books. We also know something about the different styles of these products and their content.

All print products are the result of a series of decisions about planning, researching, ideas and format. Choices also have to be made about the kind of resources available and the kind of skills and ideas that members of a team can contribute. The word **resources** will appear a great deal in this chapter. It means all the things required to do a particular job. There are different kinds of resources involved in making a print product. They include money, time, the people available to do the job as well as equipment and materials. All of these will be examined in more detail later in the chapter.

This chapter looks at the whole range of print products. It describes different types of product and provides examples. It also gives you the chance to learn about this area of the media by planning, researching and producing a print product of your own.

Element 2.1 Investigate print products

Types of contemporary print product and their purpose

In the past, a print product in the media was any product made by applying ink to paper. Most print products featured words, although some were totally image-based (see below). In recent years print products have come to include electronic publishing. **Electronic publishing** means any type of published material which is disseminated or viewed electronically. Some print products appear only on computer or TV screens – such as material on the Internet or Ceefax. These may still be regarded as 'print' products because they rely mainly on printed words and images to put over their message.

When an author makes a contract with a publisher to write a book, it is now standard practice to agree rights for possible use of the work in electronic form. Some contracts even go so far as to agree terms for the work to appear in media that have not yet been invented!

Before we investigate print products it is important to understand some definitions. Broadly speaking, there are two types of print products:

1 **Text-based** Here the material consists mainly of words, and words carry the largest part of the meaning. Examples include most books, and pages from Teletext and Ceefax.

2 **Image-based** These are based mainly on images or other visual material like graphics or simple use of colours. In image-based material the visual material carries the largest part of the meaning. Examples include posters and CD covers.

Most print products combine text and images. In some cases it is possible to define the type of product even when there is a combination. For example, an autobiography with a few pictures in the middle is definitely text-based.

In some cases, a single product such as a newspaper may combine text-based and image-based material. For example, a newspaper may have a 'problem page' that is entirely text-based whilst other areas, like the fashion pages, are image-based.

There are a number of different types of print product. Each of these types can be further sub-divided. All of these types of print products exist at the present time. This means they are **contemporary**. Types of contemporary print products include:

- **Newspaper** A news-based publication usually combining stories and photographs. Typically laid out in columns and using headlines to get attention and introduce stories

- **Magazine** A combination of text- and image-based items focusing on a set theme. Most magazines appear in a paper form and are aimed at a particular audience. The magazine format of combining written features and adverts has adapted well to other media forms like computer disc, audio recording and television

- **Electronic publishing** Print- and image-based medium, disseminated electronically. Examples include magazines and books on the Internet

- **Comic** Entertainment medium, usually consisting of stories presented in the form of graphic illustration. Most comics include text-based material, like letters pages, but they rely mainly on illustrated stories for their appeal

- **Commercial graphics** Material produced in a graphic format to promote commercially available products, services or events. Examples include hi-fi brochures or 'flyers' produced to advertise dance events.

In most cases a range of products has grown up in each category in response to consumer demand. We saw in the last chapter that the demand of audiences, combined with the desire of producers to make money, has shaped the type of media products that are available. Some of the best evidence to prove this point is found in the print media. Print products can now be produced so cheaply that it is quite easy to aim individual products at quite small audiences. As we saw in the last chapter, a printing process such as Rank Xerox DocuTech allows publishers to make a profit on a very small number of sales.

Types of print product

The list below describes the main types of print product. It is not a comprehensive list, but it gives the main areas outlined in the GNVQ guidelines at intermediate level.

Newspapers

- A **tabloid** is a small-sized paper dealing mainly in popular stories. Typical tabloid stories are based on well-known personalities, experiences and events. The tabloids usually aim for large sales and combine their writing with a lot of images. The best known examples are the *Sun* and *Mirror*.
- A **broadsheet** is a large-format paper, often published in more than one section. These papers usually base their main stories around political or economic events or issues. Broadsheets are best known for covering their subjects in a lot of detail. They sell smaller numbers than the tabloids but can still make large profits through advertising. *Times* readers, for example, have a lot of money to spend. This means companies and agencies are willing to pay higher rates for advertising in order to reach this more affluent and influential market. Broadsheets usually make more money from advertising revenue than they do from sales.
- **Freesheets** are newspapers which are delivered free of charge. They tend to be locally produced and distributed over a relatively small area. Although made up mainly of adverts, they also cover news and local issues. The

Tabloids and broadsheets often cover the same news in different ways

coverage of subjects is often linked to the kind of advertising featured in the paper. Freesheets often try to include useful information such as details of chemists' opening times. This encourages readers to keep them through the week and look at the adverts more often.

- **Local newspapers** are produced for a local area, as opposed to a regional or nationwide readership. They have more news than the freesheets and earn a large part of their income from sales rather than advertising. At the same time these papers often cover the same stories as freesheets and contain similar, often identical, adverts.

Magazines

Within the print industry, magazines can be divided into the following categories:

- **Business and related** These are magazines aimed at people in particular jobs or industries. They often rely on subscriptions taken out over a long period. They also get regular money from advertising, such as adverts for jobs and training courses.
- **Special interest** These are magazines based on a particular subject. *UFO Reality* from the previous chapter is a good example of a special interest magazine.
- **'Lifestyle'** The idea behind these magazines is that readers of a certain age or outlook will have a number of interests in common. Good examples of these are magazines aimed at teenage girls (e.g. *Sugar, J17*) or young men (*Loaded*, GQ, FHM).

Comics

Most of these are grouped by audience. Three major types are:

- **Children's** These can be intended to entertain and inform. Often they feature well-known characters and offer new stories about these characters in every issue. Examples include *Beano, Thomas The Tank Engine*, etc.
- **Action adventure** These are comics aimed at older children and adult audiences. Usually involving longer stories than children's comics, they rely on good-quality graphics and stories. Some well-established titles revolve around popular heroes like Superman and Batman.
- **Alternative** Probably the hardest category to define. Alternative comics often feature adult humour and use the comic-book format to make jokes and put over interesting and unusual ideas. The best known example in the UK is the hugely popular *Viz*.

Electronic publishing

This can be divided into two major categories:

- **Individual products** These are commercially packaged products – for example, CD-ROM encyclopedias
- **Generally available services** This is material available via machines and networks, for example Teletext and Ceefax services on television.

Commercial graphics

Material in this category may take many different forms:

- Flyers or handbills advertising events
- Inserts given away free with magazines
- Material mailed directly to homes and businesses

Classifying print products

We have already seen that it is possible to divide print products into groups. But audiences themselves do not always divide products in this way. We saw in the last chapter that it is important to understand how and why audiences use media products. In some cases audiences are interested in a range of products because all these products deal with subjects and ideas that they like.

The target audience

One way to classify print products is by the **target audience**, i.e. the intended audience for the product.

Most producers of media products have a definite idea of the kind of person they are trying to reach. They 'target' these people by trying to include as many things as possible that the audience might want. We have already seen that audiences use media material for their own needs. Most buyers of print products also buy other media material. In some cases the links are obvious. For example, people who buy magazines about the film industry are also likely to buy videos and visit the cinema regularly.

Some publications are aimed at specialist markets whose audience can be defined quite accurately. Examples include:
- Model-making magazines
- Farming magazines
- Tourist magazines and brochures

In each of these cases there is an identifiable type of person who will buy these publications. Within the target audience, certain age-groups, sexes and ethnic groups may be strongly represented. For example, most farmers are white males. In the case of a tourist guide, the target audience might be made up of many different nationalities but the information needs of the audience would be very similar.

Many products are aimed at audiences that are defined by age. For example, comics featuring popular characters like Fireman Sam and Thomas the Tank Engine are aimed at children from 4 to around 8. The letters pages of these comics often include drawings sent in by readers with the age of the reader printed beside them.

The style of print products

Style is a hard word to define. It refers to the *way* something is done. For example, if someone is known as a 'stylish' dresser, then they probably pick clothes that flatter them and make them look good. Style is the result of making a choice from a range of possibilities. In fact, all publications have their own style. The ones that stand out tend to be the ones that are presented in a very definite or distinctive way.

On the printed page, style depends on the use of certain recognisable visual features. These can include particular typefaces, page-layout styles, types of content or styles of illustration or photograph.

The extract on page 62 comes from the *Music Master* catalogue which is the main publication in the UK listing all available compact discs. Its style is very simple because it is required to list information. The use of bold type for important information like titles and catalogue numbers helps these to stand out. The listings for record labels and distributors at the bottom of each entry are important to the readers of the book. Many copies are sold to record shops who often contact labels and distributors direct to order stock.

Raksha Mancham

CHOS KHOR.
CD. . . . . **EEE 17**
Musica Maxima Magnetica / Aug '94 / Plastic Head.

Ramani. Dr. N

MUSIC IN THE RAGAS..
CD. . . . . **NI 5257**
Nimbus / Sep '94 / Nimbus Records / Cadillac / A.D.A. Distribution / Direct Distribution.

Ramases

SPACE HYMNS.
CD. . . . . **REP 4108-WP**
Repertoire / Aug '91 / Pinnacle.

Ramazzotti, Eros

TUTTE STORIE.
Cose della vita / A mezza via / Un altra te / Memorie / In compagnia / Un grosso no / Favola / Non c'e piu fantasia / Nostalsong / Niente di male / Esodi / L'ulti ma rivoluzione / Silver e missie.
CD. **74321 14329-2**
RCA / Jan '94 / BMG.

ALL THE STUFF.
Blitzkrieg bop / Beat on the brat / Judy is a punk / Now I wanna sniff some glue / Don't go down the basement / Loudmouth / Havana affair / 53rd and 3rd / I don't wanna walk around with you / I wanna be sedated / Glad to see you go / I remember you / Sheena is a punk rocker / Pinhead / Swallow my pride / California sun / I wanna be your boyfriend / You're gonna kill that girl / Babysitter / Listen to my heart / Let's dance / Today your love, tomorrow the world / I can't be / Gimme gimme shock treatment / Oh oh I love her so / Suzy is a headbanger / Now I wanna be a good boy / What's your game / Commando / Chainsaw / You should never have opened that door / California sun (live).
CD. 759926204
Sire / Aug '90 / WEA.

BRAIN DRAIN.
I believe in miracles / Punishment fits the crime / Pet Semetary / Merry Christmas / Learn to listen / Zero zero UFO / All screwed up / Can't get you outta my mind / Ignorance is bliss.
CD. . . . . .CCD 1725
Chrysalis / Jul '89 / EMI.

JAPANESE MELODIES FOR FLUTE & HARP.
Kojo no tsuki / Chugoku chiho no komoruita / Aka tombo / Chin-chin chidori / Nambu ushioi uta / Defune / Kono michi / Hanayome ningyo / Jogashima no ame / Hana cherry blossom time / Sakura sakura.
CD. C37 7127
Denon / '88 / Conifer Records.

Rampolokeng. Lesego

END BEGINNINGS (Rampolokeng, Lesego & Kalahari Surfers).
CD. . . . . LRSCD 1
ReR Megacorp / Jul '93 / Grapevine Distribution / These Records / ReR Megacorp.

Extract from the Music Master catalogue

Another example you might consider is this book. It aims to be informative and its style is intended to help you to learn. Clear type is used against a white background to avoid any distractions, and it includes pictures and cartoons to illustrate points in the text and provide light relief. The writing style uses short sentences to deliver important information. This helps you maintain concentration and learn as you read.

Structure

Two other factors have an important influence on print products:

- **Structure** is the way a publication is put together. An adult comic, for example, might have a **narrative structure**. This means that it is entirely based around one story. A newspaper, by contrast, is usually divided into different sections, each of which stands on its own.
- **Fiction/non-fiction** Publications can either based on made-up stories (**fiction**) or based on fact (**non-fiction**).

What is the purpose of print products?

All print products exist for a reason or **purpose**. Defining the purpose of a print product can be difficult, because different people can see different purposes in the same work.

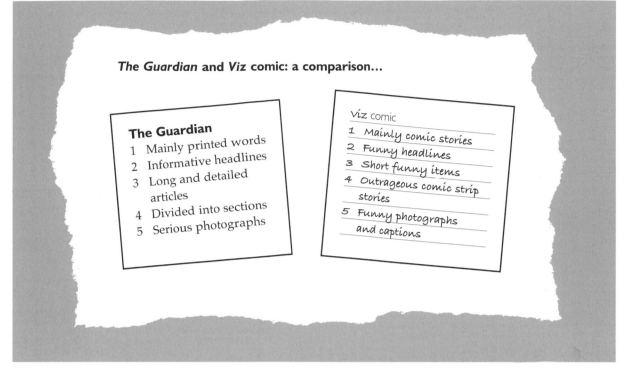

We saw in Chapter 1 that the media is an industry. The majority of media products are intended to make money. The most common purpose for print products is to make money for the people who create and produce them. In the case of a piece of commercially produced graphics material such as a mail order catalogue, the purpose is to generate sales of the products in the catalogue.

Most of the people who buy a print product see a different purpose for its existence. From the buyer's point of view, the purpose of a print product can be:

- To inform
- To entertain
- To educate
- To persuade

Some examples of print products which do these jobs are:

- **Informing:** tourist guides, instruction manuals
- **Entertaining:** children's comics, popular novels
- **Educating:** this book, specialist CD-ROM packages, encyclopedias
- **Persuading:** political leaflets, advertising posters

Print products also offer readers a range of additional benefits. These other benefits can include:

- Advice
- Humour
- A feeling of belonging to a group
- Support for opinions
- Arguments and ideas
- Surprises
- Details of products, services
- Escape from everyday problems
- Things to share with friends

The list could be extended. These benefits are the reasons why the audience buy the product. The same applies to other types of media – television and radio programmes, films and videos, etc.

It is important that you have a clear idea in your own mind of the way that print products fulfil their purpose. Some of the purposes filled by print products are quite complicated.

For example, the role of a newspaper may appear to be to inform people. But journalists often go out of their way to write in an entertaining style. Readers often appreciate this and may come to value a paper as much for its entertainment value as its informative content. Remember that the same information is often available in more than one newspaper, so the *way* a paper presents the news can be very important. People often think that newspapers should inform first and entertain second. But a newspaper's success can often depend on how well it can combine the two purposes of entertaining and informing.

It is also true that entertaining publications can educate as well. An alternative magazine like *Private Eye* has a reputation for poking fun at public figures and people in authority. But it also plays a serious role in exposing financial and political corruption and covering stories that other publications find 'too hot to handle'. Even fashion spreads in magazines can be seen as educational if they give people ideas about how to present themselves.

The important point is that people's reasons for buying and reading print products are often complicated. We all have our own reasons for making particular choices within the media. In Chapter 1 we saw that according to the 'uses and gratifications' model of audience behaviour, everyone brings their own personal needs to the media. This short discussion of the purposes of print products has shown that these needs can be very mixed, and often more than one need is met by the same product.

Why produce a print product?

As well as the obvious purpose of making money, print products also serve a number of different functions for those who produce them. Some products try to persuade people to take particular views or behave in a particular way. There are many examples of this, and some will be discussed later in the chapter.

An obvious example of a persuasive print product is found in the daily newspapers. Papers tend to feature editorials and other comments which put across certain opinions and ideas – often very forcibly.

This type of persuasion becomes very obvious during a general election campaign. In Britain in 1997 most of the daily papers told their readers to vote for a particular party. The Mirror Group, which was featured in Chapter 1 as the owner of a range of papers, used most of its titles to tell readers to vote for the Labour Party. The *Mirror* has been a well-known Labour paper for years and often puts a pro-Labour slant on news stories. However, the persuasion on election day was much more obvious than usual. The paper used arguments and particular pieces of evidence to give the best possible reasons for voting in a particular way. In 1997, the *Sun*, previously a staunch supporter of the Thatcher administration, surprised everybody by changing its mind and supporting Labour instead of the Tories.

The design of print products, including features like their size, colour, shape and number of pages, is also linked to their use. Broadsheet papers can contain a lot of information but they are not easy to pass around, read in small spaces

– like bus seats – or fold into the back pocket of a pair of jeans. A tabloid like *Sun* can be carried around in this way. Tabloids are the most popular type of paper in this country. Tabloids like the *Sun* also claim that they have many more readers than buyers. This is because the paper is passed around on building sites, in college canteens, etc. One person's paper may be read by four or five other people. Tabloid papers are specially designed with this in mind.

DANCE EVENT 'FLYER'

PURPOSE	DESIGN FEATURE
1 Advertise star DJs at event	Names are biggest items on the flyer
2 Get attention	Flyer has bright colours and strong lines in graphics
3 Provide cheap advertising	No pictures, flyer could be done on computer
4 Get the word out quickly	Flyer is easy to print and can be stuffed under windscreen wipers or handed around. Ten seconds reading is enough to get message across
5 Reach the right people	Small flyer can be left in boxes in record shops student canteens, etc.

The design of a product such as a flyer is always linked to its use

Activity 2.1

1 Gather some examples of each of the following types of contemporary print product: tabloid, broadsheet, freesheet, local newspaper, magazine, comic, electronic publishing, commercial graphics material.
2 Write brief notes to describe the classification and purpose of each one. For example, why is one newspaper called a tabloid and another a broadsheet? How would you classify the magazine? What is the purpose of each one? Compare your findings with others in your group.

Codes and conventions

People who study the media identify many patterns that keep recurring. One obvious reason for this is that successful products are widely imitated. Before long, the features that made a product successful are repeated in a range of other products.

A recent example can be seen in the area of alternative or humour comics. Most people have seen *Viz* comic which is still regularly one of the top ten magazines or comics in this country. When *Viz* sales went over a quarter of a million, a few other companies started climbing on the bandwagon. Soon over a dozen similar titles were launched. Some folded, but a few, like *Spit* and *Zit*, have survived. All these publications copied *Viz*'s ideas, such as using comic strips to show violence and bad behaviour in a humorous way.

The two terms used to describe these common features that occur time and time again in particular areas are **codes** and **conventions**.

A code is a system into which things are organised. A spoken language is one example of this because words are organised according to certain rules – like adding an '-s' to the end of a word to make it a plural. In the print media these codes include using boxes to contain images of a cartoon story, using big letters to show the importance of a headline and placing the name of a publication at the top of the front page.

A **convention** is the usual way of doing something. When things are done a particular way over and over again, we say this is **conventional**. For example, it is conventional for flyers for a dance event to use strong colours and graphic lines. This convention is based on the fact that this visual style can present a similar effect to the lights at a dance event.

Look at the extract on page 67. It comes from a comic called *The Scurvy Dog*. This was a competitor to *Viz* which ran for three issues and was wound up in 1996. The comic was doing well enough to continue, but stopped publishing because the editors were given a job by *The Daily Star* producing a humorous football feature called 'Bites Yer Legs.' The fact that a daily paper wanted to imitate the success of one of these humour comics shows how successful styles can lead to an expansion of the same kind of work.

The extract opposite shows how codes and conventions work:

Codes

The system followed in this comic fits into the usual codes of comic strips, i.e.:
- A4 paper size
- Use of boxed pictures to tell story
- Use of captions to move the story on in time
- Use of speech and thought bubbles to develop characters and action

Conventions

The style of *The Scurvy Dog* imitates a successful humour formula seen in other such comics:
- The characters are based on well-known comic 'types' from the past
- The use of modern slang words jars with the old-fashioned style of the drawings
- The characters themselves seem unaware of this

Successful publications often tend to stick with a winning formula and only update it slightly as audience needs change. This leads to the development of codes and conventions.

Some publications such as *Woman's Own* have been in circulation for years and are well established. Others – like the humour comics examined above – are a relatively new phenomenon. In both cases, however, we can see products using the same codes and conventions. These include similarities in cover style, logo, contents and even the information included in special features.

Success in this work is based on an understanding of an audience. In order to develop a successful print product, it is vital to consider the needs of audience carefully.

Masthead and extract from The Scurvy Dog *comic*

Codes	Conventions
Use of boxed pictures to tell a story	Use of characters based on other successful characters
Use of massive headline to show importance of story	Much colour in graphics and layout
Use of long paragraphs to give detailed information	Many photos of readers show them smiling and happy
Use of short paragraphs to give quick facts	Use of a lot of quotes and speech in news stories
Use of strong graphics to attract attention	Use of many details of issues and arguments in news stories
Divided into sections	Little use of colour, pictures photocopied
Built mainly around one story	Editorial items are very short
Featuring sections of comments from readers	Adverts on some pages advertise other items in publication

Codes and conventions in print products

Identifying codes and conventions

Format

This term refers to the size and layout of a publication. Different arrangements of headlines, text and pictures are used to attract readers. For example, the *Sun* uses big headlines, eye-catching front-page pictures and a small amount of text to put across a message very quickly. In other cases, different styles of type are used to separate different items.

The development of a format depends on both codes and conventions. The use of words like 'shocker' used in headlines represents a convention, whilst there are definite 'codes' in the regular appearance of dates and page numbers. In practice, it is often difficult to see the dividing line between codes and conventions. They overlap because the makers of the products stick to successful ways of presenting information and ideas. This approach builds up conventions which eventually become so familiar and well established that a system, or code, develops. For example:

Convention	Example	Reason
Much use of quotes and direct speech in news and stories	*The Daily Star*	This is a popular tabloid. Quotes and speech make it seem as if the people in the stories are speaking directly to the reader. This means the stories can be understood quickly and easily.
Use of boxes to contain action within a story	*The Beano*	The audience for this comic is young and they value the simplicity of the story telling. Framing each piece of action avoids confusion. They know what the box means.
Cross-references to other items in publication	Ceefax	Ceefax is open to people with a range of interests. Adverts remind different people in audience of their own interests. Many advert items are linked to contents of page on which they appear. For example, football league tables page sometimes advertises football transfer news. This will encourage readers to read more of Ceefax.

When studying any print product, it is worth making notes on the layout, fonts, use of headlines and size of the publication. It is also a good idea to ask readers what they feel about the use of these features.

Layout

Within a format many items are arranged in a certain way. The way columns of text, photographs and other items are laid out is an important factor when attracting readers. It is also important to remember that visual items, like photographs, are often cut down – or **cropped** – to make them fit a style of layout.

Writing style

Different publications have different styles of writing. Academic books assume a lot of knowledge from readers and often present information as if their readers are already experts. Popular magazines adopt a chatty and lively style, using a lot of direct speech and leading into points of information with a short, punchy sentence.

Writing styles present the most difficult area of investigation in terms of distinguishing between codes and conventions. In practice, much writing uses familiar styles and words which might be said to be conventional. For example, information is often presented in the form of a numbered list. At a deeper level, all writing depends on a set of grammatical rules – in this case, the rules of the English language – which in themselves are a form of convention.

The kind of writing styles you are likely to investigate also show examples of codes. To get a clear example of a code within a writing style you might have to investigate a publication such as a foreign language textbook. This might use a precise code such as writing the same sentence twice – once in each language. The Glossary in this book also follows a code in terms of writing style. It presents media terms in bold type and follows these with short explanations. The bold print and punctuation are part of the code for presenting a glossary.

The key point to look for is the way that a writing style presents readers with something they *want*. Writing styles often imitate the way that readers speak or the way that readers write. You should ask questions that check on these points.

Activity 2.2

1 Choose TWO of the print products studied so far in this chapter. Make sure they include text AND images. Identify any codes in each example. You should cover all aspects of format, writing style and structure.
2 Now do the same for the conventions in each print product. Present your written findings to the rest of the class.

Narrative structure

The word used to describe the development of stories in the media is **narrative**. It has a range of meanings. It is usually used to mean an 'account' of something. It can also be used to mean putting things into a sequence. In media studies 'narrative' means the whole development of a story, so it can include the contents of the story and the way the story is told.

In media studies narrative is often broken into two sections:
- **Plot** This is a simple outline of the story.
- **Narration** This is the point of view from which the story is told.

There are three different narrative forms: **serial**, **closed** and **multi-strand**. Their main features are as follows:
- **Serial** Built up of regular episodes, each moving the story forward and adding more information
- **Closed** One complete story where main events are all completed by the end
- **Multi-strand** An ongoing group of stories. Some events and stories may be completed within one publication; other characters and stories are ongoing.

Examples of these three different types of narrative are as follows:
- **Serial** Comic strip stories in action/adventure comics
- **Closed** Biographies of famous people serialised in newspapers
- **Multi-strand** Continuous sagas such as the *Discworld* novels by Terry Pratchett

Narratives are made up of building blocks knowns as **elements** which move the story forward. Three well-known elements which are used in a range of print products are:

1 **Conflict** Setting up some competition or conflict between characters creates tension which captures the reader's interest. Readers want to see how the conflict will develop.

2 **Development** A **development** is an incident in a story which adds important information and moves the story forward. Developments often happen with the introduction of a new character, or a discovery or a revelation of some kind by one of the existing characters.

3 **Resolution** This is the point at which the events in a story are brought to some kind of conclusion. In the case of multi-strand and serial narratives, the story will go on after the resolution has been reached. One of the first resolutions that children hear is the famous line '…And they all lived happily ever after,' which is often used to resolve fairy tales. Resolutions often explain events and make sense of the story that has gone before.

Simplified conflict, development and resolution in a typical 'picture romance'

As we saw earlier, narrative is also used to place the events in the story into **sequence**. One meaning of the word **sequence** is 'series.' **Sequencing** material, especially in a print narrative, means creating a series of events in a story.

Sequencing can be seen in both fiction and non-fiction products. There are a number of different items within a story which help to construct the sequence:

1 **Scenes** These are the basic events as seen by the viewer/reader. A scene in a print narrative is usually one complete event. At the end of a scene the story has usually moved forward.

You will be familiar with scenes from television dramas or films. These work in the same way as print narratives. For example, scenes in 'Coronation Street' are usually short and involve at least one character learning some information or making a decision. At the end of the scene, the viewer has some idea of how the scene will affect future events in the programme. Once a scene has done this, it has added to the sequence of the narrative.

2 **Chronology** This is information given within a print product that establishes a **timeframe** for a storyline or narrative. It helps to put particular events into a sequence and often sets the pace for a story.

For example, some stories use a chronology set in a very short period of time – like one day. This often suggests a series of events happening so quickly that some dramatic conclusion is inevitable. By contrast, historical novels often use a chronology that covers years and suggests slowly changing events working gradually towards a conclusion.

3 **Flashback** Flashback is a useful device for story-tellers. It enables them to describe an event which has taken place before the main period of the action. Usually this past event contains important information that helps readers to understand events which occur later in the story.

Flashbacks are also sometimes used to remind the reader of an important earlier event in the story or to show a different aspect of a character. A good example is in the *Star Wars* books, when Luke Skywalker's mentor appears whenever he is in danger and urges him to 'Believe in the force.' This strengthens him and reminds him of things that are important and good.

Colin surveyed the beach with a mounting feel of unease. The heavy dusk and strong wind reminded him that time and the weather were closing in. He shook in the numbing cold but all he could think about was Heather. The taxi driver said she had insisted on being dropped at the top of the cliff. From that point the only logical place to go was down the steep path and onto this beach. It all made some sense, but not much. Colin was wracked with doubt. Maybe if he hadn't told the police about their blazing row he would have had some help right now. If he hadn't stormed at Heather, telling her that she'd never make it as an actress, maybe she would still be with him…Perhaps they'd be in that little harbour front café enjoying the wine and the twinkling lights of the passing boats. Something skittered over the sand, blown by the wind. It hit Colin's foot. Squinting in the half light he recognized a familiar shape. It was a pair of sunglasses, mirrored and hung on a braided strap. His heart raced as his cold hands struggled to pick them up. The stiff breeze carried a faint whiff of perfume, the familiar soft scent he'd noticed when she first walked into his office. Yes, she had come down to the beach, and for the perfume to be so fresh on the sunglasses she must have been on the beach within the last couple of hours…

Notice how the extract above moves events forward in the story

Activity 2.3

1 Study the narrative structures of the two print products you have chosen. Find examples of narratives in them that are serial, closed and multi-strand and explain why each one fits each description.
2 Do the same for elements and types of narrative sequence, as described above. Explain fully your choices of each example.

Colin's hands shook. He was ashen faced and red-eyed in the cold light that broke through the café window. The staff went about their work of raising blinds, putting out signs and readying themselves for another day of noisy holidaymakers taking noisy slurps from huge mugs of tea. They looked on quizzically as Colin and the inspector regarded each other over the newly mopped table.

"I appreciate your worry, Mr Nicholson, but one pair of sunglasses proves nothing and the taxi driver wasn't absolutely sure that your girlfriend was the person he took up there."

"Wife."

"Pardon?"

"She's my wife, Inspector. Heather is my wife. We're on our honeymoon." Colin himself struggled to recognize the word. 'Wife' – yes, they were married and yet it all seemed so unreal. The last two months had flown by like the closing scenes in a cluttered dream. The parties, those candle-lit dinners, lying in until the afternoon and the pain of being apart for even one hour. In a dizzy moment of total love, Heather had pinned him to the wall of an underpass and demanded he marry her. Two weeks later, in front of two puzzled-looking cleaners – witnesses, as far as the marriage register was concerned – and a registrar, Colin and Heather promised to stay together, 'Till death' parted them. Now they were parted.

They'd been married two days, a weekend, and it had flown by in a blur of candlelight, passionate kisses on the harbour front, one mad blazing row and one cold, lonely and desperate night looking for clues on the beach…

Note how this section establishes a chronology for the events described in the last extract.
It suggests that events happened quickly, both in real time and in Colin's mind

The influence of target audience on print products

Target audiences were briefly discussed in Chapter 1. We saw that audiences have an effect on the media, and that media products are designed to allow for the way that audiences use and buy products, and to provide the information that audiences want and need.

For example, sports fans want up-to-the-minute news of events as they happen. In the case of football, there are a range of media products that do this. Each delivers content and style to suits its own audience. A few examples are outlined below.

Product	Delivers	Strengths
Major TV channel	Live action coverage	Close-up action coverage, better view than being there
Daily local paper	Lots of behind-the-scenes information	Time and space to print detailed stories, regular contact with local team
National magazine	Colour pictures, wide-ranging facts and figures, interviews	High profile, budget to print colour action shots, access to major stars
Fanzine	Attitude and opinions – sometimes negative. A fan's view of football	Honesty – written by fans for fans
Ceefax	Short, punchy news, up-to-the-minute results and tables	Technology that allows rapid access to news, putting it straight into millions of homes

The table shows that each product has its special strengths and delivers something that the audience wants. Only national TV is not a print product. Each has been influenced by audience need. This can be seen in their style, content and the way that the material is distributed.

The example of televised sport makes the point. Here, companies have fought hard for bigger audiences. One way to attract viewers is to offer views and insights into the sport that they could not get from other sources. Motor racing coverage now includes shots from inside the cars, use of backward-facing cameras mounted on cars and interviews with pit staff and ex-racing drivers recorded during the race.

The audiences have influenced this type of coverage in two ways. First, the demand for close-up views of the action was obvious from the number of people actually attending live motor racing events and from the demand for the best viewing positions around the track. Television companies could make accurate guesses about audience needs from looking at the existing spectators and their behaviour. Television managed to deliver similar views and, eventually, coverage improved as a result.

Secondly, audience figures around the world rose as car-mounted cameras and live interviews allowed them to feel more involved in the sport. One complaint from audiences in the past was that they often missed key moments in the action. With many cars now carrying cameras, this is less likely. Companies were able to use the level of response from audiences to each new innovation as a guide to how successfully their needs were being met.

Influence on print products

In a similar but rather more complicated way, readers' needs have also helped to shape print products.

For example, the broadsheet *The Times* has maintained a reputation for detailed and accurate news coverage over many years. Readers have always valued this aspect of the paper and, as a result, *The Times* has continued to use more words and fewer pictures than its rivals. The effect of reader influence has been to preserve the paper's familiar and successful style.

At the same time, competitors such as the *Independent* have been obliged to try different ploys in order to appeal to the same market. The *Independent* has developed a reputation for very good photography and found an audience that appreciates this. The success of other papers has also led to some modifications in *The Times*.

One change in recent years has been the addition of extra sections of the paper to deal with specialist interests. This is now a feature of most broadsheets. Once again, the change has come about as a result of audience demand – in this case, for more detailed coverage of areas of the Arts, such as cinema, music, theatre, etc. The paper also includes supplements on certain days for job advertisements in different sectors. This has allowed papers like *The Times* to attract a body of readers who will habitually buy the paper at least one day a week and will consider it buying on others.

Many *Times* readers hold important and influential jobs in business, public services and industry. They are used to dealing with complicated issues and gathering information quickly. In *The Times,* news is organised into 'national', 'international' and 'business'. Readers organise their reading in the same way they organise their work, by putting information into separate areas which can be considered or ignored as required.

The Times

Format	Broadsheet, small headlines with 5-10 words, same font throughout, few capital letters in headlines
Layout	Boxed items at top of front page reveal features inside paper, pages usually 7-8 columns wide, photos surrounded by text, small news items fitted in to page corners, much text and small print
Writing style	Informative, based on ideas and long explanations of facts. Not much direct speech
Content	News in most of first paper, other sections contain discussion, comment and a few review and fashion items. Much foreign news and lots on politics and business
Distribution	In all major newsagents and most small shops

Ceefax

Style	Ceefax presents simple and instant information. The writing style concentrates on facts and figures. This has been influenced by an audience that uses the pages from this product as a source of initial information. This means that they get the news first on Ceefax and expect to read or hear more detailed coverage later from some other source. Ceefax users tend to skim quickly through lots of pages: they don't want to spend 15 Ceefax pages reading about one game of football.
Content	Ceefax concentrates on markets that want quick information. There are millions of football fans in this country. Many don't go to matches very often. Those that do go to matches often don't follow their teams away from home. These people want scores, details of people who scored and basic facts to keep them up to date. Ceefax can offer this 24 hours a day. It also contains up-to-the-minute details of other stories related to football.
Distribution	Many people think twice about making the effort to go out and buy something. In the case of print products, some sales are lost because potential readers simply don't go out shopping. Other sales are lost because products are not distributed to the right shops at the right time. People often want things instantly or not at all. Ceefax services can meet this audience demand because the service is distributed into homes and is available on demand.

Representation in print products

We saw in the last chapter that the media convey distinct images of people, places and events. These images are often referred to as **representations** and each branch of the media has its own way of presenting things.

Print uses photos, drawings and other visual material to create representations or images in people's minds. It also uses words. There are some important points about the way print can represent things and people.

- **Print often uses single images** In some cases these are carefully constructed to carry a lot of meaning. When British forces were fighting abroad a few years ago, one paper superimposed a soldier's face on a picture of a Union Jack. This represented the country and the spirit of our armed forces. Readers were urged to display the picture in their front windows.
- **Sometimes images are combined with text** Adverts provide some of the best examples of this. They present images which are designed to make a particular point. In the illustration on page 76 the message being conveyed is that a particular item of sports wear makes you feel good. The representation shows a disabled person competing successfully with an able-bodied player. The two-word slogan reinforces the message.

Representations of groups and issues

The points made in Chapter 1 apply to print as much as to any branch of the media – including the media products you will create yourself.

Positive images of disabled people are rarely seen in the advertising media

In the illustration above a disabled young man is made to appear competitive, skilled and athletic. These are not qualities conventionally associated with disabled people. The advert is promoting a brand of sportswear. Similar adverts have been produced by real sportswear firms.

The purpose of this advert is to suggest that disabled people can be just as competitive as anyone else and just as likely to buy sportswear. The advert features a pair of gloves which would be needed to move a wheelchair quickly around a basketball court. Most wheelchair athletes use gloves.

The representation constructs a positive image of the disabled athlete by using conventions from sports photography. We are used to seeing pictures of famous sports stars pushing themselves to the limit and battling with opponents. The representation is strengthened by the slogan '*Think BIG* ' – a direct reference to the fact that the able-bodied player is taller than the man in the wheelchair. The suggestion is that disabled people can be just as competitive and skilled as the able-bodied if they allow themselves to think in a positive way. Buying and using sportswear like the gloves is represented as a step towards achieving that ambition.

Groups like the disabled have often been involved in campaigns about their representation in the media. Many have argued that they are not represented often enough in media products and that some of the representations are not flattering. Disabled people have very rarely been cast in heroic or romantic roles. An advert like the one in the illustration would therefore have considerable impact.

Activity 2.4

1 Choose two of the print products you collected at the start of the chapter.
2 Identify any issues of representation in them, taking care to include both social groups AND social issues. Write notes, explaining what the issues are.

Review questions

1 Give an example of a tabloid paper.
2 Give one example of a product made by electronic publishing.
3 The purpose of a print product may include e_____ and i_____.
4 A system into which things are organised is called a _____.
5 The usual way of doing things might be called a _____.
6 Explain what is meant by a 'multi-strand' narrative.
7 What is meant by 'resolution' in a narrative?

Element 2.2 Develop a proposal for print products

The rest of this chapter is concerned with developing and producing an idea for your own print product. The aim is to help you learn about research, layout, editing and other points by practical experience. This section will guide you and help you focus on the important issues.

Research for print products

Most major companies involved in the production of print products carry out **research**. Research has already been discussed in this book, and we have looked at some research methods and the uses to which research is put. You may want to check on the definition of **research** in the Glossary on page 295 or glance back to the previous chapter to refresh your memory.

The important point about research for your own print products is that it must be thorough and it must give you clear ideas about how you are going to produce your work. You have already done a good deal of your own research through completing the activities. From now on, you need to keep a clear focus on your own ideas for research, because the information you gather will help in designing and making your own print products.

Your research should consider:
- The subject matter of your work
- Production methods
- Resources
- Intended audience
- Likely competition

These are briefly explained below.

Subject matter

Everybody is an expert on something, even if it is only their own life and the area where they live. But knowing a lot about a subject does not necessarily mean you can write well about it. Your knowledge has to fit the needs of the audience and the constraints of the publication. In some cases it is easier to write about a subject on which you are *not* an expert, because you can add or subtract information without feeling personally involved in the content.

You should also consider the sources of information for your subject matter. These can be divided roughly into two types:

- **Primary sources** Information which you collect yourself from people, places or events is said to come from 'primary sources'. For example, an interview with a newly married couple for an article on romance is a primary source.
- **Secondary sources** This is material or information which has already been collected or published by someone else. Secondary material includes published information, video recordings of events or other material. For example, if you want to use secondary sources for your article on romance you might gather information on the number of couples taking romantic weekend breaks with holiday companies, or read magazines aimed at people planning to get married, or even watch 'Blind Date' on television.

Production methods

These are the methods that will be used to produce your work. A method is a way of doing something. For example, one method of getting people to read your written work is go out and sell copies of your work on the street.

In the case of a print product, production methods include the of computers, cutting and pasting pages, photocopying, printing, etc. You will have some choices about how you complete your work, but you will also have to consider some limitations. For example, the production methods may well be limited by the time and resources within your school or college.

Resource requirements

We have already considered the meaning of 'resources'. For producing your print product, the resources you will need include time, people, materials, hardware – e.g. computers – and a workplace. Make sure your requirements are reasonable. You may have to discuss them with a teacher or lecturer before making a final decision. Remember that the word 'resources' means *all* the things you will need to produce your print product, so think carefully about the expertise and time that you will need as well as things like equipment and materials. You may find it helpful to divide them up as follows:

- **Human resources** This means the people you will need to make your product successful. Different individuals bring skills to a project, but it is important to manage them well. Keeping everyone employed and happy is usually the best way of getting a job done efficiently. A skills audit sheet like the one on page 54 can provide useful information on human resources.
- **Logistics** This is a military word which is also often used in industry. In an area like the media it is used to describe the people and systems involved in moving products and materials around. You need to think carefully about this. You may need help gathering material, storing things or even bringing equipment to and from school or college. Logistics can include points as simple as organising a lift to school or college on a day when you need to bring in a pile of magazines for cutting up. Good logistics depend on planning and close communication between everyone involved.

- **Material resources** These are all the things you need to gather in order to make your print product, including paper, computers, etc. The final list will depend on the kind of product you are making and the resources available in your school or college.
- **Consumable stock** This is similar to material resources above. To 'consume' means to use up. You should allow for some materials to be used up during the production process. Good planning takes this into account. You should make sure that you know where further stocks of consumable materials such as paper can be found when needed.
- **Financial** This is the money you will need to complete your work. A good plan for print production will include knowledge of likely costs and how to meet them. At the very least you should have a clear idea of the amount of money available as you start your work.
- **Time** This is included in resource requirements because it is important to have some idea how long each task will take, and to work out a schedule in advance. Almost certainly your time will be limited. If you are working within a set timetable of so many sessions per week then your available time might be divided as follows:
  - Time available within the class sessions
  - Time available outside class for completing the work

Audience survey and market competition

Audiences are the groups of people who buy particular print products. If an audience exists for a product, we can also say there is a **market** for the work. However, as we saw in the case of *Viz* comic, this also means that other people may launch rival products on the market. In Chapter 1 we looked at models of audience behaviour and gave an explanation of markets. You may wish to turn to page 42 or use the Glossary to remind yourself of the important points.

Once you have made some decisions on material, you need to carry out a survey of your intended audience, and investigate what other material is already available. If you decide to compete with a major selling item – e.g. a national newspaper – there will be clear limits on your audience survey. You cannot reach people in all parts of the country unless you have the resources of a well-established research operation behind you.

Activity 2.5

1 Decide on TWO print products to make yourself. In a group, plan a simple four-page newsletter aimed at students thinking of taking a GNVQ Media course.
It should tell them what the course is like, what career opportunities exist at the end of it, etc. The content should be mainly text, but with some pictures.
On your own, begin to plan a CD cover for a new album by your favourite group, using mainly images.

2 Do some initial research into each print product, keeping a record of all research done. The research should include the contents, and primary and secondary sources of material.

3 Decide on the production methods and the resources to make each print product. Conduct a survey of the target audience to find out what they would like. Identify competition from other publications. Keep all your findings.

Case Study: a tale of two fanzines

This Case Study looks at two very different football fanzines. It shows that even publications with a very small circulation must get their content and planning right, and understand the needs of their target audience.

The extract here comes from a fanzine called *Nothing Borough Parks Team*. The extract opposite comes from a magazine called *Reds Review*. Both are devoted to Workington AFC, a football team which measures its regular support at just over 200 people.

THE PRIDE OF WEST CUMBRIA

WORKINGTON A.F.C

THE OFFICIALLY UNOFFICIAL FANZINE OF WORKINGTON A.F.C
ISSUE No.1 – Jan'94
PRICE...50p

Above: Nothing Borough Parks Team *cover*

WHAT'S THE POINT.....?

Why have a fanzine ? What purpose does it serve ? Does the Club actually need one ?

Well, Reds already have 2 august publications on the market in the form of the much improved Matchday Programme (more about that later) and the excellent Reds Review. However, neither of these organs (oo–erl) give a singularly fans eye view of life with the Reds – that's not to decry them in any way as both are very readable and chock full of info about our favourite team. In fact, Reds Review puts most professional club magazines to shame with its mix of detailed match reports, general club gossip, player profiles etc...coupled with interviews with ex–Reds and other blasts from the past. For £1.00, you'd struggle to find such excellent value for money elsewhere – it's just a shame that the Editor's a Barrow fan ! Sorry Martin.

Nothing Borough Parks Team aims to represent the voice of the fans. In the final sentence of the extract above, the editor even admits that he is producing the magazine to satisfy himself. The author is one of the few regular fans the team has, and he is producing a magazine to represent their views. Despite its small audience, the magazine still has to consider the same important points covered in your own print production outline.

- **Primary sources** – The fans themselves are a primary source of information for this magazine. Their opinions and experiences (including 'the lack of decent pies') is highlighted.
- **Audience survey** – The fanzine is likely to find a small and dedicated readership. The author will see most of these people standing on terraces and hear their comments as games progress. The author encourages fans to write in with their own ideas.

Case Study (Contd.)

Above: Reds Review cover

- **Market competition**
  The opening paragraph discusses the competition and goes on to explain why *Nothing Borough Parks Team* is different.

The item from *Reds Review* below is drawn from secondary sources – in this case, figures for the number of people attending games. This magazine is more of an official publication and it relies on regular information from the club, including attendance figures.

Through the Turnstiles

WITH FOUR games to go at the time of writing Reds are on course to record their highest average NPL attendance for ten years.

In the 1985-86 season Borough Park saw an average gate of 251, the best since 283 was achieved in the 1982-83 season. This season our average it at present 241 and within striking distance of what would be a notable achievement.

To reach that target we need 1,152 spectators to pass through the Borough Park turnstiles in those last four games - that's an average of 284. While the games against Great Harwood Town and Alfreton Town have no chance of reaching that target the last two fixtures, against promotion chasing Spennymoor United and Guiseley, might just top the 300 mark with both sides having healthy travelling support.

Improving attendances at Workington AFC games are important for two reasons. Firstly it provides the club with an increased income to meet the club's running expenses, and secondly and more importantly it shows businesses and potential sponsors in West Cumbria that there is a popular revival going on at Borough Park and it is something worth being a part of.

Comparing the two items helps to underline some important points about planning print material. We can see that all publications – including those which sell in small amounts – need to consider use of sources, audience and competition.

It is obvious from the attendance figures that Workington AFC attract small crowds. Not all of the 250 or so supporters will buy the magazine, and sales to people not attending games will be small. Despite this, there are *two* magazines – or fanzines – devoted to the club. They can survive because each aims for a different kind of coverage. Each considers the work of the other. Each has its own regular sources of information – primary and secondary – and each considers the needs of its audience.

When you consider your own ideas for a print product, it is important to think about your audience. A small audience has some advantages – so long as you understand your readers and present the right material. Good planning is also important. The writing style of *Nothing Borough Parks Team* may be chatty and a little cheeky, but it still follows the essential rules of successful publishing.

Preparing a proposal

Having conducted your research, the next stage in the development of your print product is to prepare a formal **proposal**. A proposal is a document that outlines all the important information about a print product. It allows a number of people to assess the likely success of the product. It also means that all of the important issues – finance, likely audience, content, etc. – can be discussed one at a time. Print products are often changed at the proposal stage as points are discussed and refined.

Proposal presentation

Proposals are usually broken down into a series of headings as follows:

- Classification
- Purpose
- Target audience
- Genre
- Medium
- Style
- Content
- Production method
- Resource requirements

There is no one 'right' way to lay out a proposal. Its appearance depends very much on the individual subject and intended reader. On page 83 you will see a made-up proposal for Ladybird books. Although the proposal itself is fictional, Ladybird is a real company which publishes a distinctive range of books dealing with true-life subjects. Ladybird has a well established reputation with an international audience of children. The proposal does not need to go into great detail about the length of the book, layout, size of pages, etc., because these will be the same as other Ladybird publications.

For your work you have limited time and resources. For this reason, a detailed proposal is very important because it will help you to make the best use of limited resources.

Now let us look more closely at the proposal headings listed above.

Classification

This includes all of the information that will help people to decide what type of product is being produced.

Purpose

This is the reason for the publication to exist. The section from 'Nothing Borough Parks Team' headed 'What's the Point?' is a good example of how to state a purpose for a print product.

Target audience

These are the people who will read/look at your product and their reasons for doing so. You should already have some useful information on this subject from the last activity.

Genre

Genre refers to the type of media products to which your product belongs. See the boxed item on page 84 for a fuller explanation of this term. Groups in the print media include tabloid newspapers, children's comics, women's magazines, special interest magazines, advertising posters and informative CD-ROM packages.

Case Study: a sample proposal (I)

Look at the proposal below for a series of books
produced by the children's publisher Ladybird.
You can see from this proposal that a number of
different points were considered.

Ladybird

PROPOSAL

Series title: **MYSTERIOUS UNIVERSE**

Classification
Three books covering popular mysteries. 48 pages,
illustrated, topic definition and three examples per
double-page spread.

Content
Common theme and approach defining mysteries, presenting
examples and exploring possible explanations.

Production methods
Author to supply 'hard' copy on paper, photocopy of
illustrations and disc copy in readable format. Books
assembled on computer prior to print run.

Purpose
Explore subject popular with target audience. Establish
Ladybird presence in expanding market for children's
books on true-life mysteries.

Resource requirements
Copy and picture reference details to be supplied by
author. Pictures from libraries and regular illustrations team.

Time-scale
Author: Deliver final copy by 31st Oct 1996. Books to
be published late June early July 1997 to coincide with
50th anniversary of first 'flying saucer' sighting and
Roswell UFO incident.

Titles
Agreed with author: 'Mysteries of Earth and Space',
'Mysteries of the Mind', 'Mysteries of the Supernatural'

What is a 'genre'?

A **genre** is a media product such as a book or film with a distinctive style and content. The word 'genre' is French and means 'type.' In the media, genres have developed because elements of successful products have been carried over into imitations. Genres may change over time as audience tastes develop, but they tend to change slowly and their style and content can remain very much the same over a period of years.

Horror fiction is an example of a print genre that has lasted for well over a century. During that time, horror material has appeared in a range of print products. Comics, magazines, books, posters, CD-ROMs and commercial graphics material have all used horror ideas in the form of words and pictures and graphics. The existence of the horror market has continued because horror material has managed to adapt. It continues to draw on our deepest fears. Because people continue to have fears, there is likely to be a future for material that understands these fears and presents them in the form of stories, characters, images and interactive material.

Medium

As we saw in Chapter 1, a 'medium' is the means of communication used by a media product. Remember that the 'print' medium also covers electronic publishing.

Style

This has already been discussed on page 61. The style of a product is the way it does its job. The term covers both images and writing, and it should be understood that style is based on choices. These choices give each print product its distinctive identity.

Structure

This is the way a publication is put together. All publications are made up of different items or elements. In a book, the structure is usually based on chapters which are similar in form. Newspapers are usually made up of a range of different items which are put together – or structured – in a certain way. This reflects the way that the readers will use the paper.

Content

Your proposal for your product should also discuss **content** and give details of the subject matter you intend to cover. You should also consider the *way* the subject will be treated – humorously, informatively, seriously, etc. It is possible to combine more than one treatment of a subject, but this needs to be carefully thought through. It is also important to plan the contents and decide which aspects of your subject you will cover and which will be left out. You should base this part of your proposal on your research. The audience research carried out in Activity 1.7 should give you some ideas for this. You may also want to carry out some more research. Before starting work on a print product, it is a good idea to compile a list of things that the audience want to see in their print product and a list of things that they definitely do not want to see.

Case Study: a sample proposal (2)

PROPOSAL
Title: Beyond the X-Files

Classification Comic, 48 pages, full-colour illustrated throughout.

Content Material relating to popular television series. Comic strip stories featuring main characters, investigative material dealing with real life X-file type mysteries, background on making of real series. Posters, games, interviews and adverts including X-files merchandise.

Production methods CD to use existing in-house production facilities including page lay-out system and printing facilities. Television companies to supply source material including production stills, publicity photos and press releases. Freelance writers and artists to produce comic strip stories. Parent TV company to have right of veto on stories.

Purpose To raise profile of CD Comics in action/adventure market. Expand range of companies advertising within CD Comics, make short term profit for company and provide platform for long-term involvement in action/adventure market.

Resource requirements Time of one full-time member of CD staff and 50% time for another member of staff. Work of accounts and advertising sales staff will increase leading to possible part-time post. Paper and software capacity sufficient to print 50,000 comics per month. Initial outlay of £125,000 to cover contracts with television company, advertising, market research and production of initial proof copies. Unspecified sum for printing of first edition — likely print run of first edition 80,000 — to be decided after market research is completed.

Timescale Market research completed within six weeks, dummy pages ready for final two weeks of market research, complete proof ready for distribution to potential advertisers within eight weeks, first edition to print within twelve weeks, in shops within fourteen weeks.

Audience 9–12 year-olds; market research to decide on other details. Company predict 60-70% male.

Price Sale price predicted around £1.95, audience research needed before final decision is made.

Production methods

This part of the proposal should describe how you will actually produce your work. It should include details of any process, equipment or particular skill that you propose to use. You may need to check on the details of software packages you plan to use before completing the proposal.

Resource requirements

This section of the proposal should include details of each of the different types of resources described earlier in this chapter, namely:

- **Human** – both in terms of time and the kind of skills required
- **Financial** – the amount of money required to achieve the aim; when it is required, and whether it is needed all at once or in stages. You should be realistic about costs. It may also be a good idea to draw up alternative plans depending on the amount of money available.
- **Time** – You have already considered human resource time but you may have to allow time for material to arrive, research to be completed, etc.
- **Consumable stock** – Consider the amount of paper, computer discs, glue, etc., that you are likely to use.

Activity 2.6

1 Develop a proposal for each of the two print products you are working on. In the group work, you should each play a full part in the production of the proposal. You will need to use the research done in Activity 2.5 to develop the basic ideas.
2 Make sure you have covered each of the different areas above.

All media products need to be produced to an agreed schedule

Planning and scheduling

Once your proposal is complete and agreed, the next step is to work out a production **schedule**. In the print industry most major products are produced to a specific timetable which lays out the whole process of production in a logical way. It states who is responsible for what and puts deadlines on the completion of tasks.

When you have a strong personal interest in your print product, it is easy to forget that the success of the project depends on organisation as well as ideas. Schedules are important because – like proposals – they break down complicated projects into a series of tasks. They also allow each task to be thought out and changed if necessary before production actually starts. Schedules provide a plan for everybody involved in a project, and each person in the team needs to be aware of them.

Your own production schedule should include details of the following:
- Roles
- Health and safety assessment
- Dates
- Times
- Logistics

1 Roles

This means who is doing what. Assigning roles involves:
- Giving tasks to the right people
- Understanding where each person's responsibility begins and ends

The actual roles given to people depend on the size of the group and the type of product. It is important that you have an **editor** who is responsible for making final decisions on what is included in your product. Editors are responsible for making final decisions on content. The word 'edit' means to polish, correct or re-arrange.

Other roles in print production are shown in the table below:

Role	Duties and responsibilities
Layout	Responsible for design and presentation. Concerned with visual appearance of the work.
Research	Responsible for finding material and gathering information about needs of audience. Also, keeping records and being able to discuss this as required.
Sub-editing	Checking and re-working material to make sure it fits the space available. Decisions made to be passed to editor for final approval.
Production	Generating original material, e.g. print, pictures and graphics. Considering alternatives, checking facts and getting right 'angle' on material.

2 Health and safety assessment

The Health and Safety at Work Act governs all places of work. It sets standards for safety procedures. The Act was introduced to protect everyone at work and it applies equally to all areas of work. You are not required to know about this Act in detail for your GNVQ, but you are expected to be responsible for having a safe working environment.

You should arrange an assessment for health and safety. In this assessment somebody should inspect the work of producing your print product and report back on health and safety issues. Health and safety are very important in a production environment because they ensure that people can work as safely as possible.

3 Dates

Dates given in the schedule form what are known as **deadlines** – in other words, times by which tasks must be completed. In the print industry this is vital because work is often passed from one area to another – for example, from writers to editors – and this has to be done on schedule in order to allow everyone time to do their job. The term 'deadline' is used because work which misses its deadline may not get produced at all.

4 Times

In many print projects, a specific amount of time is allotted to each job or task. This is useful because it keeps everyone's mind on getting the job done.

In your schedule it is important that you allow the right amounts of time for each piece of work. It has often been found that tasks 'expand to fill the time available'. In other words, if you have been given a week in which to write an article, it is almost certain that the article will take you a week to write!

5 Personnel

Most print products are produced by a range of people. Each person brings certain skills to the team. Good companies – both in and outside the media – become successful because the different team members work well together and share their skills. It is important in your work that you do the same. In Chapter 1 you completed a skills audit; if you have time, you could complete the same exercise again before scheduling production.

6 Presentation to audience

This is not included in most print schedules, but it is part of your GNVQ course. You should therefore arrange a date, time and place to present your work to an audience and get some feedback.

7 Logistics

As we saw earlier, the word 'logistics' when applied to a print product means all the organisational issues that must be sorted out before a product can appear. For example:
- Making sure equipment is available
- Making sure a safe working area is available
- Organising support for work teams such as food, transport, etc.
- Dealing with people or organisations outside the team

The logistics of different projects vary a lot. In the case of a football magazine, there are important logistical issues involved in making sure that the magazines are on sale at the football ground either before or during a game. Other products will pose other logistical problems.

Activity 2.7

1 Identify all the roles and responsibilities involved in producing the group newspaper. Allocate roles. Set deadlines for each task to be finished, and then plan the dates and times when tasks are to be done.

2 Carry out a health and safety assessment of the tasks, noting any possible hazards and action to be taken to avoid them. Plan the logistics involved at each stage, and show the arrangements on the schedule.

Content issues

One other potential problem area before you go into final production is that of **content issues**. 'Content issues' is a general term that means any issue or problem which may arise as a result of the content of your work. These can fall into a number of categories.

1 Legal

The law exists to protect people. In the print industry this protection has two important aspects:

- People's reputations are protected by the **libel law**. If something is published about a person which the Courts decide is damaging to their reputation or character, the writer or publisher must prove that what they have written is true. If they cannot prove it, then they may have to pay a very large sum in damages to the person they have wronged.

Potentially harmful allegations must be backed up by hard evidence

- Another legal protection concerns the ownership of work. If somebody writes material or creates images they usually own **copyright** in their work. In some cases the copyright is owned by the publication in which it was first used. If another publication uses this material without permission they can be sued by the copyright owner. A publication or person can also be sued for copying work too closely.

Owning or holding copyright is a good way to make money – so much so, that some agencies exist purely to hold and acquire copyright. At the start of this book you will find a list of credits for people who have given permission for the use of photos and other illustrations. These people are copyright owners. They charge a fee for people to use their pictures. Many of the photographs will have cost the publishers of this book a fee. However, this has to be a reasonable amount, or the people wanting the pictures will simply find a cheaper illustration from somewhere else.

Over the years, major newspapers like the *Daily Express* have built up extensive 'picture libraries' of photographs and other illustrations which have been used in the paper. These images are carefully filed and indexed and available for sale to other publishers to use in books, magazine articles or television programmes. Often picture libraries specialise in particular kinds of image. One of the biggest libraries in the UK is Rex Features, which specialises in pictures of famous people collected from photographers and newspapers. It is in the interests of freelance photographers to place their pictures in these libraries because when the pictures are used, both the library and the photographer receive a fee.

You will be expected to know about copyright, but in class you will not have to pay fees if you are cutting and pasting images that have been taken from magazines into a single copy of your own product. However, you should remember that if your product is intended to be sold in the shops for a profit, you will be expected to pay.

2 Ethical

The word **ethical** means 'decent.' Ethical behaviour is behaviour that respects other people's feelings and needs. In the media there are many ethical problems in the content and production of work. One major problem with the media is that much work sells because it offers an audience a chance to see into other people's lives. Problem pages are a popular feature in many magazines. In many cases the advice given can present ethical problems. For example, should an agony aunt tell someone to leave their partner or children?

Most of us have an underlying curiosity about other people. This means that work that invades people's privacy will almost certainly make money. If somebody in your local area replaced the outside wall of their home with glass, few people would be able to resist looking in. The interest which is satisfied by seeing 'juicy details' about other people's private lives splashed all over the media simply follows on from this kind of curiosity. The problem is that the people on the receiving end often do not welcome this kind of attention.

3 Discrimination

Another ethical issue is that of **discrimination.** This is when a person is treated differently because of some feature of their life such as a physical disability.

As with the privacy issue, the media tend to be pulled in two directions. Their desire for profits means that, in many cases, products such as magazines continue to present stereotypical images. On the other hand, the media have a legal obligation not to discriminate.

There are laws covering equality which apply to all areas of life. The regulatory bodies mentioned in Chapter 1 also forbid the use of material that is discriminatory on grounds of race, sex, sexual orientation, or religious or ethnic grouping.

In the case of the print media, the main regulatory body is the Press Complaints Commission, which is made up of people from within the newspaper industry. It is the responsibility of the Press Complaints Commission and other organisations to monitor the work of the print media, but many people remain unhappy with the way the print media represent certain issues. They argue that it is not enough to avoid giving offence, and that there should be 'positive discrimination' – i.e. presentation of positive images of minority groups. As we saw earlier in this chapter, disabled people are very rarely represented in the print media in a heroic or romantic light.

This is a complicated problem. As we saw in Chapter 1, an audience's view of an image depends very much on their own opinions and experiences. For this reason, it is important to recognise that your own print products – and the choices you make about content and representation – will reflect your own opinions and prejudices.

Activity 2.8

1 Working on your own, identify any legal, ethical or representational issues raised by the content of your group's newspaper.
2 Write your own notes describing each of these issues. Now have a discussion in your group comparing them with the other students' findings. Write up some minutes of the meeting as soon as possible and add them to your notes.

Review questions

1 Briefly explain how an audience might have influenced the development and distribution of Ceefax.
2 In your opinion, how does the fictitious commercial for Nibok sports wear on page 76 represent the product?
3 Name a primary source for research into your own life.
4 Name a secondary source for the same research.
5 Products which belong to the same genre have a similarity of s____ and c_____.

Element 2.3 Produce print products

By the time you have completed Activity 2.8 you should have considered all of the important aspects of pre-production. You may have made changes to your plans after some of the work above. It is now time to put your final plan into action.

This final section of the chapter is very short. This should be the busiest time of all in your GNVQ module, and you will have to think about many of the important points about print mentioned so far – layout, audiences, resources, etc. Use the Glossary on page 295 to refresh your memory if necessary.

Although you have already considered health and safety when preparing your schedule, unforeseen hazards can arise and it is a good idea to continue to keep notes on health and safety issues. These notes should be kept for all of the remaining activities until they are presented in the final activity.

Designing layouts for products

Having decided on what you are going to do and set out your proposal, you can now start designing layouts for your work. Many print products start with layouts in the form of double-page spreads. These allow people working on the material to get some idea of how the finished product will look. The points you should think about are listed in Activity 2.9 below.

Activity 2.9

1 Prepare the layouts for your final print products, including the information below.

- Size of type used
- Colours used
- Style
- Balance of images and text
- Amount of space for borders
- Number of columns per page
- Use of headlines – size, wording, etc.
- Links between image and text
- Links between different items in one publication

In the case of the group work, you should produce suggested layouts on your own, then hold a meeting with others in the group to compare suggestions. You will all have to agree on final choices – which are likely to include the best bits of everyone's work.

2 Keep your own original page layouts to hand in later.

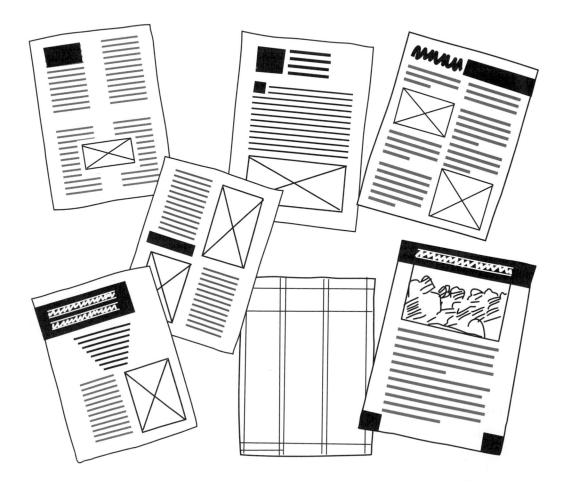

Examples of different styles of page layout

Layout issues

At the layout stage a number of important questions need to be considered:

- **'Rival' products** Look at products similar to your own that are already on the market. Make brief notes on the way they use type-size, colour and other areas listed below, then consider your own choices. When you are assessed on this work you will need to be able to explain your decisions and put forward good arguments to justify your choices.

- **Size of type** You should be aware of the range of type-sizes available to you. For example, if you are using a computer in your school/college it should present you with a list of type-sizes and styles. You may want to print some of these off to help you make decisions.

- **Colour** Budget constraints may mean that colour printing is beyond your means. But you may be able to use colour photocopiers and laser printers. There are some very cheap options available which may involve importing colour directly into your product or using images – e.g. pictures of famous people – clipped from other sources.

- **Style** Don't be vague about the style of your product. It is vitally important to define your style clearly so that everyone understands how you want to represent people, places and things, and the kind of impression you want to give.

- **Balance of images and text** You should start your work with a clear idea of the amount of space you have available. Once you know this, you can look at the ratio of images to text and compare it to 'rival' publications. You should also be aware of possible problems scanning in images, laying out areas of text, etc. This is especially important if you are relying on one specific software package to produce your final work.

- **Borders** As with the decisions on images and text, you should be aware of the way that professional products use borders. You should also be aware of any limitations in terms of equipment and time. Your decision on the use of borders should be understood within your group because this will allow everyone involved to produce work with the same appearance.

- **Number of columns per page** Your choice here will depend on the size of page you are using. It is advisable to run off some test prints which will allow you to look at the options available. Columns allow you to separate different items, but a lot of text crammed together can look very off-putting. Despite this, broadsheet newspapers often use dense pages of text.

- **Headlines** A well-chosen, punchy heading can make a big difference to a page. Headlines should be used appropriately – if you are asked why a specific headline is included or why a particular word was printed in large letters you should be able to justify your decision.

- **Links between images and text** It is important to be able to explain how images and text work together. You may be able to see a link between a particular image and the words around it, but it may not be apparent to the people assessing your work. It is important that your entire group has a clear idea of the links between images and text in the work they produce. You can check on this in advance by putting together clear sentences to explain your intention.

- **Links between items** As with the links between images and text, you should take care to explain the links between all of the items in your work. You may think some of them are obvious but you will only get credit if you can explain them in a convincing way. Some products simply bundle items together because it is assumed the target audience will be interested in a number of different subjects. In other cases products assume that an audience will make links for themselves. For example, a pop-star calendar assumes that the audience are interested enough in the performer to want to look at the same person all the year round. You may want to look at your product and make notes on the links that you feel exist between items.

Producing text and images

Once the layout has been designed and approved, the next step is to produce the text and images.

General guidance

Keep rough copies of your material and make a note of any changes of plan. Try to stick exactly to the proposal and schedule and discuss the work within your group as it progresses.

Your tutor should be able to offer some guidance as you complete your work. A well prepared plan will also help you. In addition, you should consider the kind of problems that are likely to present themselves.

Writing the copy

Almost certainly, your project will require you to produce a certain amount of original writing – known as **copy**. This will probably be based either on your existing knowledge of a subject, on research material that you have gathered, or a combination of the two. Your copy will gain you marks when it shows a clear structure and meets the needs of the intended audience.

Think carefully before you finalise your text and look at it very critically. Ask yourself:
- What am I telling my audience that is important or new?
- Why have I included this particular piece of information?
- Why have I left out that particular piece of information?
- How much can I achieve within the word limits I have agreed?

Good copy sets out with a clear aim in mind, whether it is to entertain, inform, persuade or amuse. Use facts clearly to build up an argument and only include details that really matter to the audience. Make each point clearly then move on to the next one. Don't repeat yourself. Avoid trying to do too many things in a limited space. Above all, don't use facts simply because you have them in front of you.

It is often useful to study the work of professional copywriters. If you ask the same questions about their work that are set out above, you will soon see that they use a clear structure which involves building a series of points towards a particular aim.

Thinking about structure

As well as writing clear copy, you should aim to *structure* your articles to the best possible effect. This means organising your facts and examples in a way that makes sense to the audience. You should also consider the 'angle' that the final work will take.

You will gain the most marks if you can explain that the decisions you took allowed you to present the right kind of material to your audience. It is useful to prepare this argument before you begin work – it will help you avoid being side-tracked into writing material with the wrong angle.

Sourcing images and graphics

Good pictures and drawings are always worth including, but you must be able to explain your reasons for using them. Be realistic about about what you can achieve with the equipment, time and layout skills available to you.

Again, it is useful to compare your own work to professional work which is available to buy. Images, such as photographs, help to add interest to printed work. Graphics – i.e. logos, and features such as rules (straight lines) – also help make work more attractive and direct the reader's attention towards particular items. You should be able to support your choices in these areas with arguments about the options available to you and how your choices have added to the appeal and impact of your work.

Activity 2.10

1 Select material for each of your print products.

2 Produce the raw material needed for your print products, making sure you keep to the proposal and production schedule and stick to deadlines. Consider all of the issues outlined above and follow safe working practices at all times.

Note: For the group work, everyone should have an input into the choices being made, but the final decision should be that of the editor.

The editing process

Producing text and images is only the start of getting material ready for publication. One of the most important stages in the development of any printed product is the **editing** process. Editing involves a number of activities:

- Checking for spelling mistakes and other errors
- Making sure material makes sense and is consistent
- Making sure material is pitched at the right level for the audience
- Fitting material to the right style and length

As you edit your publication you may find you have to make a number of last-minute decisions about which material to use. You may also find you have to cut and organise material to fit the demands of the proposal and schedule.

Although everyone can make suggestions and spot important changes which need to be made, the editor should have final responsibility for the presentation and accuracy of the content.

Activity 2.11

1 Duplicate some of the raw copy produced, so you can hand in examples of corrected and uncorrected text.

2 Do your share of the editing work on the copy for your group's newspaper. Think about the demands of the proposal and schedule. Keep any work rejected at this stage. Discuss decisions with other members of the group.

Case Study: editing a press release

HEAVENLYPRESSOFFICE

Heavenly Press Office 72 Wardour Street, London W1V 3HP. Telephone 0171 494 2998. Facsimile 0171 437 3317

saint etienne
"too young to die"

**Heavenly, HVN LP 10 LP/MC/CD (limited CD with remix l.p.),
released 13th Nov '95**

"Only Love Can Break Your Heart"/"Kiss And Make Up"/"Nothing Can Stop Us"/"Join Our
Club"/"People Get Real"/"Avenue"/"You're In A Bad Way"/"Who Do You Think You Are"
"Hobart Paving"/"I Was Born On Christmas Day"/"Pale Movie"/"Like a Motorway"/"Hug My
Soul"/"He's On The Phone"

Saint Etienne release "Too Young To Die", a compilation of all of their singles, on Heavenly
on 13th November 1995.

Summer 1990 is soundtracked by the lazy, breezy groove of "Only Love Can Break You
Heart" . Words borrowed from Neil Young, beat from "Back To Life", atmos by Stanley &
Wiggs. After 12 months of Madchester madness, Saint Etienne's opening shot is a Balearic
breath of fresh air. Smash Hits, Top Of The Pops and hordes of screaming fans beckon. Over
the next five years, Saint Etienne become an institution of unparalleled pop genius. Three
albums down the line, a lengthy breather is called. One year (and much breathing) later, they
are BACK with their biggest hit to date, "He's On The Phone", and the album, "Too Young To
Die".

And so, together as one, we have "Nothing Can Stop Us" with more hooks than New Order
and Revenge put together, the kandy koloured klown musik of "You're In A Bad Way", the
tears-on -the-telephone "Hobart Paving", Pedro Almodovar's fave 45 of '94 "Pale Movie", and
the latest mind "blower", "He's On The Phone". Truly an album for you, your children, and your
children's children.

Saint Etienne are still Sarah Cracknell, Bob Stanley and Pete Wiggs. During their "wilderness
years", they are recording together with Gaelic pop Lothario Etienne Daho, Sarah is working
on her first soho album, while Bob and Pete get it on with Shara Nelson, Stakka Bo and a new
project cloaked in mystery, murder and suspense.

"Too Young To Die" is Saint Etienne, end of part one. See you next year...

For more information call Robin or Chloe on 0171 494 2998.

Study this press release for St Etienne's album 'Too Young To Die.' This is a real press release from a record company. This material was forwarded to the music press and anyone else with an interest in reviewing the album.

This release has been edited for an article and then sub-edited *(see opposite)*. In the process, the release has been turned into a short news item.
Notice how the sub-editor has:
- added a different title for the news item
- changed the first sentence
- changed 'has' in the second sentence to 'contains'
- taken away the last sentence

Case Study (Contd.)

The Story So Far

It isn't the end because St Etienne are 'Too Young To Die.' On the other hand.....we've got 14 hits packed onto one greatest hits CD which marks the end of the first phase of their pop career. The album has every Etienne track that ever bothered the charts. According to the record company the band are planning a breathtaking set of projects including a solo album from Sarah and production work from Pete and Bob. We'll have them back next year. Until then we've got 'Too Young To Die.'

Edited news item

Saints Go Marching Out

St Etienne release 'Too Young To Die', a 14-track greatest hits package, next week. The album contains every Etienne track that ever bothered the charts. According to the record company, the band are planning a 'breathtaking set of projects' including a solo album from Sarah and production work from Pete and Bob.

Sub-edited news item

Now you try...

Sarah Cracknell, the singer with St Etienne, released a solo album in 1997. Imagine you are working for a paper and you have to add a picture to a story about her solo career. The only picture you can find is the one of the band featured here. Try using a piece of paper to 'crop' the photograph of the band to illustrate a story about Sarah's solo career.

A sub-editor might try the following:

- Crop picture to show singer Sarah Cracknell on her own, adding the caption 'Saint's Sarah, solo act'
- Crop the picture to show half of Pete and Bob's face on either side of Sarah, with the caption 'Pete and Bob keep an eye on solo Sarah'

Can you think of a better cropping or caption?

Sub-editing

This is the detailed process of putting the print publication into its finished form. In the case of print products made by an individual or a very small number of people it is often hard to make a distinction between sub-editing and editing. The main difference is that whereas an editor is responsible for an entire publication, sub-editors have limited responsibilities which are usually centred on one area – captions, pictures, etc. If a sub-editor does a thorough job, an editor will be able to pass the 'subbed' material with few changes.

In terms of **written** material, a sub-editor may:

- Add or delete words
- Write captions and headlines
- Structure material – for example, putting items in a different order (often called 'sequencing')

In terms of **visual** material a sub-editor may:

- Crop pictures – i.e. alter the dimensions, either to make them fit or in order to exclude unwanted material
- Scale pictures – in other words, make some bigger or smaller than others
- Sequence pictures – put them in order to make a point.

Activity 2.12

1 Do your share of the sub-editing work for the group newspaper. Think about all of the points outlined in this section. Discuss the work with other students. Use this process to produce final items and layout for the product.
2 Sub-edit your own print product.

Getting feedback and evaluating your product

Once your work is completed, you should arrange to present it to a sample audience. By presenting it to a small group of people first, you can check their reaction and make any necessary adjustments. This kind of audience research is carried out by print companies on a regular basis.

You should plan your presentation to an audience as follows:

- Arrange a date, place and time
- Prepare some questionnaires asking for reaction to your work
- Use some statistical questions that will allow people to rate their opinions **quantitatively**
- Use some questions that will allow people to state their opinions and describe their reactions **qualitatively**
- Arrange some efficient way to record your findings

The purpose of the exercise is to allow the audience to **evaluate** your work. The word evaluation means 'to give a value to something'. In the case of media products, evaluation needs to be carried out both by the audience and by the producers themselves.

Your own evaluation

For your own evaluation, there are a number of different items which can help you measure the success of your work. Some of these are listed in the table below, together with the evaluation issues that they raise:

Item	Evaluation issue
Written plans, e.g. product proposal and schedule	How well were targets met? Were production deadlines adhered to?
Rough notes and rejected material	How successful were editorial decisions about contents and ideas? Were the right choices made?
Details of production processes and equipment	How effective and reliable was equipment, esp. computer hardware (see **IT core skills** below)? Were production processes appropriate?
Safety guidelines, health and safety assessment	Could health and safety have been improved? What lessons were learnt for the future?
Notes on audience reaction	How well did the product meet audience needs?

Your final evaluation should consider the following:
- Technical quality
- Usefulness of original proposal and plans
- Production process
- Audience response

In the case of live presentations, it is important to record the event and submit as much written evidence as possible to support any points made.

IT core skills

For the the IT key skills element of your course, you are required to prepare, process and present information and evaluate the use of IT. In this evaluation, you may find it helpful to think about how useful computers were in preparing and presenting your work. You can also evaluate their usefulness in helping you to organise research findings.

Application of number

The 'application of number' key skills element of your GNVQ course requires you to collect and record data, tackle problems and interpret and present data. You will have more data at the end of this work than at any other time in the unit, so now is an excellent opportunity to tackle this aspect of the course. Calculations based on areas like audience opinions, time taken in production, etc., can all form a useful part of your evaluation. So long as the calculations are helpful in the evaluation, they will be useful in gaining a grade and helping you to acquire key skills.

Activity 2.13

1 Present both your group product and your individual product to a sample of the target audience. Consider all of the points outlined in the section above. Record the reaction of the audience and make notes on their response.
2 Use the audience feedback and the other evaluation criteria to make your own detailed notes about each print product. Your evaluation should identify weaknesses as well as strengths.

Review questions

1 'Consideration of resources should include human resources'. True or false?
2 Briefly explain the function of a production schedule.
3 What is meant by the term 'layout'?
4 Who would usually write a caption for a photo: an editor or sub-editor?
5 Name two ways in which print products might be presented to an audience.
6 Giving a value to something is called e_____.
7 How might you use rough notes to help with an evaluation?
7 Name one way in which rejected items might help you in evaluating a print product.

Assignment 2
Investigating and producing print products

This assignment provides evidence for:

Elements: 2.1 Investigate print products
2.2 Develop a proposal for print products
2.3 Produce print products

and the following key skills:

Communication: 2.1, 2.2, 2.3, 2.4
Information Technology: 2.1, 2.2, 2.3, 2.4
Application of Numbers: 2.1, 2.2, 2.3

1 Put together a 'print products' file, containing all your written work from the activities in Elements 2.1, 2.2, and 2.3, each under the appropriate element heading.
2 Include any presentation material you used or videotapes of the presentations.
3 Make a careful cross-check to make sure all the work produced is in the file, and submit the print product file to your teacher, with your name and group clearly marked.

3 Planning and producing audio products

Element 3.1	Investigate audio products
Element 3.2	Develop proposals and scripts for audio products
Element 3.3	Produce audio products

What is covered in this chapter

- Nature of audio products
- Planning for audio production
- Audio production and post-production

Your 'audio' file will need to contain the following:
- Recordings of two different radio broadcasts
- Two audio products you have made yourself
- Notes and paperwork from your own two audio products
- Your written answers from the activities in this chapter

Your teacher may wish you to make a presentation of your work, playing suitable extracts and showing key points on an OHT.

Introduction

The majority of audio production is in the form of radio programming. If you are interested in pursuing a career in audio production, the radio industry is perhaps the most obvious place to look for a job. However, the term 'audio product' can refer to other items, such as talking books, newsletters for the blind, in-store entertainment, workout tapes or even self-help cassettes for relaxation or meditation.

All professionally-produced audio material must be of a competent technical standard and in some cases, the same codes and conventions are to be found in different types of product.

This chapter begins by analysing the range of audio products available. It then explains how to develop proposals and scripts for audio products, before taking you through the process of creating your own audio product.

Element 3.1 Investigate audio products

This opening section examines the range of audio products available, looking at issues of content and style, structure, target audience and codes and conventions. The items we shall be looking at are:

- News bulletins
- Phone-ins
- Drama
- Advertisements
- Magazines

News bulletins

This genre is found on almost all radio stations, and most broadcast news bulletins 'on the hour'. They can range from around one minute on a music station such as Radio 1 or Virgin to five or ten minutes on a speech station such as Radio 4. The main purpose of the bulletin is to inform: it is meant to provide listeners with a quick, regular update on the news – which may well have changed in whole or in part since the last bulletin. In practice, only two or three of the different stories in the bulletin may have changed or been replaced by new ones, but it is the job of the bulletin editor to freshen the material whenever possible, so that people listening for longer periods do not get bored.

Activity 3.1

1 During one day, listen to a number of news bulletins on Radio 4 and on an Independent Local Radio (ILR) station. Compare bulletins as stories develop and then drop out to be replaced by new ones. Compare bulletins at the same time on the two stations.

2 Record one bulletin of two to four minutes, either on Radio 4 or an ILR station. Make notes on the purpose of the bulletin, its target audience, style and structure. Begin by noting the genre and medium.

You will notice that local happenings are much more likely to be reported on the local radio station. An overturned lorry is unlikely to make the national news – however large the traffic jams – but an incident involving particularly unusual or unpleasant deaths or injuries would make the story of interest to a much wider audience than just those in the local area. When compiling any bulletin, the news editor must be guided largely by the interests of the target audience. This means making assumptions about who they are (based upon audience research) and what is important to them.

It is usually assumed that 'upmarket' listeners to Radio 4 are more interested in international news than, say, listeners to Radio 1. Local radio audiences want to hear about what is happening in their own immediate area.

As well as the content, the target audience will affect the style of delivery: it may be fast and upbeat, such as on Radio 1, or read at the slower, more careful pace preferred by listeners to Radio 4. Listeners' appetite for up-to-date news will also influence how news bulletins are scheduled – i.e., often and at regular times, or less frequently during the day.

Case Study: James Keen – a day in the life

James Keen has been a reporter on the County Sound Radio Network since 1995. His nine-hour shift begins at 0500 hours and he is responsible for compiling and reading news bulletins until early afternoon.

On opening up the newsdesk James will check with the local emergency services in case a story has broken overnight. He will read through national stories sent to County Sound by Independent Radio News in London and decide whether there are any local angles to them that might be worth following up. He will then begin to put the stories in order of importance to the early morning listeners to the breakfast show, which is about to begin. Some of the local **news copy** (scripts) will have been written for him the evening before, by the evening news staff. There may be audio with them in the form of voiced reports (**voicers**) or short packages (**wraps**). Each item on his running order is identified by its **catch** or **catchline.** One about a dangerous building collapsing on children playing inside would probably be given the catchline 'BUILDING'. A second item about the same story – for instance, reactions from a parent – would be called 'BUILDING 2'.

Newsflash!

After reading the first bulletin of the day, James receives a call from the traffic news spotter-plane Sky Eagle One. A chemical tanker has overturned on the A31 and traffic is building up in both directions. A check call to the police reveals that the spillage is toxic and the area is going to have to be evacuated. James alerts the studio and reads a brief newsflash on air, giving the details he has. The incident is to become the lead story in the station's bulletins for the rest of the day, as it develops and different reactions come in – from police, the hospital, fire brigade and public. Luckily, another reporter arrives at 0615 and she takes over reporting the story, while a third is sent to the scene to send back live audio using the radio car.

(Continued on page 104)

Case Study (Contd.)

This is a typical hour in James Keen's day:

0715	Do check calls to all local emergency services
0725	Write brief news headlines
0730	Read headlines and sport on air
0735	Follow up lead in news diary and record telephone interview
0742	Edit telephone interview down to a good 13 second 'soundbite'
0747	Write a **cue** (or introduction) to accompany soundbite
0749	Rewrite the top line of the lead story in the bulletin
0751	Decide final running order of the 0800 bulletin
0754	Scan through new copy to check for errors
0758	Enter news booth and get ready to present the news

At 0915 James Keen attends an editorial meeting with the rest of the duty news staff. The station receives calls and press releases from different sorts of organisations wanting publicity. They include clubs and societies, companies, and pressure groups. At the meeting decisions are taken about which stories to cover, and plans may be made to send a reporter to an event or to do an interview by phone.

Activity 3.2

1 Describe how the target audience influenced the content and style of the bulletin you recorded in Activity 3.1
2 Explain how the bulletin was affected by the location of the target audience. How was it affected by the nature of the audience at that time of day (were they commuters, students, office workers)?

News bulletin structure

On each station, the structure of a bulletin is usually the same, hour after hour. It may begin with headlines and even end with a recap of the 'top' or lead story. The length and number of stories depends on the **house style**. Each story can be dealt with in a number of ways:

- **Copy read only** = the item read out on air by the announcer
- **Copy + audio** = copy followed by a short audio clip of a relevant interview
- **Copy + voicer** = copy followed by a 'voice report' from a reporter covering the story
- **Copy + wrap** = copy plus one or more interview clips, all linked by the reporter

Where copy is followed by audio, a voicer or a wrap, it is called a 'cue'. A **wrap** (known in the BBC as a **package**) is a mini-feature of about 20 seconds' length. Longer features of over a minute are called **billboards** in Independent Radio.

The different ways of reporting stories are all **conventions** used by journalists. So is the use of **jingles** (short, catchy bursts of music, often advertising products), the positioning of headlines and the weather, and the way most stations begin their bulletins with a timecheck. The ending of voicers and wraps may be signposted by a 'standard out-cue' such as:

'Carol Beale, IRN, Rome'

Bulletins often end with out-cues that are easily recognised by the next person due to speak or start a jingle, such as:

'BBC, Radio News'

on Radio 4.

The manner in which journalists speak is also a convention and a code. The tone is always authoritative: it implies that what the listener is hearing is important – it is to be believed, because it is based on proven facts that the news organisation knows to be true. Few people would bother to listen to news that sounded made-up or was not taken seriously even by the newsreader.

A news jingle is also a code: it symbolises the start of the news and says 'Listen carefully, here is the news'! There are other codes in the form of sound effects which describe where sound is coming from or what is happening. Merely saying 'Rome' in the standard out-cue is a shorthand for 'and I am telling you this from where I am standing – somewhere in the capital of Italy'.

Activity 3.3

1 Experiment with compiling your own bulletin running order. Decide on your target audience first, then give your own catchlines to stories heard on the radio or found in your local newspaper. Compare your structure with those chosen by others in your class and give reasons for any differences and similarities.
2 Describe the structure of the bulletin you recorded in 3.1 and note the use of voicers, wraps and simple audio. Identify the codes and conventions.

The narrative structure of a whole news bulletin is usually multi-strand (see page 113) because several different stories, or narratives, are being covered – as in a soap opera. Individual items may be considered to be **closed** if they report on something which has happened where the facts will not change. If a new development may be expected on a live story, that narrative is **serial**.

Bias in news coverage

Inevitably, different people and organisations respond to news items in different ways. Broadcast journalists are expected to be unbiased in the way they report news and what they cover – especially with politics. Sometimes groups and individuals complain that their point of view or cause has been misrepresented, under-represented, or not covered at all. Any story in any bulletin may raise issues of representation.

Activity 3.4

1 Analyse the narrative structure in the bulletin you recorded for Activity 3.1. Identify examples of conflict, development and resolution and make notes.
2 Identify issues of representation in the bulletin. Look particularly at any social issues raised, such as the latest unemployment figures. Are there viewpoints that are ignored? Are all possible social groups represented fairly, or has shortage of time meant some are ignored?

Phone-ins

People love to talk – and many people love to hear others talking on the telephone, particularly if they can hear both sides of the conversation! Phone-ins come in two basic forms. They can be included as part of a more general programme, alongside a mix of music, interviews, chat or competitions, or the whole programme can be devoted to a phone-in.

When the Radio 1 Breakfast Show is being planned, a phone-in competition is just the thing to add some lively extra interest in the form of a jokey conversation between the presenter and a caller.

Chris Tarrant presenting the Breakfast Show on London's 95.8 Capital FM

Most 'sequence' programmes like the Breakfast Show use the phone to get reactions from listeners to the news of the day, to run competitions or simply to add variety to the content. Some programmes will phone out to listeners who have sent in their telephone numbers, while others will simply announce the studio number and wait for the lines to get jammed with people wanting to talk on air. A producer can often see how popular a programme is by the speed and the size of the response from callers – although if nobody calls in for a competition, it is always possible the question was too tricky!

Dedications are a popular way of using the phone in a sequence programme. The caller gets the chance to say hello to friends who might be listening, as well as chatting with the presenter. Whether the friends hear it or not doesn't always matter, because many callers are just so thrilled to have been on the radio that they get quite excited anyway.

A request is when a caller asks for a particular song or track to be played. This is more difficult to arrange than a dedication, because the chosen song or track may not be readily available in the studio. Also, not many radio stations are happy to let a small number of listeners take control of important decisions like choosing what music gets played.

Many callers love hearing the sound of their own voice 'on air'

Complete phone-in programmes usually fall into one of four categories:
1 The **open line** – callers can talk with the presenter about anything they want
2 The **specific** subject – calls are taken on a subject chosen by the producer
3 **Problem counselling** – callers want help with emotional or health problems
4 **Expert help** – callers ask for advice on gardening, consumer affairs, etc., from an expert in the studio

The purpose of any phone-in material is to entertain, educate or inform, depending on the subject-matter. Radio 4 has short, specific phone-in programmes such as the current affairs discussion programme 'Any Answers' (category 2 in the list above) and the financial advice line 'Moneybox Live' (category 4). The commercial station Talk Radio, however, uses all the different categories of phone-ins round the clock as they dominate much of its programming.

The 'shock jocks'
When Talk Radio began broadcasting, the launch publicity promised 'shock jocks' in the style of the ranting, raving talk-show presenters in the USA, where 'all-talk' is one of the most popular formats. There were many complaints to the Radio Authority about bad language on air. Often the words complained of were broadcast during the daytime, when children might have been listening. There were also complaints when Anna Raeburn did a phone-in on sexual and emotional problems in the middle of the afternoon. The station has since changed its approach: the shock jocks have been replaced, and Anna Raeburn has been moved to an evening slot.

talk radio
1053/1089 am

The style of presentation and the choice of callers sets the tone of any phone-in programme. Even without the shock jocks, Talk Radio still aims to be lively and exciting, while Radio 4's 'Any Answers' programme is much more formal

At first, 'shock jocks' were notorious for their use of bad language on air

in approach – as you would expect with a totally different subject-matter and target audience. Instead of advising callers to leave their partners for somebody else, Jonathan Dimbleby is more likely to question callers about their opinions and why they hold them – often playing 'devil's advocate', i.e. strongly putting one side of an argument in order to make the caller defend their own position.

Again, producers make many assumptions about the audience and their interests. Here the content and style of the programme will be influenced not only by the target audience, but also by the time of transmission. Most radio stations would have considered Anna Raeburn's material too explicit for a daytime slot.

Phone-in structure

The structure of a phone-in depends very much on the content and the style. If it is an open line, with callers deciding what they want to talk about, all the presenter may do at the beginning is to give the telephone number and invite people to call. If there is to be a specific subject, there may be some scene-setting first – either the presenter quoting newspaper headlines or news reports, or discussing the topic with an invited guest in the studio. The guest may be called upon to make further comment as the programme progresses, or even talk with the callers as well. 'Any Answers' starts lining up its callers an hour in advance, by running trails in the programme before it, such as:

"If you're a gun owner, or you've ever been frightened by someone with a gun – or if you're just concerned by what you've heard so far, do call…"

Activity 3.5

1 Listen to two different types of phone-in on different types of radio station, and analyse what makes them different. Identify the target audience and find reasons for the style of programme chosen. What is the purpose of each phone-in, or do they have several purposes, depending on the point of view?
2 Analyse the structure used in each. How would you plan the structure of a phone-in for your own student-run radio station, bearing in mind the target audience?

Screening callers

If a phone-in programme is dominated by the studio guest or guests, it may be that there are few callers – or few the producer wants to put on air. Remember, however 'open' the programme may sound, someone is likely to be filtering the callers, chatting to them first to find out what they are going to say. The producer will want to know whether they are going to be good talkers, and warning them when necessary to keep language decent and avoid naming other people for legal reasons (see the section on **libel** on page 126). Although the programme is made up of contributions from the public, it is still the result of someone making choices – who to put on, when to cut them off, whether to question them about their views and whether or not to agree with them.

There are issues of **representation** here, as elsewhere in the media: are only certain types of callers getting access to the airwaves, and are the views being expressed representative of all the listeners, or all of society, or just certain groups? Some social issues may be thought suitable or interesting or likely to cause a heated discussion. Other issues may be ignored because they are thought to be dull or not controversial enough.

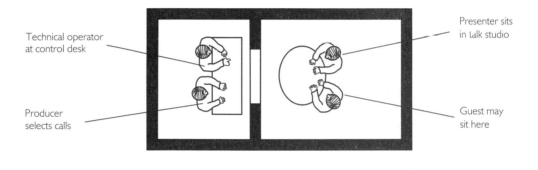

Technical operator at control desk

Producer selects calls

Presenter sits in talk studio

Guest may sit here

Typical studio layout for a radio phone-in

Phone-in codes and conventions

There are several codes in any phone-in. The format itself, whether in a one-off phone-in item or as a whole programme, involves positioning the host as the person in charge of the proceedings. The callers are allowed to take part in response to the host's kind invitation to contribute. No listener can just interrupt a radio programme of any kind whenever they want, so the invitation, '*do call…*", is a privilege allowed only occasionally. Even if callers are lucky enough to make it through the crowded switchboard and past the producer or assistant selecting which calls go 'on air', they are only allowed to speak for as long as the presenter wants them to.

Activity 3.6

1 Listen again to the two phone-ins you studied for Activity 3.5 and identify any codes in them. Is the type of language used formal or informal? Does the tone suggest they are serious or light-hearted? Does music play any part, and if so, what does it suggest?
2 Discuss your findings in class, playing examples to support your findings.

Conventions in phone-ins include the repetition of the programme's telephone number to encourage people to call. This can also be a code, because it will probably be repeated even if there are already too many callers lined up to fit in the programme. By doing so, the presenter is saying to the listeners that the programme is still keen to hear from them, and they still have every opportunity to get 'on air'. This creates an impression of open access.

The 'hellos' and 'goodbyes' at the start of each call may be brief or drawn out, depending on the style of the programme. However, it is a convention that each call is identified – that is, separated from the rest. Each caller is given an identity, too, unlike the party-style telephone chat-lines advertised in newspapers. Some programmes will use the callers' surnames, while others will just use first names. Sometimes keeping the callers more anonymous reduces the chance of someone being libelled – because it is less clear who was actually doing the talking, and who was being talked about!

Radio drama

Most drama is produced for radio, but some is produced for release on other media, such as audio cassette. Some 'talking books' for listening to in-car or by blind people are more like dramatic works than simple readings by a narrator. Electronic media such as CD-ROMs and Web sites can also contain audio drama.

People who have never heard drama on the radio often have difficulty imagining what it is like. They ask, how can we see the characters or the scenery? In fact, drama has been produced on radio since the earliest days of broadcasting – and successfully, too.

This script shows how creative sound on its own can be:

```
GIRL:      John, what're you reading?
BOY:       Oh, some story about a couple lost on a paradise island.
GIRL:      What's it like?
FX:        Waves lapping on beach (hold under)
BOY:       Blue skies, palm trees, coconuts and so many fish in the
           sea you can just put your hand in and pull one out.
GIRL:      What do they do all day?
FX:        Thunderclap 2"
BOY:       Well, they build themselves a shelter and...
FX:        Heavy rain and wind (hold under)
BOY (shouting):
           it blows down when a tropical storm comes, so they get
           soaked to the skin until...
FX:        Heard of elephants stampeding 3"(quick fade)
BOY:       they get trampled to death.
GIRL: (sarcastically)
           Mmm... sounds lovely! But don't you need pictures to enjoy
           a good story?
```

In 1938, Orson Welles and his Mercury Theatre Company terrorised America with their dramatisation of the classic tale *War of the Worlds*. They broadcast spoof news reports of strange objects landing from outer space, in between dance band music, as if they were real newsflashes interrupting the normal programmes. By the time the 'Martians' had climbed out of their pretend spaceships, many Americans had climbed into their cars and jammed the streets, trying to get away!

The BBC's radio soap opera 'The Archers' was first broadcast in 1951, long before ITV was invented and the set for 'Coronation Street's' Rover's Return was even built. Since then, the daily window on life in the fictional village of Ambridge has entertained millions of faithful listeners. For publicity purposes, the cast of 'The Archers' do dress up for photographs from time to time, but the programmes are normally recorded without a costume or make-up artist in sight.

Members of the cast of Radio 4's 'The Archers'

Drama codes

What makes radio drama believable to listeners is the large number of codes which operate in it. These can be the sound effects used – either as background 'atmosphere' (e.g. waves lapping on a beach) or 'spot' effects which are brief and describe an action (e.g. a thunderclap).

Music can have a similar effect: the combined effect of street sounds and an accordion playing may create a street scene in Paris. The theme music to a radio soap announces the start of the programme and takes the listeners all the way to the fictional location. When it fades in at the end – often on a 'cliffhanger' – it underlines the emotion or surprise in the closing words.

Other codes might be in the dialogue spoken by the actors. Compare the two lines below, to be spoken by a detective, and ask yourself which gives you the most information about what's going on – information you would need if you were listening but not seeing the action:

```
PHIL: (shouts) Hey! What do you think you're doing in here?

PHIL: (shouts) Hey, Constable! What do you think you're doing in my
               office at this time of the night?!
```

It is also a **convention** that the dialogue in radio drama is written in this way. The script must contain as much information as possible about what is happening, who is doing what, where they are, and so on. In this way, the dialogue and the sound effects combine to create a picture in the mind of the audience. Many people actually say they prefer radio to television or film because 'the scenery's better'! – that is because it isn't made of cardboard, and listeners feel more a part of what is going on because they create the scenery in their own mind.

Another convention is that the changes of scenes are indicated by a fade-out of one, then a second pause, and the fade-in of another. The passage of time can be suggested by a longer pause between scenes. Not every drama follows the same conventions, though. Some radio drama uses a fade-in/fade-out of music to mark changes of location or time. Sometimes a narrator may be used between scenes – often representing the thoughts inside a character's head. These are all codes, too, in the way they convey meaning to the listener.

Activity 3.7

1 Listen to 'The Archers' and another drama that is not a soap opera. Refer to the *Radio Times* to find out when and where they are broadcast.
2 Identify as many codes and conventions as possible, and play some examples back to the rest of the class, explaining how they work.

Radio drama genres

In terms of genre, radio drama offers a great deal more than just soap operas. You will also find one-off or 'single' plays and even serials.

Most radio drama in the UK is broadcast on Radio 4, but it is also often heard where you least expect to find it – for example, in advertisements on commercial stations, and in comedy shows on Radio 1FM or on the Steve Wright Show on Radio 2. Some more 'experimental' plays can heard on Radio 3, but drama on Radio 4 is usually aimed at a more general target audience. Their interests affect not only what kind of drama is scheduled, but when.

Although drama is expensive to produce – actors and scriptwriters have to be paid for their work – it is not necessarily what people want to hear at **peak times**. On television, the most expensive drama is scheduled during peak viewing hours, but peak time on radio is when people are on the move: at breakfast and evening drive-times. Few listeners have the chance to concentrate on 90-minute plays while eating breakfast or dashing out of the house to catch the bus!

By contrast, advertisements which use drama are so short they can be run at any time. If a radio advert uses drama instead of the more usual voice-over and music, it is because the client, or advertiser, has asked for something more creative. This often costs more money – partly because the scripting and effects take more time to prepare, but mainly because there are more actors to pay. An example of a script for a radio advert appears on page 115.

The purpose of radio drama

Radio drama can set out simply to entertain. An advertisement is intended to persuade – and in most cases to generate income for the advertisers, who in theory should sell more of their product. Corporate advertising can be just about improving a company's image, or about spreading information. When 'The Archers' was first created, it was intended to teach farmers about new farming methods in a way that would appeal to them – so drama can be educational, too. It often is, because BBC Schools Radio produces drama as well.

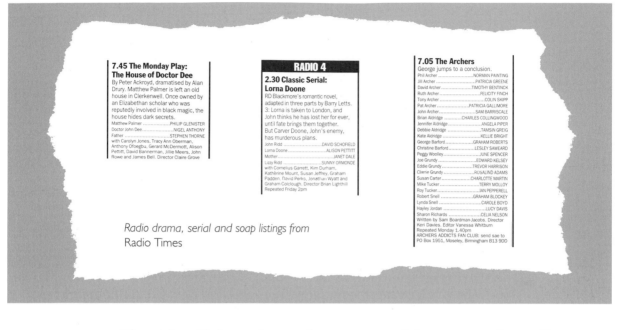

Radio drama, serial and soap listings from Radio Times

The style will depend upon the purpose and the target audience. Drama can be funny, serious, moving, exciting, depressing, inspirational, challenging or many other things, depending on what is intended by the scriptwriter. The scope for playing to all the different human emotions is also limited by the time available and the time-slot: it may be difficult to work a radio audience into a passion in a 30-second advertisement for a used-car dealership – but there are plenty of talented creative copywriters who would like to try!

Activity 3.8

1 Compare the styles of different advertisements using drama to put their message across. Now write a short script for a 30-second advert of your own, deciding what atmosphere, effects and music would be needed to make it come alive.
2 Do the same for a soap opera and a short play. Present your findings to the rest of the class, using tape extracts to help make the most important points.

Narrative structure
Narrative structures differ, depending on the nature of the drama. Soap opera is normally **multi-strand,** because a number of different storylines are being developed alongside each other in each episode. The final episode of a soap would be **closed**, because all the different storylines would be wound up and there would be no cliffhangers or mysteries left to unravel. Most single plays will also be closed, because there is nothing to follow on the next week. The narrative structure of a drama series is serial.

Representation
Drama raises many issues of representation. In 'The Archers', the Grundy family are the working-class types – and they are the ones who are usually up to no good, except for the mother, who, being female, tries to keep the men on the straight and narrow! Some producers argue that stereotyped characters are necessary to allow the listeners to imagine them as 'like' someone they know.

The storylines in 'The Archers' are not always about farming – they often touch on social issues. For example, the people of Ambridge have often agonised over issues such as women priests, New Age travellers, drugs and homelessness.

Activity 3.9

1 Work out the narrative structure of each item of radio drama you have considered so far, and briefly give reasons for your choice.
2 Identify any issues of representation raised by them. For instance, are any ethnic minorities represented? By what codes do you know they are there? Why? Are there gender or class issues in any of them? For example, are the doctors white, male and middle class, and all the unemployed people underprivileged? Explain your answers.

Advertisements

There are many different styles of radio advert, as well as those involving drama. The simplest is the single voice. This is a simple announcement with nothing but the voice and the script to put across the message about the advertiser's product. Used sparingly, it can be very effective. If every advert used the same style, though, commercial breaks would be very dull.

Many clients ask for their message to be read over what is called a 'bed' of music. A voice over music is a 'voice-over' or 'v/o'. Even more creative clients (with bigger budgets) might want the advert to feature a specially created jingle. The idea is that, just as people hum along to catchy songs they hear on the radio, so they may well get hooked by a catchy lyric advertising the company's name or product . Here are two examples:

Two Mills – just another way of saying Honda.

Where in the world?... PC World

Some scripts call for two or more voices in conversation; others demand very creative drama production. The more people involved in the production process, the more it will cost the client to produce. Some very well known actors and actresses now voice radio adverts, and they may charge much higher fees to appear because they are endorsing a product. Otherwise, many of the voices you hear are those of the professional voice-over artists who record for several different radio stations a week.

Alphasound in Manchester produce adverts for several stations, sending them from their studios to the radio stations over quality ISDN lines, ready for almost immediate transmission.

Purpose

The main purpose of any advertisement is to persuade – i.e. to sell the advertiser's message to the listener – and thus generate income. It may also entertain, as the message may be remembered more easily if it has been amusing.

Since advertisers have to pay for the production of the advert and for transmission of the advertising campaign, they are usually very careful about the target audience. The content must be carefully designed to appeal to the likely customers. It must also be scheduled at a time when that kind of person is likely to be listening. If the advert does not appeal to the target audience it can hardly be expected to work. Likewise, if it is not even broadcast when they are listening, it has been a waste of money.

COPY

DIET COKE
RADIO 30" 23.1.96
'SATURDAY'

GIRL 1:	It's eleven thirty.
GIRL 2:	It's eleven thirty.
GIRL 3:	It's eleven thirty.
GIRL 4:	It's eleven thirty. Diet Coke break.
SFX:	SILENCE
GIRL 1:	He's not there ...
GIRL 2 :	Not there ? ...
GIRL 3:	... look, he's not there ....
GIRL 1:	But ...it's eleven thirty.
GIRL 2:	It's eleven thirty ...on Saturday!
GIRL 3:	Oh we forgot it was Saturday ...
GIRL 2:	...wonder what he does on Saturday ..!
SUNG:	I JUST WANNA MAKE LOVE TO YOU ...
ANNCR:	Diet Coke. Just for the taste of it.
	Can help slimming or weight control only as part of a calorie controlled diet.

Script for 'Diet Coke' radio advertisement

Scheduling issues

Many local commercial radio stations schedule sports programmes on Saturday afternoons. That is because they expect lots of male listeners will want to know the latest on their favourite football team. Since lots of males tune in on Saturday afternoons, it is also an ideal time for advertisers wishing to target a male audience to schedule their adverts.

Breakfast time is the largest audience of the day, but mid-morning audiences usually include a higher proportion of housewives. Many will be about to go out shopping, and they may be encouraged to buy products they have heard advertised on the radio when they get there.

In terms of structure, the simpler the message is, the more effective the advert. Usually a product will have a 'unique selling point' (USP); the advertisers' main aim will be to put this across, together with the name of the product and how to obtain it:

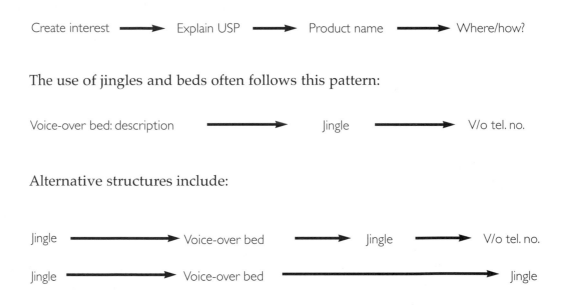

Create interest ⟶ Explain USP ⟶ Product name ⟶ Where/how?

The use of jingles and beds often follows this pattern:

Voice-over bed: description ⟶ Jingle ⟶ V/o tel. no.

Alternative structures include:

Jingle ⟶ Voice-over bed ⟶ Jingle ⟶ V/o tel. no.

Jingle ⟶ Voice-over bed ⟶ Jingle

The musical bed may not be used for the whole of the advert, but will begin or end somewhere in the middle.

Codes and conventions

All the structures shown above follow conventions about how radio adverts should be created – but there will always be the creative commercial producer or copywriter who will come up with something dazzlingly different – no easy task when they have to write perhaps dozens of adverts every week!

As we saw earlier in our discussion of radio drama, careful choice of music can create a very powerful sense of mood and place. This applies as much to the simplest of adverts, as to the most complicated pieces of radio drama. Codes play a large part here. The commercial producer will have a library of musical tracks created for just this kind of production – called 'library music'. A large part of the creative process is being able to select from hundreds of tracks the one which sounds right for the mood the producer wants to create. The recording companies try to make the job easier, by calling the various compilations, say, 'Industrial' or 'Pastoral' to indicate how the tracks will sound – and what coded messages they will convey about the product.

Another code may be in the voice used: is it serious, or light-hearted? Does it sound authoritative, as if the person speaking knows what they are talking about and can be trusted?

Representation

It can be argued that representation in adverts is largely in the hands of the advertisers – after all, they are the ones who are paying for the message to be produced and broadcast: the commercial producers and copywriters simply create the adverts they want. Any under-representation of ethnic minorities is because the advertisers want to create mainstream images which have the widest possible appeal.

However, some radio adverts deliberately target what are known as 'niche markets' – often quite small audiences made up of a narrowly defined group of listeners. Stations such as Kiss 100FM in London, for example, have a high listenership among the capital's black community. Many advertisers on Kiss 100FM are probably targeting that community, as they are seen as likely customers.

Most voice-over artists are white and male – but there are many successful female ones, too. You will probably notice that most voices on adverts are middle-class. That doesn't mean, though, that the advertisers only want middle-class customers.

Activity 3.10

1 Record six different adverts from different commercial radio stations, noting down the day and time each one was broadcast, as well as on which station. For each one, match the style and structure to the target audience for the product.
2 Decide whether the audience being targeted in each commercial is likely to be listening in large numbers at those times, and if so, why. Decide whether that target audience matches the general audience of the radio station as a whole, or is just a sub-section of the total listenership.
3 Now find as many codes and conventions as you can in the adverts, and note your findings. What issues of representation are raised in them? Discuss your findings with the rest of the class, using the tapes as examples.

National magazine programmes

A radio magazine programme is just as the name suggests – a collection of different items wrapped up in a single package. Like print magazines, they can be general in content or specialised – with a name that indicates what they are about and who they are likely to appeal to.

The table at the top of page 118 shows a number of national magazine programmes past and present on Radios 4 and 5 Live. The content is determined by the target audience, and so is the time they were broadcast. 'Medicine Now' and 'Does He Take Sugar?' were for very specialised audiences, which is why they were broadcast at very off-peak times, around 9pm. In theory, lawyers and doctors who want to keep up with the latest developments in their fields will make the effort to tune in on the right evening at the right time in order to catch 'their' programme. In practice, some people outside the target group will listen too, perhaps because they have a particular interest in the subject.

Station	Magazine title	Content	Target audience
Radio Four	Today	News/current affairs	General Radio Four
	Moneybox	Financial matters	General Radio Four
	Does He Take Sugar?	Disability/the disabled	Disabled and their carers
	Sport on Four	Sports features	Sports fans
	Kaleidoscope	Arts	General Radio Four
	Medicine Now	Medical issues	Medical profession
	Law in Action	Legal issues	Legal profession
	Mediumwave	Media	General Radio Four
	You and Yours	Consumer/family matters	General Radio Four
Radio Five Live	The Magazine	General	General Radio Five Live
	The Big Byte	Computing	Computer fans
	Top Gear	Motoring	Motoring enthusiasts

Specialised magazines will 'inherit' fewer people listening to the programme before than a general programme, because people are more likely to switch off with such an abrupt change of subject. The more general magazines are more likely to contain something to interest everybody listening, so they are scheduled in peak times. Radio 5 Live has fewer specialist magazines, mainly because of its high content of rolling (i.e. continuous) news and sport.

Magazine style

The style of a magazine depends upon the content, because specialist audiences expect to be spoken to as if they know something about the subject. More general audiences are likely to need more explanation before items. This is particularly true if the subject is less everyday.

There are a number of different types of items found in a magazine. A programme might regularly use some or all of these:

- **Feature, package, wrap or billboard** – a report linked by a single reporter
- **Live or recorded interview** – by the presenter or a reporter on location
- **Two-way** – presenter talks to a reporter on location
- **Double-header** – presenter chairs discussion between two guests
- **Debate** – presenter chairs studio debate
- **Review or talk** – guest in studio reads prepared script
- **Music**
- **Competition**
- **Weather, travel, business updates**
- **News headlines**

Which items find their way into the programme also depends upon its purpose. It may be intended only to inform or to educate – or entertainment could be the main purpose. If so, music or competitions may well be included.

Activity 3.11

1 Listen carefully to a national magazine programme, noting down its transmission times. Identify the target audience, based upon the network, day, time and content. Use the information to explain the style of the programme and why it is broadcast at that time. Write down all your answers.

2 Identify the programme's purpose, and explain how the style chosen helps it to fulfill that purpose. Why is the style suitable for the target audience?

Magazine structure

The structure of a magazine depends upon its purpose, target audience, content and duration. Shorter magazines are unlikely to repeat items because many of those listening at the end of the programme will have been listening at the beginning. The longer magazines, for example, 'Today' at breakfast time on Radio 4, run for a number of hours, and so some early items may be repeated or updated later on. All the items in the magazine will be linked together by one or two presenters.

The role of the presenter is crucial in keeping the programme flowing. A typical presenter's role would be as follows:

- Introduce programme
- Menu of items
- Cue to item 1
- Back announcement to item 1
- Timecheck and signpost
- Cue to next item
- Back announcement to item ◀
- Timecheck and signpost   *Optional loop*
- Cue to next item
- Signpost next programme
- Farewells

The **narrative structure** of a whole magazine is multi-strand because a number of different items run through the programme. However, each item may be either closed (because it is finished) or serial (because there is more to come later or in a different programme as a follow-on).

Codes and conventions

Certain conventions apply to magazine programmes – such as the use of a 'menu' at the start, to list the items coming up. Regular 'signposting' through **links** provides a reminder of what the programme is called and what items are still to come. Often a weekly or daily magazine will end with a brief mention of items coming up in the next edition.

It is a convention that the presenter, as the central linking figure in the programme mix, is identified as a personality – rather than taking the more neutral role of a newsreader in a news bulletin. Friendly, off-the-cuff chat with contributors is very common – even in Radio 4's 'Today' which is listened to by top politicians and academics who you might expect to be too stuffy to want to hear jokey comments made about the sports reporters!

It is usual, too, for items to last no more than around four to five minutes, although there will always be exceptions. Jingles or 'idents' to identify the programme may be used, too, depending upon the programme (for example, 'Nationwide' on Radio 5 Live).

In terms of codes, the informality of the magazine presenter is a deliberate attempt to draw the listeners in to the programme by making them feel part of it. The informality suggests friendliness, which can encourage loyalty. With the listening figures in mind, the producers want the listeners to remember to tune in again next time. The way whole items are reduced to brief summaries in the menus and the signposting are also codes: listeners hear five words from the presenter which summarise a forthcoming five-minute feature; they decode them into an understanding of what the item will be about and will be like – and then decide whether to carry on listening or switch off.

Individual items, especially features or packages, also use sound codes in the form of atmosphere to paint audio pictures just as in drama, or music to suggest locations, subjects or mood.

Activity 3.12

1 Analyse the structure of the magazine programme you recorded earlier. Write down the different types of item, and identify where the menu and signposting are used. Also describe the narrative structure of the programme.

2 Identify any codes and conventions you hear, noting down your findings. Do the same with any issues of representation raised by the choice of presenters, reporters or guests. What social issues are covered by the programme, and whose side of the story gets the most favourable coverage? Is there any bias in the programme?

Review questions

1 Why do news bulletins run for different durations?
2 What is meant by 'target audience'?
3 List four ways telephone calls might be used on radio.
4 What are the conventions of radio drama?
5 Describe the structure of three different radio commercials.
6 What is a magazine programme?

Element 3.2 Develop proposals and scripts for audio products

Proposals and planning

Any new audio product must begin with an idea – one which is fully worked out in terms of who, what, when, where and why. Each of the audio products we have looked at so far in this chapter started out with a proposal. Some proposals are rejected and never get further than the idea stage, but many go on to be developed – and some, such as 'The Archers', become famous and run for a long time.

For Element 3.3, you are required to produce two audio products:

- A **radio drama** – to be done in a team of three to five people
- A **feature** (also called a 'wrap', 'package' or 'billboard') – to be done on your own

But first you have got to plan them properly. Before you begin planning the detailed content, you must first decide on the **classification** of the products you are going to make. Will you make a radio programme or some other audio product, such as a talking book or a promotional tape to play in a shop?

The next step is to decide on the **purpose** – is it to persuade, entertain, inform, educate or to generate income? Check back over what you have read so far in this chapter to help you match purpose to product.

Now decide which **genre** will be most suitable – taking care to bear in mind the target audience of the product, because they are the people you want it to appeal to.

The **style** will depend upon the genre and the target audience – it is no use making a promotional tape using rap music if the people who hear it are too old to appreciate your choice of music!

Next you can make some decisions about the **structure.**

Activity 3.13

1 Make two copies of the proposal sheet below and fill them both in. One copy is for your drama and one is for your feature. Some suggestions have already been filled in for you. As the drama is to be produced in a group, you will need to hold a meeting and decide amongst yourselves how to fill the sheet in. For the feature, you should complete the proposal sheet on your own, but you should discuss all your decisions with your lecturer when you have finished.

2 For both products you should begin a production log. An example of a production log is shown at the top of page 122. A lot of the evidence for completion of Element 3.3 will be found in the log, so it is important you keep it carefully and accurately, noting down everything you do towards making the products. In the group project you should make sure the work is spread evenly among you and that each of you does some of each task.

Name/s

Product: *Drama/feature*

Medium: *Radio*

Purpose: *Entertain/persuade/inform/educate/generate income*

Genre: *Soap opera/single play/bulletin item/magazine item*

Target audience:

Style: *Serious/funny/light-hearted/matter-of-fact/...*

Structure:

Audio product proposal form

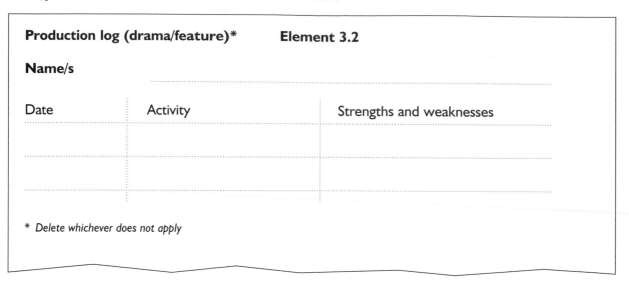

Production log (drama/feature)*   **Element 3.2**

Name/s
....

Date	Activity	Strengths and weaknesses

* *Delete whichever does not apply*

Example of a production log

Recording progress

You will continue to build up the proposal as you work through this section of the book. Remember to log every activity connected with the project. You are collecting important evidence about what you have done and how well it went.

It is also important that you **evaluate** everything you do – that is, identify the strengths and weaknesses of every action. **Strengths** are all the positive things which went right about what you did, and the **weaknesses** are the things that could have turned out better if things had been different. Reasons *why* something is a strength or a weakness are just as important.

Planning the content

Your product must appeal to the target audience and be suited to the context in which it is to be played. The context is the type of radio station – or, in the case of a talking book or promotional tape, the situation in which it is to be heard.

You need to think about the purpose and style of the item as much as the genre and the structure. The most successful people in the industry are those who can come up with workable ideas that have maximum appeal to the target audience, without sounding out of place next to the material which comes before and after.

Planning your feature

When choosing content, it is important to think about how easily you can gather the material. If you *must* include an interview with a member of the Royal Family, bear in mind that they are only very rarely available, even to the professionals. Can you really afford to get to Hollywood to interview a film star – and get back in time to meet the deadline? Every part of the content has to be something you stand a realistic chance of getting. You should try hard to get interesting material, though – one 16-year-old radio student 'doorstepped' footballer Paul Gascoigne until he got an exclusive interview with him which the newspapers would have fought over! Now that student is working full time as a qualified journalist.

The content is a vital part of any feature, wrap or package. Once you have thought of a subject you wish to investigate, consider what angle you will explore it from. If you chose dogs as your subject, you could fill hours of radio time covering everything from what they eat, to what to do if you are bitten by one, or how to deal with a neighbour who lets their dog bark all day. Choosing one angle for your five-minute feature allows you to home in on a particular aspect, and cover it in enough depth to make some impact.

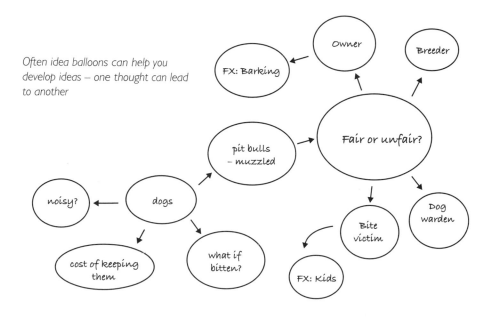

Often idea balloons can help you develop ideas – one thought can lead to another

Dangerous dogs

For example, suppose you chose as your angle the law that says certain dogs should be kept muzzled if they are out in public. Next you would have to decide on a **treatment**. The treatment is where you explain how you are going to cover the angle: who you are going to interview and what the listener is going to hear. Now the proposal would have the following extra information:

Audio product proposal	**Part 2**	**Element 3.2**

Subject	Dangerous dogs	
Angle	Muzzling pit bulls in public – is it fair?	
Treatment	Interviews:	Pit bull owner
		Council dog warden
		Pit bull breeder
		Dog bite victim
	Atmosphere:	Barking, snarling dogs recorded at dog pound
		Children playing in playground
	Linking script:	'Reporter' links all audio clips together

The only way to build up an idea is to do some preliminary **research**. The angle may only come once you have done some finding out about the subject.

Likewise, you may not begin to fill out your treatment until you have considered what information will be needed, and whose viewpoints ought to be heard. The research will also begin to tell you how realistic your idea is. If you find it hard to get answers, perhaps you are looking in the wrong place – or it might be that the subject you have chosen is just too difficult. Successful media producers also know when to cut their losses and move on!

Activity 3.14

1 Continue to develop your own feature proposal as shown in Part 2 of the audio product proposal above. Your own ideas should be different to the example shown, but they should be worked out in a similar way. You should also now cross-check your content ideas with the first part of your proposal, to make sure you have not strayed too far from the original brief.

2 Begin researching into the idea. What aspects do you need to cover? What will interest the target audience? Who will you interview and where will you get the atmosphere or sound effects (fx)? How much time and what resources are you going to need to gather the material for the feature?

Research into an idea is not just collecting facts and interview material – important as they may be. You should also be investigating *how*, *when* and *where* as much as *why* and *what*. Facts and interview material, as well as any music and sound effects you wish to add, will all come from either primary sources or secondary sources.

As we saw in Chapter 2, **primary sources** are the people you speak to at first hand, either on the phone or in person. They are considered reliable in as much as you, the reporter, are in a position to make judgements about whether they are telling you the truth. Of course, it may be difficult to tell immediately if someone is lying to you – and a good reporter checks facts before using them, particularly if they stretch the imagination a bit.

Secondary sources are the ones where the information has been passed on to you by someone, or written down in a book, document, archive, record, on the Internet, or in a newspaper. Facts from secondary sources may also come from radio programmes, television programmes or some other kind of recording – such as a CD-ROM. Here, it is up to you to decide whether the source is reliable or not. You must consider whether the writer of the news article or the producer of the video has quoted the information accurately, or whether it may have been taken out of context.

Content issues

Research and content planning always raise a number of content issues about legal matters, ethics and representation. The legal matters which most trouble radio producers are **copyright** and **libel**.

Copyright
Copyright is about a person's right to have their work protected from theft and plagiarism. The full details are in the Copyright, Designs and Patents Act 1988. Once a work has been created – for example, a book, article, photograph, song or radio programme – the right to make money from it belongs to someone.

That someone may be the writer, photographer or journalist, or it may be the person or company they were working for when they did the work. So, one reporter cannot just record someone else's interview with a pit bull owner off the radio and then use it in their own feature.

Paying copyright fees
If an audio extract such as a recording on a CD is used in someone else's programme, the composers, performers and sound recordists who made the original extract will all want to be paid for their work. Radio stations pay royalties to use music off disc – usually by making payments to the Performing Rights Society, Phonographic Performance Limited and the Mechanical Copyright Protection Society. Each organisation represents a different group of people who own copyright in recorded work.

PRS represent composers – when you broadcast their work

PPL represent record companies and performers – when you broadcast their work

MCPS represent publishers and songwriters – when you make recordings of their work

This usually means that a piece of music *may* be used – but the details on the label or sleeve will have to be noted down carefully and submitted on a logging sheet to the different organisations. These returns are made all together at fixed points in the year.

Copyright piracy is on the increase

This all may seem tiresome, but copyright law is there to protect *you* as well – because it means that your work is copyright, and no one can use it without your permission. You may use a recording of someone's voice if you get written permission to do so from the copyright-holder, but remember that the penalties for breach of copyright are heavy– it is important to get this 'clearance' to use copyright material or you may find yourself having to pay large sums if you are caught out!

There is no need to add the word 'copyright' to your radio broadcast as if you were producing a video, or writing a book or a magazine article. The law assumes that a broadcast radio item is someone's work and therefore belongs to someone: the person or organisation who has invested time, money, and use of equipment in creating the piece. However, if you are producing an audio book or a tape of any kind, you should print the word 'copyright' and your name and the year on the sleeve or label.

Libel

The other legal issue concerning content is **libel**. The Defamation Act 1996 covers audio products, just as it covers the other media, both print and audio-visual. It is there to protect people's reputations from being unfairly harmed.

For example, if a radio item makes 'right-thinking people' think less of someone unfairly, that person can claim in court that they have been 'defamed'. Juries in libel cases can award huge sums in damages to the person who has been wronged, depending on how damaging they think the untrue statement has been.

Libel actions against radio stations are quite rare. They happen less often than with newspapers, mainly because newspaper journalists take greater risks than broadcasters do: they can afford to, if it will mean greater publicity and extra sales. Radio stations are always keen to increase their listenership, but not at the possible expense of libel damages. So while a tabloid newspaper might happily libel someone, gambling that the extra sales earned by a juicy story will be worth it, few radio stations would do the same. There is also the worry of complaints to the BBC Governors, the Radio Authority for commercial stations, or even the Broadcasting Standards Commission.

The libel actions against radio stations tend, therefore, to result from accidental defamation, rather than from calculated risk-taking. In 1988, Radio City in Liverpool paid £350,000 to someone over an item the court agreed was defamatory. The journalist involved must have felt pretty bad about costing his employers so much money over a mistake. Journalists' own professional reputations will suffer if they do not understand about libel and make mistakes as a result. For example, if in a feature a reporter calls the owner of a pit bull terrier 'irresponsible', and mistakenly accuses him of letting the dog roam around children's playgrounds without a muzzle, the owner may well sue for libel once the piece has been broadcast.

Defending libel suits

In a libel action, a broadcaster can defend him or herself in a number of ways. If, for example, they can prove to the satisfaction of the court that what they said was true, then they will be safe. But there is a large difference between knowing something to be true and being able to prove it in court.

Another defence is 'fair comment'. In the case above, the broadcaster might be able to argue that they were justified in calling the dog owner 'irresponsible' simply because he keeps what many people agree is a dangerous dog.

However, that would not allow the broadcaster to accuse the owner of letting the dog out in public without a muzzle. If a court decided that the claims (or 'allegations') were made maliciously, then they might find him or her guilty of malicious falsehood.

The general rule about avoiding problems over libel is that, before identifying someone and saying they have done wrong, *you must be sure of your facts*. It is good professional practice to check with the news editor or programme controller before putting the claims on air – and they might want to consult the lawyers first. It is no defence to repeat a libellous statement made by someone else and blame them. If in doubt – leave it out!

Ethical issues

Ethical issues over content include discrimination and privacy. Discrimination would involve not using someone in an interview because they are from a certain ethnic group. It could also be called discrimination if, in a feature about the NHS, you only interviewed male doctors and female nurses.

Whatever your intention, you need to consider very carefully your choices of who you are going to interview in case it even *appears* that you have been discriminatory. Racial discrimination is only a legal issue if you actually cause hatred against a racial group or persons because of their racial origins – for example, colour or religion. Otherwise, issues of discrimination over sex or race are 'ethical' issues. That means that you are expected to be responsible enough not to discriminate, and if you do, your conscience should be troubled.

Invasion of privacy

It is also considered unethical to invade someone's privacy unless it is in the public interest. Investigations like those carried out by Roger Cook, who began his doorstepping of crooks and double-dealers on Radio 4, are generally regarded as justified, because exposing people who break the law and cheat others is clearly 'in the public interest'. But relatively few invasions of privacy can really be justified on ethical grounds. An example would be trying to discover what a well-known public figure wears in bed – you would not be acting in the public interest then, because the public does not have a right to know!

Invasion of privacy is unethical unless genuinely carried out in the public interest

In order to record on someone's private property, you need to gain permission first. You should also always check whether you may record in privately-owned places such as shopping precincts. Planting secret microphones and secretly recording telephone calls for on-air use can land a reporter in trouble if they are caught – unless it can be proved to be in the public interest.

Representation

Issues of representation are also important when planning your content. Consider the three different ideas for the feature on dangerous dogs, shown below:

Treatment 1	Interviews:	Pit bull owner
		Council dog warden
		Anti-dog campaigner
		Dog bite victim
Treatment 2	Interviews:	Pit bull owner
		Pit bull club member
		Pit bull breeder
		Council dog warden
Treatment 3	Interviews:	Pit bull owner
		Council dog warden
		Pit bull breeder
		Dog bite victim

In Treatment 1 the choice of interviewees is heavily weighted against pit bull owners – three anti-dog campaigners against one pit bull owner. In Treatment 2 it is the pit bull enthusiasts who are three to one against the dog warden whose job it is to keep unmuzzled pit bulls off the streets. Treatment 3 is the only one where both sides of the argument get equal coverage. Of course, it would be possible to balance out Treatments 1 and 2 by dividing the time equally between the two sides – giving the three interviewees on one side of the argument only as much time as the one person disagreeing with them. However, that might sound less natural than interviewing two people from each side in the first place.

Avoiding bias

Where there is a disagreement about an issue, it is important that responsible broadcasters present social issues in a balanced way. That means giving both sides equal and fair treatment. Otherwise, the broadcaster will be accused of bias, and a complaint may be made to the BBC Governors, the Radio Authority (for commercial stations), or the Broadcasting Standards Commission. The BBC has to be particularly careful over accusations of bias, because it is funded by public money from the licence fee. Independent stations also have to follow the Radio Authority *Codes of Practice*, which have strict rules about being impartial – that is, not showing bias to one side or another. The BBC's rule book is the *Producers' Guidelines*, and ignoring it is a serious offence.

Social groups should also be fairly represented. To do so is as much an issue of representation – and what kind of a picture of 'reality' you are presenting – as it is an ethical issue. As a professional reporter, what you describe (or the image you create by your choice of interviewees) should be as true to life as possible. It should not be a work of fiction as if you had discovered a world in which all doctors are white and all criminals are black. A reporter is in a very responsible position, having the power to present a distorted picture of the world. It is important that you use the power of your position to present as truthful a representation as possible of what you find.

Choosing production methods

Your research into production methods will need to cover the availability of the material, and how you are going to access it. In television, it is normal to do a 'recce' to make sure a location is suitable for recording, because the 'look' of a scene often has to be just right. On radio, this is not usually necessary. If there is some background noise that might disturb your recording, or if the acoustics are too resonant, you can fairly easily move to another place.

Logistics
The equipment you need to take with you is also fairly standard – a portable recorder and a microphone. However, you will need to consider **logistics**, e.g.:
- Where are you going to meet the interviewee?
- Is there somewhere you can record without being disturbed by unwanted noise or other people?
- When is the interviewee available?
- Do you need permission to enter premises – for example, a factory or a shop?

Atmosphere
Another consideration is atmosphere. The atmosphere for the item on dangerous dogs is needed to make the feature sound more interesting: it is the added 'colour' in the piece which will make it come alive. Imagine a report about a new police helicopter with no noisy helicopter sounds to be heard. What would you think of a piece about stormy weather wrecking boats in a harbour if the only sounds to be heard were seagulls and ice-cream sellers? So, how are you going to get your atmosphere, and when?

Production facilities
You also need to decide what production facilities will be needed. Will you mix sound effects or music in with the other audio material in the radio studio or will you just edit the audio together?

Either way, you will need to record your own voice links. But will they be recorded while out on location, or back in the studio when you have had time to select what material to use and how to structure the content? Look ahead to Element 3.3 to decide what will be most appropriate.

Bear in mind that you can change your schedule for production if really necessary, but the more carefully you plan, the less likely it is that you will meet unforeseen problems. The deadline for production is rarely a moveable one. If there is a slot reserved for your feature, you miss it at your peril!

Codes and conventions
The other area of research you will need to do is into the codes and conventions of feature production. A professional radio producer will want to create features which will be interesting and lively, but which will not sound out of place. That is, you should not be trying to copy every other feature you hear broadcast, but the more you listen to other people's work for a similar target audience to your own, the more ideas you will get about how yours should sound.

Activity 3.15

1 Listen to a number of features on the radio station for which you have decided to produce your product. Using the points raised in Element 3.1 for reference, identify any relevant codes and conventions you should keep in mind. For example, how should you sound on your links between the interview clips? Serious or light-hearted – and why? How is atmosphere actually used? Is it allowed to run for a long time or is it played at the beginning of items to establish a location, and then faded?

2 Analyse three different features by doing a running order (or structure plan) for each one. Why have the items in each feature been put in that order? Identify any legal and ethical content issues. What might have been left out to avoid legal or ethical problems? How balanced is each feature? How have social groups and social issues been represented – fairly, or unfairly? Discuss your ideas, to see how many agree with your findings.

Writing the production script

All the work you have just done will help you write your production script. For example, you will often notice that in features, interview clips are introduced in certain ways. It is quite rare to introduce an interview by saying:

> `'I spoke to John Carpenter about his pit bull terrier.'`

It is much more common for the reporter to say:

> `'John Carpenter owns a pit bull terrier.'`

Or, better still, the link may sum up the first part of what the interviewer has to say:

> `'John Carpenter is proud of his pit bull terrier.'`

In this way, something more interesting has been said than in the first example, and in fewer words. If you have to listen to the words '*I spoke to…*' over and over again, you will soon find them very boring.

Script layout

What you cannot tell from listening to the radio is how scripts are laid out. There are conventions of format which you are expected to follow. The feature consists mainly of a linking script – read by you, the reporter – and the interview clips taken from the interviews you will be recording. You probably will not be able to complete the script until you have recorded most of the interviews, because you cannot predict exactly what the interviewees will say and how they will say it. But you should be able to start building up the script as you go along, because the structure you have decided upon and the choice of interviewees will determine the content for you.

The only scripting you can do for interviews is to identify key questions you are going to ask. There is little point in recording long interviews with each person, when your whole feature will only be five minutes long. That leaves a maximum of 1.5 minutes per interviewee, if you are to have time to include some information in your own linking script. Therefore, you need to decide what you particularly want from each interviewee, and decide how to get them to say it.

This does not mean putting words into their mouths, or distorting the truth by only asking them to explain part of what they think. It does mean that in your initial research, and when arranging each interview, you should be finding out what areas each interviewee ought to be asked about, and what they are likely to say.

Writing interview questions

The next step is to write key questions which will encourage each interviewee to explain what they think in the clearest and most interesting way. Avoid closed questions which really only allow the interviewee to answer 'Yes' or 'No'. For example:

```
Q: Did you feel frightened when you found out?
A: Yes, I did, really.

Q: Were you once a street busker?
A: Yes.
```

The answers above are not very interesting, although there are times when a closed question is needed to corner the interviewee into confirming whether or not they did something:

```
Q: So, did you break your promise to the voters?
```

A good politician will probably be able to duck a question like that anyway:

```
A: I'm not in the business of breaking promises.
   What I said was...
```

Usually, though, you should think of open questions using 'who', 'what', 'when', 'where', 'why' and 'how':

```
Q: How did you feel when you found out?
A: I was shocked and frightened, like I'd never been
   before in my life.
```

That is a much more interesting reply. Now you will want to ask for more information, so you can follow up with:

```
Q: Why?
```

Conducting the interview

It is a good idea to write your key questions down in case you forget them when you are setting up the tape recorder. If you want to look really professional you can memorise the questions so that you seem to be asking them 'off the cuff'.

Don't rustle papers during the interview and avoid sticking rigidly to the questions in the order you have written them down. If the interviewee says something strange or unclear, don't be afraid to ask for an explanation. If you don't understand the answer, it is a good bet the listeners won't either!

```
A: I'm doing an Intermediate GNVQ in Media. Next year
   I hope to go on to the Advanced GNVQ.
Q: What does that mean?
A: Oh, it means General National Vocational Qualification...
   Intermediate is the first step to an Advanced GNVQ,
   and one of those is equivalent to two A levels. They're
   much more 'hands on', and they're industry oriented.
```

Avoid asking 'double' questions – that is, two questions rolled into one:

Q: What are you doing now, and why are you doing it?

The problem with double questions is that some interviewees will use the opportunity to answer the question that they *want* to answer, and ignore the other one. Both parts of the question above are good enough to deserve answers, so ask each one in turn – on its own.

The editing process

When you have recorded all your interviews, you will need to decide which parts of each one you actually want to use. These should be the answers that are most relevant to the feature, where the interviewees are being interesting and can be clearly understood. Each bit of interview is an audio 'clip'. Putting the clips into an order that makes sense, and writing a script around them, is probably the hardest part of producing the feature.

The script should link all the different clips, explain anything that is unclear, and give the whole feature its direction and purpose. 'Direction' means that the feature should actually 'lead somewhere' – so, as you write the script, think carefully at each stage, 'Where is this going?' If the direction is unclear, that is exactly the question the listener will be asking – except they might be about to switch off, because they can't follow the item at all! **Purpose** is about what you first intended the feature to do when you planned it – to inform the listeners about the subject, from the angle you intended.

Fortunately, when you write your script, you do not have to write out all the words used in the interview clips you use. What is important is how each clip begins and ends. You also need to know how long each clip is.

```
Catchline: Pit bulls

FX:          Snarling dog 4"

ME:          BUSTER IS A PIT BULL TERRIER. LUCKILY HE'S ON THE OTHER SIDE
             OF THE DOOR, HERE AT THE RSPCA'S HEADQUARTERS WHERE HE'S
             BEING KEPT UNTIL HE'S PUT DOWN. HIS OWNER IS STEPHEN KING.

I/V KING:    "It's outrageous...

             ...decision of the court"   DUR 17"

ME:          BUT THE COURT'S DECISION CAME AFTER THE DOG WAS FOUND
             WANDERING IN A CHILDREN'S PLAYGROUND WITHOUT A MUZZLE.

FX:          Playground, children playing. (fades under)

ME:          IT WAS HERE THAT PAMELA TAYLOR'S CHILDREN WERE PLAYING WHEN
             SHE SAW THE DOG COMING OUT OF THE BUSHES. SHE SENSED DANGER
             IMMEDIATELY.

I/V TAYLOR:  "I was shocked and frightened...

             ...called for help straight away." DUR 19"

ME:          THE POLICE OFFICER WHO WAS FIRST ON THE SCENE...
```

How to lay out a production script

Activity 3.16

1 Write key questions for each of your chosen interviewees.
2 Begin your production script, leaving gaps where necessary, until the interviews have been recorded. Show any sound effects and music you want to include.

Preparing the production schedule

Health and safety

If the interviews you have chosen need to be recorded on location, you must find out if there are any special risks involved. When you are fixing up interviews – probably on the telephone – ask whether there are any special safety requirements about the location.

For example, you must have permission to record on private property, and dangerous places such as building sites or factories will have strict safety rules about who can enter, and when. There may also be rules about wearing special protective clothing, such as hard hats or ear protectors – and you may have to be accompanied by someone while you are on the premises. (Check, though, that where you are going will not be too noisy to make a decent recording.)

Even going to the location and coming back may present safety problems. Be careful not to place yourself in any danger on the way: dark streets, back alleys and busy roads can be very dangerous, and you want to get back to the studio with yourself and your equipment in one piece.

Logistics

The **logistics** of the operation are the detailed arrangements for getting to the right place at the right time with the right equipment. Plan your route carefully, making sure that you are on time for any appointments you make – and that you have left yourself enough time to meet your deadline. Remember, scripting and post-production will take time, and on a real radio station it is vital not to miss your broadcast slot. Read through the next element to get some idea of how much time you will need.

Two other important issues are:
- **Human resources** Do you need to take someone else with you as an assistant? If safety is a special concern (see above), your teacher may insist you do so. However, radio is a very individual medium – it is very unlikely you would need as many people to work on a five-minute radio feature as you would in television to make an item of the same length.
- **Equipment and hardware** Booking the right equipment is essential: it is no good arriving to collect a tape recorder and microphone if there are none in the store. Have some tape ready, too.

Evaluation

By now you should have gathered some information about your subject, arranged the interviews and sorted out the logistics, taking care about all possible health and safety issues. At this stage, if you are to avoid problems later, you need to identify any weaknesses in your material and your plans:
- Have you got enough information to work out sensible questions to ask your interviewees without getting important facts wrong?
- Have you chosen the right interviewees?
- Are they knowledgeable enough about the subject to be worth listening to?

It is a very good idea to speak personally to the interviewee on the telephone beforehand if you can. That way you'll get to hear how they sound – and if they mumble or stammer, it will be worth politely finding out if there is anyone else who might sound better on your tape. Rather than cause offence, you might make the excuse that you already have 'too many male/female voices' lined up.

Date	Time	Place	Activity	Personnel/equipment	Evaluation

How to lay out a production schedule

Activity 3.17

1 Complete your production schedule, adding all the details. Write notes for your audio file, evaluating your research findings against the original proposals. You should note down strengths and weaknesses, as well as making any necessary changes to your plans.

2 Identify any legal, ethical and representational issues you came across, and say how you dealt with those issues. You will be producing your feature in Element 3.3. Go straight to that section of the chapter if you are ready to go into production. Otherwise, you will also need to develop your proposal and script for your group drama.

Planning your drama

Researching a play is likely to be quite different from researching a feature. Instead of finding facts and interviewees, you will be researching a script, locations in which to record, music and sound effects to add, and actors to play all the characters.

From the basic information in your drama proposal, you will have to develop the idea with the other members in your group. You need to make group decisions about the **content** and **style**, and then begin work on the **structure**. All these decisions must relate back to the purpose and target audience in your original proposal: were you planning to entertain, inform, or both? Who are the target audience – and what kind of play will appeal to them?

Drama can be complicated or simple; often it is the simplest ideas that are the most effective. It can be funny or serious, too. You need to be fairly creative to write fiction, but it is also possible to write a fictional play based upon real people, or on events that you know about or can find out about through research.

For example, a drama set during the Second World War can be very realistic if you check facts about people and events first. You will need to find out what happened, what people did then, what they used to eat, where they used to go, and so on.

A different approach is to be deliberately avant-garde and create odd situations that will make listeners sit up and take notice. For instance, you might take characters from a play by Shakespeare and set them in an air-raid shelter in wartime London.

The main problem with basing drama on real people is that you may libel somebody accidentally. Libel law is just as tricky when you have identified somebody by accident: although you may have had no intention of depicting a living person, if they are convinced they can be identified in your work, they may be able to convince a court that you deliberately misrepresented them.

Plot and characters

The two main ingredients in a drama are the plot and the characters. The plot is the storyline, or what happens. The characters are the people involved in the plot – although not all of the people mentioned have to be heard. Imagine hearing this scene from a student's play:

```
TITLE: TAKING SIDES              WRITER: JOE BLOGGS
SCENE ONE


1       FX:       Distant shouting then door slams



2       TEACHER:    Quick, hide me, please. Or those students'll
                    get me!


3       PRINCIPAL:  All right, Matthews. Get under the desk and
                    I'll see you're alright.


4       TEACHER:    (grunts) Thank you, thank you.
```

The layout here is a convention of drama scriptwriting. Sound effects are underlined so the technical operator or studio manager can easily see where they are. Each item has a number so the actors and the production staff can easily find their way around the script during rehearsal and production.

Notice how the words are written as people would speak – not as they might appear in a school essay! 'Those students will get me' becomes 'Those students'*ll* get me', and 'I will see you are alright' becomes 'I'*ll* see you'*re* alright' to make the speech sound more natural and therefore more believable. You may not have the greatest actors in the world to do your own recording for you, but if you can help them sound more lifelike and less wooden, you are making their work much easier.

The sound effects ('FX' in the script) can either be recorded specially, or can be found on one of the many sound effect discs available. Apart from this, all the script requires are two actors – although a number of other characters have been suggested. The script may continue with more information about who is doing the chasing, how many students there are, and why they are angry, but only if the writer decides. The whole play as it develops is the product of the writer's imagination, and the freedom to create the action and characters the writer wants is one of the best things about writing fiction.

Activity 3.18

1 In your group, research and write a ten-minute radio play based upon the proposal you wrote earlier. You may decide to continue the script started above, developing the plot and creating more characters – or you could write something totally different. Bear in mind the target audience and what they would like to hear. Make sure your script is correctly laid out as in the example above. Make notes of your research findings and add them to your audio file.

2 Identify any music or sound effects needed. Check back over the work you did for Element 3.1 to help you remember how words, sounds and music can 'paint pictures' in the listener's mind, often creating scenery you could not hope to build.

Your research should cover codes and conventions, too. By listening to other dramas you will get good ideas of your own – without having to copy the plot or characterisation. Remember, copyright also covers other people's radio scripts, so you cannot just record chunks of other people's plays and pretend they are your own. However, you can get inspiration from other people's ideas and the way they have created codes to set up meanings in listeners' minds.

When you are being creative, take care over issues of representation. Are you just repeating racial, class or gender stereotypes? What are you actually saying about any social issues you may be dealing with – and are you telling the 'whole' story, or just part of it? You ought to think about regional accents, too – and make sure the dim people and the unemployed do not all sound like the creation of stand-up comedians.

The production schedule

When you are beginning your script you will also need a **production schedule** which will help you meet the deadline set by your teacher.

As with the feature, the schedule for your radio drama should:

- List dates for the completion of each of the different stages
- Identify who is doing what at each stage and where
- Give details of resources required
- Specify any important health and safety issues

Recording on location

Drama can be produced in quite a simple radio studio, but some producers decide to record on location. Usually this costs more money, but to have sound effects and acoustics laid on can be a good idea. Remember that you can trick the human ear with your choice of location, because the eyes cannot see where you really are to spoil the picture you have created. In this way, you could create the atmosphere of being in a cave, when you are really in a cellar with lots of echo. If you add seashore effects afterwards, it will sound as if you are truly at the seaside!

If you do decide to record on location, you will have to plan the logistics of getting the right people and equipment to the right place at the right time.

With the right equipment, it is possible to add echo in the studio, but you will need to research production methods and add equipment requirements to the schedule. Somebody will also need to book the studio and get hold of any extra microphones or other equipment that may be needed. Check under Element 3.3 to see what you will need.

When you have researched and written the script, and planned the production in your schedule, you will need to evaluate what you have done so far. Again, you need to match the work with your original proposal, and make sure that what you are about to produce will appeal to your target audience. Only when you have done all that will you be ready to go into production.

Activity 3.19

1 Complete your production schedule.
2 Make notes on any legal, ethical and representational issues you may have had to deal with. Evaluate your script and schedule against the proposal, identifying all strengths and weaknesses and any changes you need to make. Add your notes to the other evidence in your audio file.

Review questions

1 Explain the differences between a wrap and a documentary.
2 List a number of primary and secondary sources.
3 Explain one legal and one ethical problem in reporting.
4 What are logistics?
5 What should be in a production schedule?

Element 3.3 Produce audio products

Health and safety issues

Activity 3.20

1 For this section, carry out a risk assessment. That means you should judge what health and safety hazards there may be at each stage. For each hazard, decide what action to take in order to avoid putting yourself or others at risk.
2 Make a list of all possible hazards you can think of. Now plan how to cope with those hazards and add to the list all actions taken.

Safety can cover many different aspects of production. It concerns you and your team members, as well as members of the general public – that is, anyone you ask to be involved, or anyone who might get in your way or find you in *their* way during the production process.

- If recording on location, you should make sure you do not cause an obstruction or cause other people to step out into traffic to get round you.
- Wherever you record or edit, you must always have an escape route in the event of a fire or other emergency. You must also always take care with electrical equipment because of the risk of fire and electric shock.

- Studios have a lot of mains-powered equipment, and editing is usually either done on a mains-powered tape machine or a computer. No liquids should be taken near these items – no matter how thirsty you are – and nothing should ever be poked into them: fingers, objects, jewellery or long hair.
- Razor blades or sharp knives such as scalpels for editing should be handled with care and always stored safely after use in a sheath or metal tin. Used blades should be carefully wrapped in thick sticky tape or dropped in a sharps disposal box.
- Spinning reels on tape recorders can be dangerous, too. Never try to stop metal spools spinning with your hand or any object. Let them stop in their own time. Be careful, too, about things dangling into the spools as they turn: long hair, jewellery and ties can get caught by the spools and pulled hard, causing injury.

Choosing recording equipment

Studio recording should be done without connecting or disconnecting leads. A teacher or a technician should be able to help you here. Use one microphone per person for the drama, or all gather round one microphone at the same time.

Cassette or CD players can be used to play in sound effects or atmosphere you have recorded beforehand. Listen carefully through headphones to check that the levels are balanced correctly and nothing is too quiet or too loud in the mix. A simple drama does not need any mixing, and it is common for sound effects to be created 'live' – by bringing door knockers or coconut halves into the studio. Most drama studios have different-sized doors to open and close, and probably a tray of gravel for people to tread on to create the sound of feet tramping up a path.

Recording on location and in the studio are different in many respects. Usually recording on location is done with a portable tape recorder, while studio equipment is larger and heavier. The studio will often be set up more or less ready for your own recording needs, whereas on location you must make sure you have the correct equipment with you.

Some portable tape recorders are reel-to-reel machines which use quarter-inch tape. Others, used in industry as well as in colleges, are broadcast-standard cassette tape recorders. If you use a quarter-inch machine such as a Uher, you will be able to edit the tape you record on without further work. However, if you use a cassette machine, you will need to 'dub' the audio material onto a format that can be edited more easily.

The first problem with cassette tape is that it is thinner and less easy to handle. It also plays at a slower speed and finding the exact place to make a cut is very difficult indeed.

If you have a MiniDisc recorder, you will be able to edit on the disc by simple button presses – but because this newer technology is more expensive it may well be beyond your reach. Some radio stations – but certainly not all – have already invested heavily in buying new 'non-linear' editing systems which enable you to edit and even mix sound on a computer screen. However, re-equipping with the latest technology is too costly for some radio stations, and for the foreseeable future at least, it will still be necessary for people joining the industry to be able to edit quarter-inch audio tape.

Microphone technique

Microphone technique is basically the same whatever the equipment being used. You must record the correct amount of sound onto the tape or MiniDisc

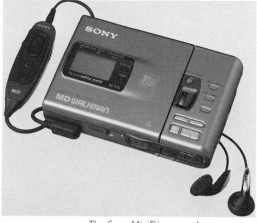

The Sony MiniDisc recorder

– not too much because it will overload the system and distortion is likely to occur. Too little will cause the wanted sound to be lost in the background noise (or hiss) that you will hear only too loudly if you turn the volume up high on a very quiet recording.

Activity 3.21

1 Experiment with the portable tape machine which you will be using for your recording. You will find the position of the microphone and the recording level affect the read-out on the level meter. Record your own voice so that the meter needle moves but does not enter the red or 'danger' zone. Now position the microphone further away from and closer to your mouth, watching the effect it has on the needle.

2 Try interviewing someone else so that the needle moves as much it can without crossing into the red 'danger' zone.

You will have noticed that if the person you are interviewing is softly spoken will need to move the microphone closer to their mouth if they are to be recorded at the same volume (or 'level') as your own voice. Likewise, you will need to hold the microphone further away from a louder person's mouth. Recording a drama may mean further experimenting with the microphone position. It may be best placed between all the different actors, or if it is closer to some than to others it will make them seem further away than the rest.

If background noise is a problem, bringing the microphone closer to the speaker and lowering the recording level will lower the amount of background sound when you play the tape back. Always make a test recording before you leave for a location recording – and another one when you arrive, to hear how the finished recording will sound. Check the battery level before you set off, too, and make sure there are no loose connections in the microphone lead.

Using background noise

Some background noise is useful as atmosphere, but there are times when the noise of a heater or a machine in the background is just a nuisance. Always listen carefully for unwanted background noise before you record, and turn off the source of the noise if you can. If you can't, try moving somewhere quieter and doing the recording there.

Avoid unnecessary or distracting background noise when recording

Even a clock ticking will cause you problems when you edit – because cutting bits of the tape out will make the clock's ticking seem to stop and start very noticeably. Two students once recorded a parrot at the same time as their interview – and later they wished they had put the cage outside the room! It can be a good idea to take the telephone off the hook and even put a 'do not disturb' notice on the door to prevent unwanted interruptions. Keep an eye on your recording level while you record – and on the time, so that you know how much you have on tape and how much tape is left.

Checking the recording

Always check the recording after you have finished, just to make sure the equipment or your own technique haven't let you down. If you are still on location you may be able to record again, but if you have already returned to base, it will take a lot more effort to fix up the recording all over again. Make sure you have recorded all you need to record, following the proposal, script and schedule. It is industry practice to record a 'wild track' while on location. That is, just record a minute or so of the background sounds to have at your disposal in case you need to mix it later with other material to create an effect.

On your way back to the studio, you can spend time constructively by sifting through the recordings while they are fresh in your memory. Recording on MiniDisc is so flexible that you can even begin editing the recordings – if you are not driving. If you use a tape recorder, you can still listen to the recordings you have made and start choosing which pieces are going to be the most useful. For the feature, some parts of each interview will stand out as being very useable, while others will be less interesting. If you have recorded the drama on location, you may well have recorded alternative 'takes' of some scenes.

When you get back to base, you need to carefully log all the material you have recorded. Tapes should be labelled from the start, then you should be able to find any part of any interview quite easily, by fast-forwarding to the right place on the right tape. Having a detailed log of all your material will make it easier to make the decisions about what to put in and what to leave out. This will make scripting the feature easier, too.

Check the material for recording quality: if it sounds wrong in some way, you will probably have to leave it out, unless the problem can be sorted out in post-production.

Tape	Counter no.	Item	Details	Quality
A	005	King i/v	cross about court decision (23")	OK
A	048	King i/v	plans to get another dog (16")	OK
B	011	FX: dogs snarling	At RSPCA (23")	Some distortion after 16"

A log of recorded material

Activity 3.22

1 Listen to all the recordings you have made, and compile two logs, as described above – one for the feature and the other for the drama. Check each log against the proposal and the production script, identifying any changes and any new recordings you will need to make. Write a report to go with the log, detailing strengths and weaknesses.

2 Identify any new legal, ethical or representational issues that you find, and say how you plan to deal with them.

Post-production

Once you have checked your raw material, and done any replacement recordings, you are ready for the **post-production** stage. You should still be working to the deadlines in your production schedule. Any finishing touches to the scripts should be made now – for both the feature and the drama.

You may find you need to add or delete material in order to run to time, or to make the finished products make more sense to the listeners. This is the time to prepare any **additional material**. You should think carefully about the structure you planned, and whether it works as expected. It is not too late to make changes – providing what you change means your finished product will match the proposal better. Think in terms of **fitness for purpose** – is the product going to do what you promised in your proposal?

Once you have done your 'paper edit' – i.e. deciding on paper what to include and what to leave out – you can begin to record the voice links for the feature and do the actual edit on tape or computer, assembling all the different parts of the production in the correct order.

The feature will sound awkward and unprofessional if the sound levels jump up and down on playback, so at this stage you must make the greatest effort to make sure the levels are as even as possible. If you recorded your interviews on cassette, you must dub – or copy – the parts you wish to use over to quarter-inch tape. If you recorded them on a portable reel-to-reel tape machine such as a Uher, you will be able to miss out this stage. You may do the dubbing either in the studio, through the mixer, or direct from cassette machine to quarter-inch by connecting the two with the correct lead.

Whichever way you choose to dub, you should take great care with the levels. The aim is to record onto the quarter-inch tape enough of the sound for it to be clear on playback, but not so loud that it will distort. Watch the meters on the tape machine and set the recording levels before you begin to record. Make any adjustments to the level as necessary, to keep the needle on the meters peaking at around the same place, but without making any changes too quickly.

You should record your voice links onto quarter-inch tape at the same level as you dub your interview clips. If you have recorded your links on the portable cassette machine, you can dub them across at the same time as the interviews, putting everything down on the tape in the correct order. If you are going to edit on a computer, using software such as DAVE 2000, or Fast Edy, you will need to load all your audio onto the PC at the same level too.

The final edit

This is the stage at which you tidy up the tape, removing all the gaps between items. Chapter 6 describes editing on computer. If you are using a razor blade to edit quarter-inch tape, you must take great care over razor blade safety (see opposite).

It is very important to listen carefully to every edit you do. If you are editing out a mistake, (for example, a cough, as in the example) then you should evaluate the success of the edit. A good edit is one which is not noticeable to somebody who does not already know it is there. The aim is not to make somebody seem to say something different from what they really said or meant to say – that would be deceitful on your part, and they would quite rightly complain that you misrepresented them in your work.

Even where you are editing two different items together, you must consider whether you have done so in a way that sounds natural to the human ear. Cutting quickly from a very soft sound or voice to something very harsh might give the feature an uneven quality that would be better avoided. Some loud background sounds are better faded in at the dubbing stage, so that they do not cut in suddenly. You may have to consider re-dubbing them to get a better result.

You will need to edit the drama, too. (If you did the recordings on cassette, again, that means dubbing onto quarter-inch tape first.) Rather than editing-in inserts, as with the feature, in the case of the drama you will need to check that the scenes are in the correct order, add in any missing material, and cut out any problems, such as where the actors fluffed their lines or had to re-speak them. While you are editing, you must be evaluating what you are doing at every stage.

Finally, the tape should have yellow or green leader tape spliced onto the start, so the sound begins just where the magnetic tape begins. This way, for transmission (or 'TX'), the studio staff can quickly line up the tape right at the start of the item, without having to play it through to find the beginning.

At the end you should splice on some red leader tape. Again, this gives the studio staff a clear indication by sight as to when the end of your item is coming up. Some tape machines will stop automatically when red leader tape passes a light-sensor. If your machines do this, take this into account when splicing on the red leader and leave a little extra amount of blank audio tape in place before the red.

Editing audio tape

Here is an example of how to cut out a cough between the words 'good' and 'morning'. Remember, the tape goes from left to right so the words appear reversed!

1 Decide where to edit. Play the tape through several times to identify where to cut.

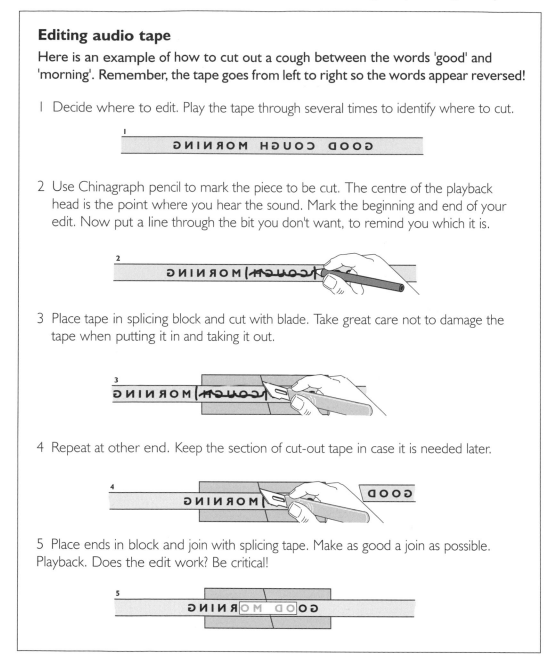

2 Use Chinagraph pencil to mark the piece to be cut. The centre of the playback head is the point where you hear the sound. Mark the beginning and end of your edit. Now put a line through the bit you don't want, to remind you which it is.

3 Place tape in splicing block and cut with blade. Take great care not to damage the tape when putting it in and taking it out.

4 Repeat at other end. Keep the section of cut-out tape in case it is needed later.

5 Place ends in block and join with splicing tape. Make as good a join as possible. Playback. Does the edit work? Be critical!

Activity 3.23

1 Dub and edit all the material needed for your feature and drama – one at a time! Mark off every edit as you do it against its entry on the log and the script. Check that you have dubbed and edited everything you need to make the product sound as it should do according to the script. Make notes at the end of the log about any additional material you have had to record for each product.

2 Write brief notes about any further legal, ethical or representational issues you have come across – especially when you had to make decisions about what to cut out and what to leave in when editing or creating additional material (check back over Element 3.2 for details).

Writing the cue sheet

Every tape made for radio should have a **cue sheet**. This is a sheet of paper which has all the essential details of the tape written on it. The cue sheet for the feature stays with the tape until after transmission, so that the producer, presenter and technical operator (or studio manager) working on the programme can find out all they need to know about the tape at a glance. It is much quicker to check the duration and how a tape ends by looking at the cue sheet than lining the tape up on a machine and playing it through.

The cue sheet also provides the programme presenter with a line or two of introductory script about the feature before it is played. Often there will be a back announcement ('back anno') as well. A back anno is a line or so of script to be spoken after the feature, giving a credit to the reporter and perhaps adding some additional information or details of a helpline to call.

```
RADIO XYZ          THE LUNCHTIME MAGAZINE
CATCHLINE:         PIT BULLS
TX DATE:           16/10/97

INTRO:             Being attacked by a pit bull terrier must be one of the most
                   frightening experiences possible. But if you were the owner
                   of a dog that hadn't bitten anyone, and a court ordered the
                   dog to be put down, you would probably not be too happy — as
                   Simon Partner has been  finding out.

TAPE IN:           fx DOG SNARLING 4"
                   "BUSTER IS A PIT BULL TERRIER...

TAPE OUT:          ...MEANS CERTAIN DEATH FOR BUSTER."
DUR:               4'57"

BACK ANNO:         Simon Partner reporting. There is a helpline for pit bull
                   owners in similar circumstances. I'll give you that number
                   after the next piece of music.
```

Cue sheet for a feature

When writing cue sheets, accuracy is vital. Note how inverted commas (") are used to indicate where speech begins and ends. The dots are used to show how the speech continues between the 'Tape in' and 'Tape out' cues.

The details of how the tape begins and ends must match up exactly with what is on the tape. Any difference between them may cause confusion in the studio when the programme is on air, and precious seconds may be wasted, checking that the tape is the correct one to be played. Your own professional reputation is at stake every time you make a mistake – so take the time and trouble to make sure you get the details right.

The duration must also be correct because the programme may need to run exactly to time, and the amount of time left for other items after your own feature needs to be worked out in advance. If your feature overruns, there may be a problem fitting the next item in. If it under-runs, there may be a gap left for the presenter to fill – and you are unlikely to be thanked for that!

The cue sheet for a drama would be very similar, except that it is for a complete programe in its own right, rather than an item in a longer magazine programme. It therefore has continuity announcements instead of the intro and back anno.

```
RADIO XYZ          THE PLAY OF THE WEEK
TITLE:             INTO THE UNKNOWN
TX DATE:           16/12/97

CONTINUITY IN:     Now it's time for our Play of the Week. 'Into the
                   Unknown' takes us back to the second world war, and an
                   air raid shelter in Coventry.

TAPE IN:           fx SIREN 6"
                   "Here they come again...

TAPE OUT:          ...Happy Christmas, everyone!"

DUR:               9'57"

CONTINUITY OUT:    Into the unknown was written by Jenny Thomas. The part of
                   Rachel was played by Sarah Smythe.
```

Cue sheet for a whole programme, such as a play

You will also need to label the tape with all the following details:
- Catchline (or title)
- Duration
- 'Tape out' cue
- Your own name (a good idea in a college but probably not necessary in a small radio station)

Activity 3.24

1 Play your tapes through, checking that there is no more work still to be done. Make up a cue sheet and a label for each tape, making sure that the details are the same on the label as on the cue sheet.
2 Write a brief evaluation of the quality of your taped material.

Evaluating the result

Once any audio product is completed, there comes the moment when it is listened to by others. A radio reporter or producer has a boss to keep happy – that is, the news editor or programme controller. There are also colleagues who will hear what they produce, and will be making judgements about their work.

Perhaps most importantly, any audio product is made to be heard by its **audience** – that target audience you identified when planning the proposal. Audiences make or break producers – because if their work is not well received, they may not be given a second chance. That means your own job prospects depend on how good the work is thought to be.

Activity 3.25

1 Play your own tapes to an 'audience' of your fellow students. Begin by explaining to them who the real target audience was meant to be. After playing each tape, ask them to give their reactions. Be prepared to answer questions.

2 Write up a brief report on the audience's reactions to each product.

Review questions

1 What dangers are there in location recording?
2 Describe good microphone technique.
3 Why would a radio producer want atmosphere on a tape?
4 How should a reel of quarter-inch tape be prepared for broadcast?
5 What is a cue sheet for?
6 What dangers are there in the studio and when editing tape?

Assignment 3
Planning and producing audio products

This assignment provides evidence for:

Elements: 3.1 Investigate audio products
3.2 Develop proposals and scripts for audio products
3.3 Produce audio products

and the following key skills:

Communication:	2.1, 2.2, 2.4
Information Technology:	2.1, 2.2, 2.3,
Application of Numbers:	2.1, 2.2, 2.3

---

1 Put together an audio file containing all your notes, logs and production paperwork from the activities in Elements 3.1, 3.2, and 3.3, each under the appropriate element heading.
2 Include your two tapes: the individual feature and a copy of the group drama, all properly labelled and with the cue sheet attached.
3 Add to the audio file all the reports and evaluations you have done.
4 Check to make sure all the work produced is there, and submit the audio file to your tutor with your name and group clearly marked.

4 Planning and producing moving image products

Element 4.1	Investigate moving image products
Element 4.2	Develop treatments and scripts for moving image products
Element 4.3	Produce moving image products

What is covered in this chapter

- The nature of moving image products
- Planning for moving image products
- Production and post-production of a moving image product

Your 'moving image' file will need to contain:
- Recordings of two different video products
- Two treatments for a video products – one fiction and one non-fiction
- One production script
- Notes and paperwork from your research and planning
- Your written responses to the activities in this chapter

Introduction

We are all constantly exposed to moving images. We are also media 'consumers' – whether of soap operas, advertisements, the latest computer games, party political broadcasts, national and local news programmes or chat shows. These are just a few examples of a vast range of moving image products which have their own styles and are produced for different reasons for different audiences.

In this chapter we will look at some of these different moving image products, their particular styles and audiences and how they are put together. You will be required to think about the moving image products you watch, and about the viewing habits of other audiences.

Having examined a range of products, you will have the opportunity to plan and produce a moving image product of your own.

Many people are involved in producing moving image products, including scriptwriters, presenters, camera-persons, costume designers and make-up artists. We will be looking at their work. Planning, communication and co-operation are all essential skills required for a successful final product, and you will need to practise these skills in the roles you take within your own production team.

Element 4.1: Investigate moving image products

A TV make-up artist at work

Most of the products that we look at on TV, film or video have certain charac-teristics and rules, or codes and conventions, which allow us to put them loosely into groups or **genres** (see Glossary). Each of these genres uses conven-tions that we all recognise and which help us to identify it easily. To begin this chapter, we will investigate the particular conventions used in chat shows, soap operas and advertisements.

The chat show

This is a very popular television genre which reaches many different audiences. Well-known chat show hosts include Kilroy, Oprah Winfrey and Clive Anderson.

The content of these programmes can range from serious social issues as in the Esther Rantzen show to the more entertainment-based topics dealt with by personalities such as Frank Skinner.

The conventions of a chat show will include a presenter who hosts the show, a range of guests and a live studio audience. The subject-matter, guests and audience will differ according to whether the purpose of the show is to educate, to inform or to entertain.

Discussion between studio guests, presenter and audience on Central's 'Kilroy'

Activity 4.1

I Look at a number of chat shows on television during one day and make a note of the following elements and characteristics:

– Presenter/host
– Target audience
– Subject matter
– Studio design
– Use of 'roving microphone', chairs on stage
– Transmission time
– Guests

2 Record one of the shows and make further notes on the subject matter, the structure (what are the items in the programme? Are there other features such as singers or comedy acts?) and style. Try to clarify who the audience is, paying particular attention to the time of the programme's transmission and the topics dealt with.

Target audiences
Producers of chat shows are very aware of their target audience, and this will guide their choice of subject matter, host and style of programme.

Consider the shows listed below and try to identify the target audience for each one, taking into account the transmission time, the pace of the programme and the choice of host and subject matter:

● The Esther Rantzen show
● 'Kilroy'
● The Oprah Winfrey show
● 'Montel Williams'
● 'Question Time'

You may also like to consider how the studio audiences participate in these shows. Is it through asking questions, pressing buttons to express their opinions or physically moving from one part of the studio to another?

Structure and conventions

Although the structure of chat shows may vary slightly, most follow roughly the same format or conventions:

- The presenter introduces him or herself in front of the camera, addressing both the audience at home and in the studio. This introduction will include the subject matter, the guests and a general chat to the audience.
- The first guest is introduced. The presenter chats to put them at their ease.
- The presenter highlights the guest's reasons for being on the programme (e.g. to promote a film, a new television series, a book or a current affairs issue).
- The guest talks.
- The discussion is often opened out to the studio audience.
- Often the programme features guests representing both sides of an issue, in order to stimulate a debate.

Other chat show conventions are as follows:

- The show is often recorded live in front of a studio audience.
- The atmosphere is relaxed and informal.
- The host and guests are usually on stage, sitting in comfortable chairs.
- Sometimes, as in 'Kilroy', the presenter moves around the audience to get a more 'intimate' feel to the show.
- The camera discreetly observes the conversation, giving close-up views of the person talking and the presenter's reactions.

The style of the show is much like an everyday conversation. The skill of the presenter is to make the show seem as relaxed as possible, but in fact a live recording puts great pressure on both the presenter and the guests, and unexpected events may – and sometimes do – occur. Similarly, although presenters appear to be effortlessly well-informed about the guests and/or the topic under discussion, they are well-briefed beforehand by teams of hardworking researchers.

Chat show presenters need to be well-briefed about their guests

Case Study: Julie Estefan – TV researcher

Julie Estefan works as a researcher for a weekly TV discussion programme. She is usually at her desk from 9.30 to 5.30 unless she has to go out on an assignment.

As soon as the producers and programme planners have decided on the topics for the next show, Julie is allocated a research area to work on. This week it's 'teenage mothers'. She has been asked to find out the statistics on teenage pregnancies for the region and to interview teenage parents. She will be given particular angles to look for, e.g. whether the mothers' own family were involved in the decisions made, whether the father became more or less involved after the pregnancy, the average age of the girls, whether they returned to school after the confinement. Finally, Julie will look at support groups for young parents, legal bodies, religious groups, and the role of the DSS.

Julie's day

9.30 – 10.30	Julie starts her work by reading magazine and newspaper articles on the subject
10.45 – 11.30	Phone calls to gather information from headteachers of schools, hospital personnel, the Town Hall and other bodies already mentioned
12.00 – 2.00	Interviews with hospital personnel on the health status of young mothers, the birth and post-natal reactions
2.00 – 4.00	Julie transcribes her findings and makes a list of preliminary suggestions to discuss with the director of the programme
4.00 – 5.00	Production meeting and discussion with the director. Julie talks about her findings and discusses a possible angle that the programme will take. She may also suggest appropriate studio guests.

Presenting the findings

Throughout the day, Julie takes notes, including both the information that she is sifting through and her own reactions and observations. When the research is complete, Julie presents information to the producer on:

- How many babies are born to teenage parents in a particular city over a year.
- How many teenagers decide to bring up their children with or without the help of their parents.
- The views of doctors, parents, teachers, and representatives of pressure groups.
- The views and experiences of teenage parents.

(Continued on page 152)

Case Study (Contd.)

Now the production team have to decide which guests to invite on to the show and the running order of the programme.

Not all the first choice guests will be able to come, so the team have to draw up a reserve list to make sure a full range of opinions and types of people are represented.

A number of issues arise at this stage. For example, guests with particular reputations may want to reveal a completely different side of their personality. It will also be important to make sure that individuals with strong views are not allowed to monopolise the discussion.

Julie's job will now be to telephone all the guests and confirm the time and date of their arrival for the recording of the live show. Then a final running order can be drawn up. This will show when the guests talk, for how long, and at what point the presenter opens the show up to the studio audience.

Activity 4.2

1 Look at the chat show you recorded in Activity 4.1 and describe its structure and conventions. Explain why you think the choices of guest, subject matter, schedule time and studio design were made. How did the target audience influence these choices?

2 Identify any issues of representation. Are there any viewpoints that are ignored? Does the show include as wide a range of social groups as possible? Are there any which you think are left out?

Soap operas

Soap operas are a very popular form of television drama, covering issues and topics to suit all generations and social groups. They not only deal with relationships and communities in regions of England and abroad, but also include current issues which affect many levels of society, such as homelessness, conflict between generations, attitudes to homosexuality, etc.

Narrative structure

One of the main characteristics of soap operas is that they deal with several stories at the same time. Rather than following the adventures of a single family or group, viewers go from group to group, often watching three or four continuing stories within the usual half-hour time-slot. As we have seen, this kind of structure is called **multi-stranded**.

Soap operas also appear three or four times a week and can be scheduled for day-time or evening viewing. The separate stories are open-ended and leave the audience looking forward to the next episode to see what will happen. Another device that is sometimes used in soap operas or drama series is the 'flashback' where an episode or incident from the past is shown to give information about what has already happened.

TV soaps often use storylines based around contemporary social problems

Activity 4.3

1 Look at three soap operas at different times in one day and make a note of the following elements and characteristics:
   – time of transmission
   – how many stories are woven into one episode
   – what issues are covered
   – at what point the story ends, and what viewers expect to happen in the next episode
   – target audience
2 Record one of the soaps and make more detailed notes on its structure. How long is spent on each section of each story? How many times do the characters reappear?
3 What are the relationships of the characters to each other within each story segment and what are their relationships to the people in the other segments? How much do they overlap? What are the issues raised? Where is it set? What are the locations and sets?

Codes and conventions

The main storyline in a soap opera is often linked to a location – such as Brookside Close, Albert Square, or Ramsay Street. The sense of place is very strong and is reinforced by the characters' accents, dress and attitudes.

Other codes and conventions are:

- Two or three dramatic events usually happen in the course of a 30-minute episode – anything from a child falling over and cutting her knee, to the theft of a character's necklace, or the diagnosis of an acute illness.
- To work well, the drama usually involves conflict of some kind.
- The storylines are often based around the characters' feelings and the way they interact with one another.
- The characters in soap operas are often presented very realistically – they usually talk to each other in informal everyday language.
- The audience is drawn into the situations by being shown intimate scenes and conversations from the lives of the characters.

Activity 4.4

1 Watch the soap opera you recorded in Activity 4.3 and make notes about production style, codes and conventions, using the following questions as a guide:

   – Where is the camera positioned when the characters are talking?
   – Does this make you feel that you are eavesdropping on their conversation?
   – What makes you feel that the action and speech are realistic?
   – Describe the different sets and locations used for each scene and storyline.
   – How do they contribute to establishing a sense of place?
   – How does the lighting affect the mood of the scenes?
   – Do the characters have regional accents?
   – How do they address each other – is it in an informal or formal style of speech?
   – How realistic do you think it is? Does it reflect your own life in any way?

2 Identify any issues of representation. Make a list of all the groups that you think are represented, e.g. children, single parents. Are there any groups which are *not* represented at all? What are the issues that are dealt with?

Advertisements

We are all familiar with TV advertisements. Their purpose is to inform an audience about a particular product, service or issue and persuade them to take action – usually by making a purchase. The style of advert varies according to the message that needs to be portrayed and the target audience.

An advert is made by a production company which is hired by or belongs to an advertising agency. The agency is employed by a company to advertise and communicate their product, service or message to a particular audience. The advertising agency will work with the client to develop an approach and style for an advert. Television advertising may be part of a major campaign which could include adverts in magazines, posters and radio commercials, all communicating the same message to a target audience.

Television adverts are expensive to produce and to broadcast. The most expensive advertising slots are during programmes with high viewing figures such as 'East Enders', and 'Coronation Street', as they will reach the largest audience. However, if the advertiser wants to sell to a target audience such as children from 5 to 10 years of age, the best time to advertise would be during children's television, when their target audience will be watching.

Style

The style of adverts can vary depending on their purpose and target audience. They fall roughly into the following categories:

- **Humorous adverts** These use jokes and comic situations, often fronted by TV personalities, to create bright, upbeat images that make an impact and stay in the audience's mind. Humorous adverts are often used to promote products which are bought on impulse such as fizzy drinks, snacks and chocolate bars.
- **Adverts based on celebrity endorsement** These aim to project an image of quality and style by associating a product with a well-known figure, often from the world of sport or the performing arts. Celebrity endorsements are often used to advertise products such as trainers or sportswear.

- **Adverts based on scientific or professional endorsement** Typically, these involve an 'expert' (recognisable by their white lab coat or dark suit) talking to camera about the 'new, improved formula' of a product such as a washing powder or hair shampoo.
- **Adverts based on emotional appeal** These deliberately play on the audience's feelings – for example, making mothers feel guilty if they do not use the latest domestic products to protect their family from household germs.

Activity 4.5

Record ten advertisements and use the details to fill in a table based on the one shown below. Make notes on and include any other styles of advert you have noticed.

Product	Category			
	Humour	Celebrity endorsement	Scientific/professional endorsement	Emotional appeal
Tango	✓			

Structure and conventions

In terms of the structure of the advert, often the simpler the message, the more effective it is. Almost every product will have a 'unique selling point' (USP) that will need to be conveyed to the audience. This is a feature that makes one product different from others in the shops, such as the 'bagless ' Dyson vacuum cleaner, or the 'gentle action' bleach that removes stains without affecting the colour of your clothes.

Many adverts tell a story and have to convey the essential elements in a very short time – typically anything from 10 to 15 seconds. The creative team working on an advert have to communicate quickly so that the audience can instantly recognise and understand the message.

Many advertisements rely on the audience's recognition of famous people, and on their knowledge of existing genres. For example, styles and conventions from films such as the Western, science fiction and adventure genres are often quoted and parodied in adverts.

Some adverts work like soap operas, each one continuing a story and ending with a cliffhanger – the best known example being the saga of the 'Gold Blend' couple. Others, such as the Oxo ads, use a regular cast of characters to build familiarity and increase audience identification.

TV advertisements often use 'story appeal' and romance to sell products

Activity 4.6

1 You have already identified different styles of advertisements by sorting your ten recorded advertisements into different types. Try to take this a step further and identify the characteristics of each type. For example, in the advertisements that tell a story, what techniques do the advertisers use to compress the action into such a short timespan?

2 Look at the camera work – how does it help move the narrative on?

3 Do the advertisers use famous people in the story? What do we know about these people that helps to reinforce the message of the advertisement?

Note: Make notes on all these questions.

Representation in adverts

Because of the need to tell a story in a very short time, adverts often portray characters in terms of regional or cultural stereotypes. This kind of representation is often criticised, but the advertisers would respond by saying that they need to do this in order to convey meaning and recognition in seconds.

Activity 4.7

Go back to your recorded advertisements and pick out as many stereotypes as you can. Make notes on examples of the representation of old people, people who come from different regions in Britain or from other countries, women, young people etc.

Review questions

1 Name one specific example of each of the following types of moving image product:
   - non-fiction
   - fiction
   - promotional.
2 What is meant by 'codes and conventions' in moving image products?
3 Would you describe the narrative structure of a soap opera as serial, closed or multi-strand?
4 Name four purposes of moving image products.
5 Give examples of products that meet each of the four purposes you have identified in question 4 above.
6 What is the single most important factor influencing the scheduling of a TV programme?

Element 4.2 Develop treatments and scripts for moving image products

In the previous section we investigated three different types of moving image products. Each started life as an idea and a proposal. In this section and the next, you are going to plan and produce two moving image products of your own. But before you choose which type to produce, you need to think carefully about the following:

- The **purpose** of the product – is it to persuade, entertain, inform, educate or to generate income?
- Your **target audience** and the **genre** or type of product you wish to create.
- The **style** of your product – this will be determined by its purpose and target audience.

The planning stage

There are three major stages in the planning of a moving image product:

1 **Pre-production** – This covers planning everything for your production. It includes research, writing a treatment, preparing a production script, organising the budget, designing and making costumes, hiring actors/actresses or presenters, setting up the production team and booking or hiring equipment.
2 **Production** – Making the moving image product, using appropriate technology.
3 **Post-production** – Editing, adding music and sound effects, and putting on captions or credits.

Element 4.2 takes you step by step through the pre-production processes, and Element 4.3 will take you through the production and post-production processes. By the end of Element 4.2 you will have produced two treatments: one for a fiction and one for a non-fiction product. You will also need to produce evidence of research carried out for your two programmes, plus a production script and a note of any issues that may relate to the production.

The production log

Every stage of your planning and production needs to be recorded, from the initial idea to the evaluation of the finished product. The document that contains all these records is your **production log**. This is your individual record. It will contain all the documents and research you have carried out for your production, and your comments on your own role and the progress of the project.

A production log is like a diary which records everything you do before and during the production. The log should be started at the very beginning of the assignment and should include the following:

- How your film was recorded, logged and checked against the treatment and the script. Each shot must be written down.
- A record of material prepared which does *not* appear in the final product, e.g. notes of discussions, and any production planning sheets.
- Notes about the planning of the editing, and decisions made during the editing process.
- A risk assessment sheet with actions taken – see the Health and Safety checklist on page 168.

In fact, every decision that you make and every activity that you work on should be recorded in your production log. It should also include your own assessment or evaluation of each activity (your own strengths and weaknesses, the success of your team, how teamwork could be improved, etc.). Your production log should be headed like this:

| Production Log | Element 4 | (Your name) |

Pre-production planning

Think about the programmes we investigated in Element 4.1 and decide which kind of programme you would like to produce yourself. You can use all the activities you have carried out so far as a preparation for your product. For example, as you have carried out a considerable amount of research on chat shows, soap operas and advertisements, you might like to continue the work you did earlier by producing one of your own.

Remember that you have to write *two* treatments, only one of which you will actually produce. One treatment must be for a fiction product and one for a non-fiction product. You could therefore take a soap opera and an advertisment as your fiction products and a chat show as your non-fiction product. However, you do not need to restrict your choice to the programmes that you have looked at already.

Other ideas might be:
- A music video
- A party political broadcast
- A college or school video
- A community video

Are there any others you can think of?

If you choose to make an advertisement, you could refer back to the table you produced for Activity 4.5 and choose one particular style of advertisement.

Before you start you need to decide what the product is, who is your target audience, and what codes and conventions you are going to use. Will you use recognisable 'types' to convey meaning very quickly, or will you avoid this by using other methods?

When you have decided about which moving image products you want to work on, make sure that every decision you make is recorded in your production log. You can design this for yourself. The first page of your log should be a project proposal sheet showing the following information:

- Your name
- The medium you have chosen (e.g. television, video)
- The purpose of the product (e.g. to entertain, inform, persuade, educate, generate income, etc.)
- The genre (e.g. soap opera, quiz show, video, advertisement, documentary)
- The target audience
- Style
- Structure
- Budget

Remember also that all the work you have completed so far should be logged and placed in your 'moving image' file.

Activity 4.8

Design a product proposal sheet and complete copies for your two product ideas, one fiction and one non-fiction.

Writing a treatment

The proposals that are submitted for moving image products are called **treatments.** This term is used throughout the film and television industry. A treatment is written at the very start of a film's or television programme's life. It is used to convey the message, storyline, location and characters to the producers, investors or client.

It is very important to produce a treatment before you start production work, because as well as conveying the idea to other people, it also gives you a chance to test out your own ideas.

The main function of the treatment is to give detailed information about the subject and style of your product. You need to cover:

- **Research –** Include any audience research you have done, such as questionnaires, interviews and results of any other research, such as leaflets and brochures, which you have collected for information. Later on you will also include notes on research into location, lighting, etc. (see page 167).
- **Content issues –** Include notes on any legal, copyright and ethical issues connected with your products. For example, do you need permission to reproduce copyright material? If you want to use music, or clips from films and television programmes you will need to write and ask permission from the copyright-holders.
- **Representation –** Give details of who will be appearing in your products and how will they be represented.

The above items apply to both fiction and non-fiction products. We are now going to look in more detail at how you write each separate type of treatment.

A fiction treatment

For a fiction or dramatic product, the treatment will consist of an outline of the story, with some description of how it is to be told or presented through moving images. It will also include details of genre, characters, locations, time, lighting, period and any possible special effects, casting or sound which will help the reader to visualise the end-product.

ONE BAD TURN

Cast
Rebecca (14) is the eldest of a large family, and takes responsiblity for her younger brothers and sisters. She is a neat girl, who is seen as trustworthy by staff and friends.
Jo (also 14) is her friend. Jo's grandparents have looked after her since her parents went to work in Hong Kong four years ago. She is indulged, seen as a princess, and always gets what she wants. She is great fun, boisterous and popular — as long as she is not crossed.

Story outline
Jo and Rebecca are both in the same class at school. Jo is the class comedian and bully; Rebecca is seen as a goody-goody, who always hands her homework in on time. In the registration period Rebecca bravely stands up to Jo, and refuses to give her the answers to last night's Maths homework. Jo steals Rebecca's homework book and now Rebecca is in trouble…

Setting
Action takes place outside the headmaster's study. The scene is empty except for two chairs which Jo and Rebecca are sitting on. Jo is sitting nearest the door, on which can be seen a sign which says 'Headteacher'. Rebecca looks upset and nervous and her eyes are lowered. Jo looks confident and finds Rebecca's nerves amusing — she is obviously a bit of a bully.

Synopsis
Jo and Rebecca talk about why they are there. Jo persuades Rebecca to take her cigarettes for her whilst she goes in to see the headteacher 'to save her getting in trouble'. The headteacher's door opens slowly. The girls both look apprehensively at the door. A loud haughty voice calls Rebecca into her office and she enters nervously. As the door closes the last shot is of Jo looking smug.

Style
This scene will be in the realistic style of a soap opera. It will be shot during the day and the lighting will reflect a light and airy school corridor…

Example of a TV drama treatment

Activity 4.9

Write a treatment for your fiction product.

Writing a fiction script

One of the differences between fiction and non-fiction products is that fiction products have a script which is written down before shooting begins. The words of the script are learned and performed by actors. In non-fiction products this is not usually necessary, as the product will be made up of real people speaking for themselves – for example, in interviews.

If you are producing fiction or drama it is very important to write out the entire script or screenplay in detail before shooting begins. The script should include the spoken dialogue and the stage directions i.e., instructions to the actors on where to move, etc. (*Note:* The script or screenplay for a fiction product must not be confused with the production script. You will learn about this on page 164.)

Here is an example of a script to help you get the idea:

SCENE 10   EXTERIOR PAUL'S HOUSE   EARLY EVENING

Sixteen-year-old Paul Fraser is sitting on the wall outside his house, swinging his feet and throwing stones on the floor. He looks miserable and is chewing gum, staring into the distance. The garden and the house are obviously not cared for, and the shell of a car is in the driveway. Mrs Fraser, Paul's mother, a woman in her early forties, walks along the pavement. She is returning from work. She is wearing a business suit and is carrying a briefcase and a shopping bag.

MRS FRASER (sarcastic):

        I hope you didn't wear yourself out today Paul, sitting there all day must be very tiring.

Paul jumps off of the wall.

PAUL: Are you speaking to me? Do I exist? Let me pinch myself. Oh yes. 'Hello Paul, did you have a good day today? What did you do with yourself?'

MRS FRASER: You don't do yourself any favours, love, I mean you are a young man, with your whole life ahead of you, you should be out there making a name for yourself.

PAUL: Change the record. Here we go. Look, I'm going to Phil's. See you later.

Paul exits suddenly leaving MRS FRASER flabbergasted. She opens the front door, watches Paul disappear into the distance, then closes the door slowly.

ENDS

You will see that the scene heading gives an at-a-glance guide to the scene. It contains four pieces of information:

- The scene number
- Whether the setting is interior or exterior
- The location
- Whether the action takes place during the day or night

There are also certain conventions which apply to script layout:

- When characters first appear, the script gives a short description of them including their name, age and appearance.
- Each time a character speaks, their name appears first, then their lines.
- Any actions by the characters are inserted (usually in a different type style to make it easy to see them) at the appropriate point in the script.

Activity 4.10 ————————————————————————————————————

Write the script for your fiction proposal.

————————————————————————————————————

A non-fiction treatment

There are different issues to be considered when writing a treatment for a non-fiction product. Non-fiction products are based on fact and involve real people who appear as themselves and speak their own words – as in a chat show or a documentary. This means that you do not have to write a word-for-word script, but you do need to find people willing to appear in your product and draw up a detailed plan of what they are going to talk about.

You may decide to make a non-fiction documentary-style programme about your school or college. If you like this idea, you could brainstorm with your group and see how many ideas you can come up. Possibilities might include a promotional video to sell your college to local school leavers; or you could film a documentary about the resources in the new Technology block, or show a typical 'day in the life' of a particular department in the college, such as Performing Arts.

Researching a non-fiction product

Once you have decided on the style of programme you are going to make and the subject you are going to cover, you need to think about research. For example, you will need to find out:

- What aspects of your chosen subject you need to cover
- What is going to interest your target audience
- Who to interview
- Where would be a good location
- What lighting and sound facilities are available
- What time and resources you will need

You will also need to investigate **primary** and **secondary** sources of material for your project (see page 78).

Constructing questionnaires

In order to get the information you require, you will need to prepare your questions very carefully and practise your interview techniques beforehand. Questionnaires are a very useful tool for gathering information. A questionnaire is a list of questions on a particular subject which you want someone to answer. Details of how to construct a questionnaire are given in Chapter 1, page 39.

You need to be very clear about what information you want, and about the kind of question which will draw it out from your interviewees. For example, if you want to find out how a student travels to and from college and how long it takes, and you ask:

'Does it take you a long time to get to college?'

you may simply get the answer:

'Yes'

This is not very helpful, because 'a long time' can mean different things to different people. In order to get a really clear picture, you would need to ask more specific open questions which encourage the interviewee to respond. For example:

'When do you get up?'

'When do you catch the bus?'

'What route do you take?'

'How long does the journey take you?'

Activity 4.11

Make a list of the questions you want to ask your interviewees and try them out on a classmate. Discuss the questions and amend them so that they obtain the information you want.

Collecting written information

If you are doing a treatment for a documentary – for example, about your school or college – you will need to collect written information about it, such as brochures, statistics and publicity material. You then need to decide how much of the material is relevant and how to work it into your programme.

Legal and ethical issues

During the research stage for any non-fiction product, it is essential to find out whether you need permission to use the material you have collected and if so, who to ask.

You also need to plan carefully to make sure that no-one will say anything on your programme which could be seen as **libellous** by a viewer (see page 126 for more information about this).

You will need to seek permission to film people and sites in the college. People you may need to get written permission from include:
- Everyone you film (they will need to sign what is called a 'release form')
- Parents of young children who appear in the film
- Owners or property or land used in the making of the film
- Police and highway officers (if filming in a public place)

This is something you should do well in advance of your filming. Your schedule will depend on this efficient preparation.

You should also think about **representation** issues. Does your programme include a fair range of views on the subject being covered?

Locations

You will need to carry out research into locations. If you are doing a documentary about your school or college, what aspects of the building do you want to show? Which particular student or staff activities do you want in your programme?

Codes and conventions

Before you start your non-fiction treatment, you need to be familiar with the conventions of the particular type of programme which you are planning to make. We have already looked at a range of chat show programmes in Element 4.1. If you are planning to produce a documentary-style programme, you should look at a range of programmes which involve interviews, discussion, locations (both interior and exterior) to see how your programme could best be produced.

When you look at the programmes, make a note of the **sequence** of the items presented. Why do you think the scenes appear in this order? Look at the interview and discussion sections. Are they interesting? Are they too long? Is there a balance of views represented? Do you see as many aspects of the subject as possible? If not, how has the programme-maker decided what to include and what to leave out? Are there any content issues over legal and ethical problems? Have social issues or groups been represented fairly?

You don't have to *copy* any particular style, but there may be aspects of the programmes which you think are attractive or interesting and which you want to use or adapt for your own purposes. It is a good idea to record two or three documentary programmes and have a look at their structure, how the subject matter has been selected, and how they represent the issues.

Activity 4.12

Write a treatment for your non-fiction product, either using the ideas discussed here, or your own ideas.

The production script

Now that you have decided on the content of your programme and carried out the research, you are ready to write your **production script**. This is the written plan of your programme, including dialogue, sound and shots, which will be used by the production team when they produce the video footage.

The layout for production scripts for drama and documentary programmes is the same – two columns, one with information about the images and the other with information about the sound.

The information contained in each column will differ depending on whether you are working on a fiction or non-fiction product.

For a fiction product, the production script will contain details about the camera shots, all of the dialogue, the action and any special effects and music which will be included.

For a non-fiction product, the production script will contain the images that will be used, the narration (or voice-over), the people chosen to be interviewed and the key questions that will be asked. An example is shown opposite.

Camera Shot	Scene / Action / Sound
1. Exterior 'college' showing the college sign (LS)	Music Fade to Narrator 'Hello and welcome to Framley College...'
2. Cut to (CU) of college sign	'... Framley College has a wide range of courses and options for young people.'
3. Close up (CU) of student/ presenter standing outside entrance, next to the sign	'... We are going to investigate some of the choices that students make ...'
4. Medium shot (MS) of students going in and out of the college, talking to each other	'... And talk to them about their hopes and ambitions.'

Extract from a production script

Activity 4.13

Choose one of the two treatments you have developed and write a production script for it, based on the layout shown above.

Shot types

There are many different types of camera shots you can use. Not only will a variety of shots make your video more interesting to watch, but the type of shots you use can make a difference to how your audience react to your video. Illustrations of different shot types are shown on page 166.

Camera moves

Don't forget that you can *move* the camera too. Here are some of the things you can do:

- **Pan** – turn the camera to the left or right whilst mounted on a tripod
- **Tilt** – tilt the camera up or down while on a tripod
- **Zoom** – move in towards your subject using the zoom lens
- **Track** – move the camera forwards or backwards using the 'dolly', a piece of equipment like a trolley which allows the camera to move smoothly across the ground. In school or college you could improvise, using a chair with castors
- **Crab** – move the camera sideways, usually on a dolly attached to the tripod.

Shot types

Where's the camera?
Placing the camera in different positions can create some interesting effects. Putting the camera on the floor gives a 'mouse eye view'.

Having the camera upside down gives the impression of walking on the ceiling, while shooting with the camera sideways gives the impression of walking up walls.

Establishing shot (ES)

Medium shot (LS)

Long shot (LS)

High level shot

Two shots (2S)

Close up (CU)

High angle shot

Big close-up (BCU)

The production schedule

Once the production script has been written, the next stage is to organise a **production schedule**. This involves working through your script, dividing it into scenes and filling up a chart with the following headings:

Scene no.	Location	Actors, costumes, props	Equipment needed

From this chart you will be able to work out your shooting schedule. Remember that films and programmes are not shot in sequence and it is possible to shoot all scenes in one location at the same time, even if they appear at the beginning and end of the film.

Good video production and programme-making depend on detailed planning. Work out at an early stage what you are likely to need. Do you have the necessary props and equipment, or are you able to borrow or hire them?

Production schedule

Title ....

Location .... **Date/Time** ....

Personnel ....

....

Production ....

In shot ....

Equipment

Video/camera ☐

Tripod ☐

Dolly ☐

Tapes ☐

Batteries ☐

White cards ☐

Storyboards ☐

Lights ☐

Microphones ☐

Props ....

....

How to lay out a production schedule

The production schedule should be distributed to all members of the production team in advance of the planned shoot. This will allow them to organise themselves and get hold of any necessary equipment. Make sure all members of your team know their roles in the production and agree to be responsible for the tasks allocated.

The production team

As well as thorough planning, communication is important when filming your video. A production team should consist of a number of clearly defined roles:

- **Director** – Working from the production script (sometimes called the 'shooting script') the director will control the movement of the actors and the action. The director should be a good listener and be able to communicate ideas to the team. S/he must also log all the shots, keep the paperwork up to date and make sure the production team keep quiet during filming!
- **Camera operator** – The camera operator has responsibility for shooting the film using the camera in the best possible way for each shot. S/he is responsible for the equipment, which could include booking it and making sure that the batteries are charged.
- **Sound recordist** – If you are using microphones external to the video camera, this person will be responsible for the successful recording of sound. This will involve adjusting levels, and giving direction to presenters/performers regarding volume levels.
- **Editor** – After filming, the editor pieces together the separate shots using editing equipment, referring to the production script.

Risk assessment

Throughout the production of a film it is important to make sure that hazards are kept to a minimum, and that team members and equipment are protected and safe at all times. This process is known in the industry as 'risk assessment'.

When shooting your programme there are two main considerations – people and equipment. People behind and people in front of the camera must not be put in danger and there must be rules about the condition of the equipment and the way it is used. Follow the health and safety checklist below.

Health and safety checklist

Leads

- Never disconnect a plug by pulling on its lead
- Before closing case lids, ensure no leads will be trapped and pinched
- Never tie knots in leads
- Never tie cables over the heads of lamps. Lamp cables can often be coiled and hung using the chains or lugs provided on the lamp stand
- Always coil and pack away leads neatly

Videocassettes

- Always label your cassette and its protective container as soon as possible
- Use the tabs provided to prevent accidental erasure of important recordings
- Avoid dust, dirt, moisture, heat and magnetic fields
- Fully rewind your cassettes when finished and store vertically
- Do not drop or knock cassettes

Cameras

- Do not drop or knock the camera and always make sure that camera is mounted securely on a stable tripod
- Never point camera at the sun or a bright light source
- On finishing a shot, close down the iris and replace lens cap

- Avoid dust, dirt, moisture, heart and magnetic fields
- Protect from rain or drizzle
- Do not touch the lens
- Do not disconnect viewfinders from the cameras
- Do not replace cameras into their case upside down
- Remove a camera from the tripod by loosening the correct tripod mountings and NOT by twisting the camera

Activity 4.14

Carry out a risk assessment for the product which you are going to produce. Make a list of health and safety hazards at each stage. For each hazard, decide what action to take to minimise risks and avoid placing yourself, or others, in danger.

Review questions
1 Define and give examples of primary and secondary research sources.
2 Name two legal issues which you should consider when developing your moving image products.
3 What sort of information should you include in a treatment for a moving image product?
4 Who in a production team would refer to the 'treatment'?
5 What are the main differences between a production script written for a non-fiction product and one written for a fiction product?
6 What factors should you consider when scheduling a production?

Element 4.3 Produce moving image products

You should by now have planned and prepared all the appropriate pre-production documents and be ready to start shooting. Here is a reminder of the documents you should have for the product you are going to shoot:
- Treatment
- Production script
- Production schedule
- Risk assessment list

If you have not already done so, you should familiarise yourself with your video recorder and equipment. Practise setting the equipment up and loading the camera. Practise filming and moving the camera, creating different types of shot with the zoom and panning the camera from left to right and right to left.

Moving the camera
When performing any camera movement, remember the following points:
- Operate all camera movements smoothly and slowly
- Begin and end the camera movements with a static shot of a few seconds – this improves the look of the shot
- When following a moving subject, keep the camera slightly ahead of the subject to allow for walking space.

Framing

Decide what it is you want your audience to see in the frame. Keep the subject that you are filming in the centre of the frame and avoid leaving either too much or too little headroom. If there are two people in the shot, avoid too big a gap between them. Sometimes you may find that you get a better shot by moving the camera position, or, if you are filming people, by positioning them in a certain way. Do not be afraid to experiment until you find the camera position that gives the best results.

Here are a couple of exercises which you may like to try:

Exercise 1

Sit your group on chairs in a semi-circle. Set your camera on a tripod in the middle of the circle. Frame the head of the person on the extreme left, making sure that the whole head is visible and is in the middle of the frame. Start recording and pan slowly and steadily from left to right across the semi-circle, so that each member of your group in turn is framed.

Exercise 2

Carry out the same exercise, asking each person to say their name and the name of their favourite pop group. This will allow you to test the microphone levels on your camera and discover how the distance from the microphone affects the actors' voice recording and volume levels.

Shooting your moving image product

You will be editing this film, and so don't forget that you can have several attempts at each shot if necessary, then select the best one at the editing stage. To make things easier, it is a good idea to mark the beginning of each shot. A clapperboard is ideal, but a folder or a sheet of paper held up to the camera before the action starts is a perfectly good way to mark the beginning of each shot.

Logging the shots

One member of the team (usually the director) should be assigned to log the shots and keep a note of the length, number of takes and outcome of each shot.

Pre-roll

Always leave the tape running five seconds before and after your shot. Pre-roll recording is very important – you will never be sure of an accurate or clean edit if you try to edit too close to where you have paused or stopped the tape.

Discipline on set

Filming can be an extremely frustrating activity, but all members of the production team must concentrate on the task in hand. This means listening to each other and being quiet during filming. Camera people must know what actors and presenters are going to do, and when they are going to do it.

The following is a drill used by professional production teams to make sure that there is complete discipline on set. It ensures that everything happens in the correct order and that no vital material is missed at the beginning or end. The verbal cues can be cut out at the editing stage.

Verbal cue	Action
'STANDBY'	Everyone to their places: sound ready:
	camera balanced: framed up: focused and in pause mode
'RUN TAPE'	Start video recorder by releasing pause
'ACTION'	Action begins (two seconds after pause is released on VCR)
'CUT'	Stop video recorder by engaging Pause or Stop control

It is a good idea to use this in your own productions.

Activity 4.15

1 Record your moving image product, based on the production script which you have developed.
2 Make sure that you clearly label the tapes and that they are stored in a safe place. It is not a good idea for one person to take them home, as if this member of the team is absent, it will delay the next stage of the production.

Post-production

Editing

Editing takes place throughout the production process, as you decide:
- What to include in the script
- What to leave out of the script
- What to record
- What not to record

At the post-production stage, however, editing means selecting the material you want from the video footage you have shot, and putting it together, using the structure you planned in your original production script. With the help of editing equipment, you will select sequences from your original recording and copy them, in order, on to a new tape. At this point, you can also make decisions about any additional material you may wish to include in your programme – for example, sound effects, music and credits.

The first stage in the editing process is to log each shot. In order to do this you have to watch all of the video footage shot. This is known as 'viewing the rushes.' As you watch, make a note of each shot, the point where it occurs in the footage (known as its 'time code'), the length of the shot, and a brief description of its content.

Time codes

Professionals use special equipment to register time codes. If you do not have this equipment, you can use a clock with a second hand to time each shot from the beginning of the film, and log its length.

Activity 4.16

Watch all the video footage you have shot and log each shot, noting its time code, length and content.

Making an Edit Decision List (EDL)

Once you have logged all the shots, you are ready to select the shots to use in the final film. This is called preparing an **Edit Decision List (EDL)** or a 'paper edit'. You will need to use your original production script as a guide and select the best quality shots which most closely match what you originally planned.

The EDL starts with the first shot to be used and continues in order of shots to the end of the video. It should include the time code of each shot to be used. This will allow you to find the shots quickly and start them accurately. You should also include in your EDL any music, sound and fades, mixes or special effects required. An example of part of an EDL is shown below.

Activity 4.17

Make your own EDL for your moving image product, following the layout of the example below.

Shot	Time code	Item	Details	Quality
1	0000	College sign	Pan to sign	OK
3	0035	College stairs	Zoom in on front door	Good
6	0060	Students sitting in	Pan common room	
		common room		OK

Example of an Edit Decision List

Completing the EDL

When you have completed your EDL, you may identify new legal, ethical or representational issues. You should say how you plan to deal with them. This may mean re-recording or recording additional material and incorporating the new or additional shots in your EDL. Once you are happy with the final version of your EDL, you are ready to edit your material.

The editing process

Editing equipment can vary, but at the simplest level it is possible to buy a lead to link your video camera to a video recorder which in turn is linked to a television. Using the 'play' and 'record' buttons, you can copy sections from your original footage on to a new tape in the video recorder. This method is perfectly workable, though not always accurate. Professional editing is done on an edit suite which consists of two recorders with a control pad which allows editing to be done with precision and accuracy.

Whatever your equipment, the most important aspect of video editing is the selection of material which will be used in the final video.

Activity 4.18

1 Edit all of your material as planned in your Edit Decision List, using the equipment which is available to you.

Activity 4.19

1 Show your finished video to some representatives of the target audience which you identified in your original product proposal.
2 After the screening, record the reaction of the audience to the product. This can be done by either an audience questionnaire, post-screening interviews or a discussion about the video.
3 Make notes about the audience's response to your video.

Evaluation

As part of your assignment, you need to write an evaluation of your final product. In this, it is important to be honest and reflect on your project, highlighting problems you encountered and how you dealt with them. The evaluation should include the following information:

1 Evaluation of your product

Compare your finished product with your original plans such as the script and the treatment:
- What changes are there, if any?
- Why were these changes made?
- With hindsight, would you make any other changes to the way you worked?
- Explain what these would be.
- What codes and conventions did you use? Were they appropriate to your product?

2 Evaluation of your production team
- How effective was the production process?
- How did you work as a group?
- How successfully did you manage to operate the equipment?

3 Evaluation of the audience reaction
- How did the audience respond to the video?
- Was their response favourable?
- Considering their response, what changes would you make to the video?

Activity 4.20

Write an evaluation of your product using the following headings:

- The product
- The production team
- The audience reaction

Review questions

1 Briefly describe the role of each of the following members of a production team: the director, the editor, the camera operator, the sound recordist.
2 Name three different shot types and describe them.
3 Describe what is meant by 'logging' the shots during filming. Why is this important?
4 What is an Edit Decision List? Describe how it is made.
5 What should you evaluate your finished product against?

Assignment 4
Planning and producing video products

This assignment provides evidence for:

Elements: **4.1** Investigate moving image products
4.2 Develop treatments and scripts for moving image products
4.3 Produce moving image products

and the following key skills:

Communication:	2.1, 2.2, 2.3, 2.4
Information Technology:	2.1, 2.2, 2.3, 2.4
Application of Numbers:	2.1, 2.2, 2.3

1 Put together a 'video' file containing all your notes, logs and production paperwork from the activities in Elements 4.1, 4.2 and 4.3, each under the appropriate element heading.
2 Include your finished video production on a labelled videotape.
3 Add to the video file all the reports and evaluations you have done in the different activities.
4 Check carefully to make sure all the work produced is in your file, then submit it to your tutor, with your name and group clearly marked.

5 Video production

What is covered in this chapter

- Working to a programme brief to plan a video production
- Producing and editing a video product
- Presenting a video product to an audience
- Evaluating a video product and the production process

Your 'video' file will need to contain the following:
- A production log detailing your own contribution to the projects (see page 176)
- Records of research undertaken in the planning of your video productions
- Pre-production planning documents for two video productions, one fiction, the other non-fiction
- Two edited video productions, one fiction, the other non-fiction, neither more than five minutes long
- A report on both video productions, reviewing each against the aims of the original brief and commenting on the strength of the ideas, the technical quality of the production and the audience's reaction
- An evaluation of your own and the production team's performance in the planning and production of your video products

Introduction

In Chapter 4 we examined a number of the processes and issues involved in planning and producing a video product. This chapter will develop the skills learned earlier and give you further opportunity to apply them in practice.

You will be working as part of a team to plan and produce two video productions, one fiction and one non-fiction. You will take on different roles within the team for each production and you will need to keep a careful record of everything done by yourself and by your team.

At the end of the chapter you will be asked to evaluate the two video productions. Did they achieve what they were supposed to achieve? You will also be required to evaluate the way in which members of the team worked together to produce the videos.

The production log

Both assignments in this chapter require a **production log** to support the finished product. As we saw in Chapter 4, a production log is like a diary which records everything you do before and during the production process. The log should be started at the very beginning of the assignment and should include the following:

- A written record of each shot
- Details of how your film was recorded, logged and checked against the treatment and the production script
- Where each scene was recorded and who was in it
- What went wrong, or did not go according to plan
- How problems were tackled and resolved
- A record of material prepared which does not appear in the final product, e.g. notes of discussions and any production planning sheets
- Notes about the planning of the editing, and decisions made during the editing process, with justifications for any changes made in style or content
- A risk assessment sheet, together with actions taken – see health and safety checklist, page 168
- Notes reporting the final presentation of the finished product to an audience, describing the audience response, the technical quality, original intentions of the treatment and the effectiveness of the production process

Element 5.1 Plan video productions

In this chapter you will be working as a member of a production team. Each person in the team will take on a specific role and you will need to conduct regular production meetings to co-ordinate the planning of your productions and to canvass the opinions and ideas of the group. We will be looking later at specific production roles and responsibilities within the production team, but first let us look at how to conduct a production team meeting.

Production team meetings

The quality of the communication which takes place during production meetings can be affected by a number of things:

- **The size of the group** – In a large meeting some people may hold back from contributing, even if they have something valuable to say
- **The formality of the meeting** – A very formal set-up may be intimidating for some people and prevent them from making a proper contribution
- **Individual personalities** – Meetings can easily be dominated by one or two personalities; it is important to ensure that proceedings are properly conducted so that everybody has a chance to have their say

Meeting procedure

At the initial production meeting it is a good idea for the team to exchange telephone numbers and addresses, and agree on a time and place to meet.

An 'agenda' should be drawn up in advance to give group members a clear idea of decisions to be made at the meeting and action to be taken.

The 'minutes' are a record of what was said and decided at a meeting – for example, notes of further action to be taken, with details of who is responsible for doing it and when it needs to be done by. Minutes are based on notes taken during the meeting by the secretary. They are sent to all members of the team in good time for them to be read before the following meeting.

Roles within a production team

At the first production meeting, the group should draw up a list of preferred roles, based on their experience and personal preferences. As we saw earlier, a production team should consist of a number of clearly defined roles:

- The **director** directs the action, logs the shots and generally supervises the production team
- The **camera operator** shoots the film and maintains the camera equipment
- The **sound recordist** is responsible for everything to do with external sound recording
- The **editor** pieces the programme together after it has been shot

More details of these roles are given in Chapter 4, page 168.

It is a good idea to take on at least one new role during each production. This will enable you to learn new skills.

The production brief

A 'production brief' is produced when a programme or a video product is first commissioned by a client. The production brief clearly states the required outcome of the video, including the target audience, the theme and the deadline for the finished product. In a commercial situation this would be used by the video production company to develop ideas and pitch for the job. The term 'pitch' means to present a proposal to a client in order to secure a video production contract. Several different production companies may pitch for the same contract, and the client will choose the one they like best.

Activity 5.1

1 With your production team, look at the briefs on pages 178-9. Choose one person to be the note-taker and then as a group, brainstorm initial ideas for each of the briefs. 'Brainstorming' means that everyone puts forward their ideas quickly and all ideas are written down – there is no discussion or criticism at this stage. You will eventually have to produce two of these products and note-taking at this stage is essential, as quite often initial responses to ideas can be the strongest.

2 Each member of the team should choose a different one of the briefs and take some time on their own to think about their ideas for the video, including the following:

   - Target audience
   - Type of product
   - Style
   - Genre
   - Length
   - Content/narrative

3 When everyone is ready, take it in turns for each person to describe their ideas for the brief they have been working on. Then as a group, agree on two of the briefs which you will actually produce – one fiction and the other non-fiction.

   Make sure that each member of the team has a note of the ideas for these two briefs – you will need them for later activities.

Case Study: production briefs

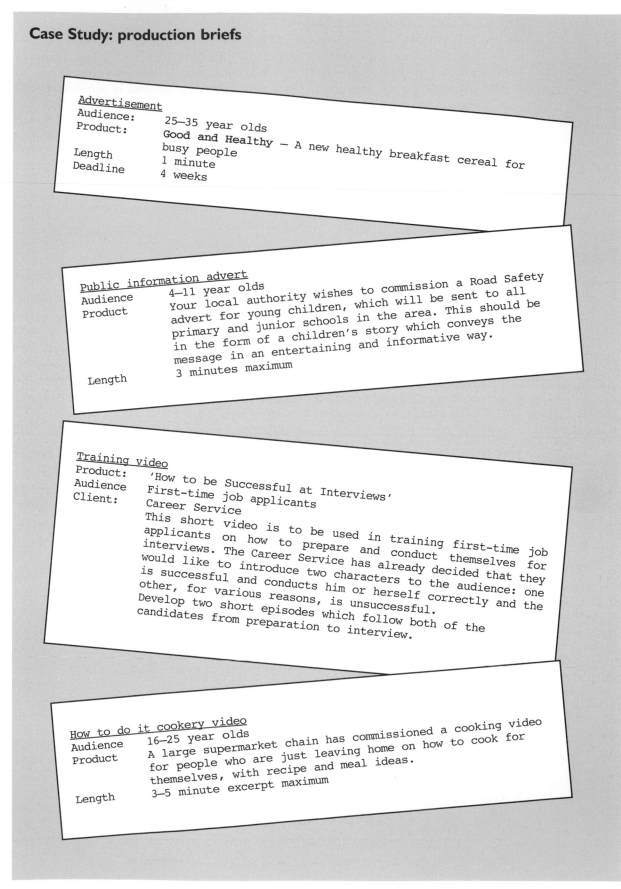

Advertisement
Audience: 25—35 year olds
Product: **Good and Healthy** — A new healthy breakfast cereal for busy people
Length 1 minute
Deadline 4 weeks

Public information advert
Audience 4—11 year olds
Product Your local authority wishes to commission a Road Safety advert for young children, which will be sent to all primary and junior schools in the area. This should be in the form of a children's story which conveys the message in an entertaining and informative way.
Length 3 minutes maximum

Training video
Product: 'How to be Successful at Interviews'
Audience First-time job applicants
Client: Career Service
This short video is to be used in training first-time job applicants on how to prepare and conduct themselves for interviews. The Career Service has already decided that they would like to introduce two characters to the audience: one is successful and conducts him or herself correctly and the other, for various reasons, is unsuccessful. Develop two short episodes which follow both of the candidates from preparation to interview.

How to do it cookery video
Audience 16—25 year olds
Product A large supermarket chain has commissioned a cooking video for people who are just leaving home on how to cook for themselves, with recipe and meal ideas.
Length 3—5 minute excerpt maximum

Production briefs (Contd.)

Magazine programme
Audience: 16–18 year olds
Product: The college authorities wish to commission a magazine
            programme which will be screened in the common room and
            other public areas of the college. It will include
            information about the college, leisure and entertainment
            opportunities, local promotions for events and issues
            concerning the student population. It will be
            broadcast weekly.
Length: 5-minute video excerpt
Deadline   4 weeks

Soap Opera
Audience: 35–50 year olds
Product: A new television channel is seeking to launch a new late-
            night chat show for people who have just returned from a
            night out. The content and style should appeal to the older
            audience.
Length: 5-minute excerpt

Research

Before a production company produces a video it will almost certainly do some research. This is in order to make sure that the video fulfils the client's needs, attracts the target audience, and also that the information it contains is accurate.

You have already been introduced to the basic research methods in Chapter 4, page 162. Here, we go into a little more detail about how to conduct good, effective research.

Sources of information

Primary sources of information are the people you speak to directly on the phone or in person. Methods of getting information from primary sources include the following:

- **Structured questionnaires** These allow you to collect information from a number of respondents or members of your target audience and to compare and study responses from a range of people to a set of fixed questions. Questionnaires can be completed in writing by the respondent or they can be used as the basis for a telephone or face-to-face interview.

- **Interviews** These can range from casual 'vox-pop' street encounters to friendly chats and in-depth interviews. You need to be clear in your own mind why you are interviewing a particular person. Is she an expert? Is she a famous personality? Has she seen something unusual? Whatever the reason, this will form the basis of your questions and guide your approach. Any interviewer needs to be clear about what it is he or she wants to find out and to prepare questions accordingly.

  At the planning stage you need to think about where the interview is going to take place and how you can make the interviewee feel at ease. It is a good idea to get to know them a little and make them feel comfortable before the interview.

Secondary sources of information are usually written – for example, books, documents, archives, records, newspapers or the Internet. A secondary source could also be someone who passes on a message to you from someone else. Secondary research methods include the following:

- **Analysis of content** This involves looking at particular texts and categorising aspects of them. For example, you may want to investigate the number of advertisements on television in a particular time slot which show men drinking beer or lager or taking part in sporting activities.
- **Analysis of documents** This is research using information which is published and in the public domain. For example, you may need to go to the library to find out about diets or the properties of particular foods.
- **Statistical analysis** This involves looking at government and other research figures, for example, Department of Health statistics from 1986–1996 on heart attacks in women between the ages of 35 and 50.

No one method is better than another. Different methods suit different purposes and it is advisable to use more than one method when researching your video products.

Carrying out research

Once you have decided as a group on the briefs that you will be working with, you need to organise your research. For example, each person could take responsibility for one of the following areas:

1 **Target audience** One approach might be to write a questionnaire and conduct a survey to investigate your target audience (see Chapter 4, page 162). The kind of things you need to find out about your target audience might be:
   - What kind of images or messages do they respond to?
   - What are their tastes?
   - What concerns this age group?
   - Do they have any opinions about the subject matter you plan to cover?

   This information will affect your final product. For example, if you are working on the healthy breakfast cereal advert, you may find your audience would like to eat healthily but does not have enough time to get organised. This could be reflected in the way you create your advert.

2 **Subject matter** If you need to find out more about your chosen subject matter, it may be worth going to the library, collecting leaflets or contacting pressure groups. For example, for the advertisement for the healthy breakfast cereal, you could contact the Health Education Authority to see if they have any research on the benefits of healthy eating. You may also want to explore the links between healthy eating and relief of stress.

3 **Competitor analysis** You may want to look at and compare products which are of a similar nature (either in terms of subject matter or audience) to the product you are researching. You could also analyse the effect these products have on their audience by including a question in your questionnaire. This will help you to decide on the style and structure of your final product.

4 **Production research** You will need to find out the budget, facilities and equipment available for your video. Ask your tutors to produce a rate card to help you assess the cost of equipment and materials.

Activity 5. 2

1 As a group, decide which types of research need to be done for each of the two briefs you have chosen to work on. Allocate the research tasks so that each member of the group carries out at least one of the above types of research.

2 When all the research is done, meet as a group and share what you have discovered. Each member of the team should have a copy of all the research which has been done by the team for each of the two briefs. Keep a clear record of which research was done by you and put this in your unit folder.

Pre-production planning

Using the results of your research, the next step is to create pre-production documents for the making of your video. In professional video and film production a lot of emphasis is placed on planning before the costly process of production begins. Pre-production planning includes producing the following documents:

- Treatment
- Production script
- Storyboard
- Production schedule

Treatment

The **treatment** is a description or outline of the content of the video. For a fiction or dramatic video, it will consist of an outline of the story, written like an essay with details of how you intend to tell or present the action through moving images. In the case of a factual video, the treatment literally *is* the story. For example, if you were making a documentary on the effects of screen violence, the treatment would explain whether you intend to show violence in films as a bad influence on the audience, or show that the audience has a choice and is able to distinguish between real life and 'entertainment'. It would also explain how you intend to develop and present your point of view.

In preparing a treatment, the following questions should be answered:

- Is the subject going to be treated seriously or humorously?
- Is the video going to be factual or fantasy?
- Are you going to be critical of the subject or sympathetic?
- Are you aiming to inform, teach, entertain, provoke or reassure?
- Will you be using actors or real people?
- Will you be using pictures with voices and sound effects over the top, or will you hear voices as people speak on screen?
- Who is the intended audience?

Examples of treatments are shown in Chapter 4, pages 159–162.

Activity 5.3

1 Working on your own, use the notes on the two chosen briefs from Activity 5.1, and everybody's research notes from Activity 5.2, to prepare a treatment for each of the two video productions you will be working on.
2 When everybody has completed their treatments, make sure that copies are distributed to each member of the group so that everyone sees the treatments for each brief.
3 Working with your group, choose ONE of your two briefs. Each person in the group should present their treatment for this brief to the other members of the group. Then, as a group, decide on one treatment for this brief which the whole group will develop into a finished product. Make sure that everyone agrees on the choice of treatment to be developed.

Activity 5.4

For this activity, you will need the brief which you did NOT choose for Activity 5.3 above.

Ask your tutor to act as a 'client'. Arrange a time when each member of the team in turn can present their treatment of this brief to the 'client' and the other team members. Remember that you will need to give your tutor a copy of the original brief and also a copy of each person's treatment for that brief. At the end of the presentation, the client will choose which treatment is to be developed into a final product.

From now on, you will be working as a group on two specific treatments, one of which will have been chosen by the 'client' (your tutor) and the other of which will have been agreed on by your group. *All the activities from now on will need to be done for both products.* If possible, you should try to ensure that you carry out different roles in the production team for each one.

Writing a fiction script

For your fiction or drama product you will need to write a complete script. For help on scriptwriting and an example of a fiction script, see Chapter 4, page 161.

The production script

Once you have written the treatment plus a full script for your fiction product, a production or shooting script must be prepared for each one. This gives details of the shots required in each scene.

The production script should be divided into two columns, one for camera and the other for dialogue and sound. Each separate shot should be numbered and details of shot type and any other camera instructions should be written in the camera column. Music, dialogue and sound effects should be written in the sound column.

Even if your video is to consist largely of interviews, you will still need to write a draft script so that you know the overall direction the programme will take. Your interview questions should be written carefully to extract the responses and information you need for your video. Avoid questions that lead to 'yes' or 'no' answers. Chapter 4, page 165 shows how to lay out a production script, and page 166 gives descriptions and abbreviations for camera shots.

Activity 5.5

1 Working in a group, organise a script meeting in which each person expresses their script ideas and a rough production script can be created.
2 One member of the group should then be responsible for translating these ideas into a production script and circulating it to all members of the group.

Creating a storyboard

As well as a production script, many production teams develop a 'storyboard' during the pre-production planning stage of a project.

A storyboard is the first step towards visualising a script. It is a necessary stage of getting the ideas for a film on to paper. The storyboard is a visual plan of each shot in terms of camera angles, sound and what each frame contains. It is referred to by the director and the camera-person during the filming of a programme.

In the pre-production stage storyboards are especially important. Every picture is worth a thousand words of explanation and interpretation. With pictures everyone can see what is meant to be going on. The rule is: the more time spent achieving the right look and style at the storyboard stage, the less time and money spent in production and post-production.

You do not have to be a great artist to produce a good storyboard – 'matchstick' people are enough to communicate the type of shots you want. An extract from a storyboard is illustrated on page 184.

Activity 5.6

Working as a team, prepare a storyboard for your video based on the production script. Circulate copies of the storyboard to all members of the production team.

Extract from a storyboard

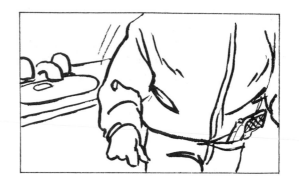

15 MS. The man picks up a gun, tucking it into his waistband.

16 The man turns and exits frame.

17 CU as the boy quickly turns and hides behind the wall.

18 Extreme CU (ECU) of scared boy. He tries to remain unnoticed as we see the man in the background turning up his collar. The boy whispers to himself, 'Oh my God'. The man turns and approaches.

19 Reverse-angle MS of boy. The man walks into shot towards the boy. He speaks, 'Hey boy'...

20 The boy turns to face the man.

Budgeting

Once you have prepared your production script and your storyboard, you will be able to work out how many days' filming and editing will be needed. In a real production company, this would be done in discussion with the producer and director. On the basis of this information, a budget for the project can be drawn up.

Film and video production can be very costly and it is important for finance managers to work with producers to make sure that productions stay within budget. Clearly your own budget will be very limited.

You may be interested to know that the actual costs per day of a three-person film/video crew are as follows:

Costs per day

Camera-person	£150–200
Sound recordist	£150–200
Director/producer	£200–400 (drama)
Equipment broadcast standard	£150–200

Your tutor should have given you a total budget for each of your projects, plus a rate card detailing the cost of, for example, hiring equipment, video cassettes and photocopying costs. Using your production script, and this rate card, you should be able to estimate the cost of your production. You may find it helpful to break the costs down under the following headings for each scene:

- Scene
- Equipment
- Tape/film stock
- Performers
- Costumes and props
- Set/location

Activity 5.7

As a group, work through your production script using the system explained above and work out the total costs of your production.

Health and safety considerations

Before you start filming you should assess the health and safety issues concerned with producing your video. When filming, the two most important considerations are people and equipment. People behind and in front of the camera must not be put at risk. Video equipment is expensive, often shared by a number of students and should be treated with care and respect.

Your college or school should be able to give you further information about insurance of equipment and safety of students. It is very important to clarify the position, especially if you are filming on location, as you may not be covered by the college insurance policy.

The risks of filming on location are different from those of filming in a studio or a classroom. A list of health and safety considerations to take into account during filming appears on page 168.

Always consider health and safety when filming

The production schedule

Having planned the production, you should now produce a **production schedule**. This will divide the production into sections, taking into account equipment available, personnel and performers available, transport, time of filming and time of meeting.

The production schedule divides the script into the most convenient order for filming so that all shots in a particular location can be done at the same time. See Chapter 4, pages 166–7, for further information on how to lay out a production schedule.

Activity 5.8

1 Prepare a production schedule for the filming of your video. This should be circulated to all members of your team, and equipment, performers and location should be booked and arranged.

2 Arrange a meeting of the production team in order to organise responsibilities during the filming of the video. Since two video products are to be made, you have an opportunity to experience more than one production role. It is a good idea to vary your role on each production so that you learn new skills and develop a greater understanding of the production process.

Review questions

1 List the four different roles within the production team.
2 Briefly describe the term 'production brief'. What information should it contain and what would a production team use it for?
3 Name two primary sources and two secondary sources of information.
4 Explain the term video 'treatment'?
5 List three of the costs that you may need to budget for when producing a video product.

Element 5.2 Produce and edit video productions

Basic production communication

During the production process good communication both behind and in front of the camera is essential. Presenters and actors must know when the camera is running and when to begin. Camera people must know what actors and presenters are going to do, and when they are going to do it.

To ensure that everything happens in the correct order and that no vital material is missed at the beginning or end, use the verbal cues listed in Chapter 4, page 171.

Preparing for filming

Lighting

Check your lighting conditions, then 'white balance' your camera. Some cameras have an automatic white balance, in which case you only need to check you are on the correct setting (outdoors or indoors). Others need to be balanced by holding up a piece of white card (or a white T-shirt), zooming in and then pressing the white balance control until it is set. It is important to do this, since light has different 'temperatures': indoors it is more reddish in colour, and outdoors it is more blue. In order to get balanced colours, you must follow the above procedure every time you change light conditions, or turn off the camera.

For more about lighting, see pages 274–5.

Sound

Although the camera may have a microphone attached, it is better to use a microphone that plugs into the camera and picks up sound from only one direction, especially if you are conducting interviews, or performing drama. This ensures good, clear recordings.

Final preparations

Before you start, it is a good idea to film a short 'vox pop' by asking five or six of your fellow students a simple question like 'What did you eat for tea last night?' or 'Who's your favourite band?'

Make sure that each of the shots is MCU (medium close-up). Check that the sound quality is clear and that the shots are even.

Finally, make sure that each person in your team is able to answer the following questions:

- Do you know what your role is and are you prepared?
- Do you have the correct equipment?
- Are you clear about your roles? (if necessary refer to the list on page 168)
- Are you clear about procedures on set?

Discipline and good communication on set are essential. Be sure to use the production drill mentioned above, and observe health and safety precautions.

Organising the filming

To organise the filming you should refer to the treatment and script prepared earlier. All shots should be logged by the director in the production log. Also each shot should be marked on the tape by a clapperboard. If you don't have a clapperboard, mark each shot using a piece of paper with the following information on it:

Production title	....
Shot no.	.... Take ....
Date	....
Production group	....

These marks will be useful when you are editing. If you use them along with the shot log you can easily find the shots you wish to use.

If you have time, it is useful to rehearse the scenes you will be filming. This will allow the camera-person to see the scene, and it will also give actors the opportunity to run through the script and their moves. At this stage, the director can also give comments on the scene and suggest any alterations and additions.

Activity 5.9

Record your video with the production team performing the roles allocated.

Editing

Once you have completed filming, watch all of the footage and prepare an **Edit Decision List** (see page 172). From this you will be able to make a paper edit of your video. At this stage you should also assess whether there are any issues regarding representation of characters, people or issues which need to be addressed. This may mean filming extra footage.

To refresh your memory about editing techniques, see Chapter 4, page 172.

Activity 5.10

Prepare an EDL, and use it to edit your film.

Adding a title sequence and closing credits

Very often you can be so busy on the main body of the video that you forget about the title sequence until the end. If you watch television or films, you will notice that items such as the title and closing sequences are very important. They tell the audience about the title of the programme, the actors and performers, and production staff. Also, the choice of lettering or typeface used can tell the audience about the kind of programme they will be watching.

Item	Function
Opening titles	Announce the show
Sub-titles	Identify people and places
Credits	Identify those appearing in, and contributing to the programme
End titles	Draw the video to its conclusion

To give you some ideas for your own video products, you should look at a range of television title sequences and graphics. Pay particular attention to the way in which they complement or enhance the genre of the programme.

There are many different ways in which you can create title sequences. 'Character generators' are graphics tools which are regularly used in video and television production. Letters are created using the character generator's computer-type keyboard. These can then be electronically inserted directly into the video picture. Alternatively, you can create wordprocessed or handwritten title cards, video them and add the footage to your video.

Activity 5.11

Design credits and a title sequence for your video. If you do not have the technical facilities to put the graphics on to your video, draw or type the words onto paper and place this in your 'video file'.

Review questions

1 What do you do when you 'white balance' a camera?
2 Why is it helpful to use a clapperboard when filming several different scenes at a time?
3 What do the initials EDL stand for?
4 What are 'character generators'?
5 How might 'character generators' be used when making a video product?

Element 5.3 Review and evaluate video productions

Once you have finished your video, it is time to test it out on a sample of your target audience. Professional feature films are regularly tested on an audience to check the clarity of characters and storyline. Before the product is previewed to the press, it is usually screened to a sample of the target audience, who are asked to complete a questionnaire or report card like the one shown on page 190. This tells the distributor whether they have pinpointed their key audience correctly and can proceed with their marketing campaign.

In order to evaluate your own video, you will present it to an audience and ask them to respond to your production, so you need to plan how to collect the responses. You can either use a written questionnaire, or you could record a post-screening discussion on video or audiotape.

Activity 5.12

1 As a group, identify a sample audience and arrange a time to show them your video product. Plan how you will record their reaction. If necessary, draw up a questionnaire or book the necessary audio/visual equipment to record their reactions and comments.
2 Present your video to a sample audience which reflects the target audience you identified in your treatment for the video. Collect feedback from the audience about their reaction to your video.

'Bears On the Run' – **Test screening**

Name . . . .

Age . . . .

Sex . . . .

1 How often do you go to the cinema (Tick box)

Once a week ☐   Once a year ☐

Once a month ☐   Less than once a year ☐

Once every six months ☐

2 What was the last film you saw in the cinema?

. . . .

3 Did you enjoy 'Bears on the Run'?

Yes ☐   No ☐

4 What were the things you liked most about the film?

Extract from a test screening report card

Activity 5.13

1 Write a report about your video production including the following information:

– How the final video compared with the requirements of the original brief
– Comments on the strength of the original idea
– Comments on the technical quality of the final video
– An assessment of how you performed as an individual in the pre-production, production and post-production stages
– An assessment of how the team as a whole performed in the pre-production, production and post-production stages

2 When you have completed all the activities in this chapter for both your fiction and your non-fiction videos, you should have all the evidence you need for your portfolio for Chapter 5

Assignment 5
Video production

This assignment provides evidence for:

Elements: 5.1 Plan video productions
5.2 Produce and edit video productions
5.3 Review and evaluate video productions

and the following key skills:

Communication:	2.1, 2.2, 2.3, 2.4
Information Technology:	2.1, 2.2, 2.3, 2.4
Application of Numbers:	2.1, 2.2, 2.3

---

1 Put together a 'video file', containing all your notes, logs and production paperwork from the activities in Elements 5.1, 5.2 and 5.3, each under the appropriate element heading.
2 Include your two video productions on labelled videotapes.
3 Add to the 'video file' all the reports and evaluations you have done in the different activities.
4 Make a careful cross-check to make sure all the work produced is there, and submit the file to your tutor(s), with your name and group clearly marked.

6 Plan and produce sound products

Element 6.1	Prepare and plan sound products to a given brief
Element 6.2	Record and edit sound products
Element 6.3	Evaluate completed sound products

What is covered in this chapter

- Planning and preparation for audio products
- Recording and editing sound products
- Evaluating sound products

Your 'audio file' will need to contain the following:
- A report on the planning of one sound product
- The script and production schedule for that product
- Two edited audio tapes, source tapes and edit lists
- Two evaluation reports – one for each product

Your teacher may wish you to make a presentation of your work, playing suitable extracts and showing key points on an OHT.

Introduction

This chapter follows on from the work you did in Chapter 3, with the intention of increasing your knowledge and ability in the field of sound production. The main themes are audience, location, equipment, editing and cost. You will plan two sound products, and produce them. You will also evaluate them.

Element 6.1 Prepare and plan sound products to a given brief

The requirements of a brief

As we have seen in previous chapters, a **brief** is set of requirements given to you as a producer, telling you what sound product to make. If you are working full or part-time, the brief will come from your line manager – and in a radio station, that may be the news editor (or head of news) if you work on the newsdesk. If you work in the programme department it will be the programme controller – unless you are working for a BBC network, such as Radio 1, when it is the network controller or senior producer who will give you the brief. If you are working as a freelance, your boss is a 'client' – and to get further business, you need to keep him or her satisfied!

If you are making sound products outside the radio industry – say, for a tape-slide sequence – the brief is likely to come from somebody who has not actually produced any sound products themselves. The brief for a training tape, for example, may come from the author – and they may have only a vague idea of what is involved in producing the soundtrack they want.

Following the brief

A good sound producer or journalist always pays full attention to the brief. If you do not produce a product which meets your client's needs, next time they will probably give the work to someone else. That is why you must later evaluate what you plan and produce, to make sure it follows the brief.

The brief will specify what the function of the product is to be. It may be part of a presentation, or be played in a static display (such as in a shop), or even form part of the programming of a radio station. The subject should be stated in the brief too. A training tape will be *about* something, and a radio feature or documentary will be on a specific topic.

Check over the information in Chapter 3 about the **target audience** – because that will be decided for you as well. How you plan and produce the programme in terms of style and content will depend on the target audience.

The budget

The **budget** is the total amount of money allocated to a project – and the *way* the money is to be spent could also have been decided for you. Radio 4 might offer around £6,000 to £9,000 to a staff producer to make a half-hour documentary, but there are certain costs that are unavoidable, and the producer will straight away have to set aside amounts for studio hire, personnel and office space. Independent producers working for the BBC are allowed to use their own staff, studios and offices, so they are freer to make their own decisions. Royalty payments for the use of copyright material – music, sound effects and archive recordings or film soundtracks – also have to be paid for. The producer's own time and expenses have to be budgeted for. In local radio, there will be a lot less money offered for producing the same length of programme.

Equipment and resources

The brief may mean certain types of **equipment** are necessary. Producing an outside broadcast such as a commentary on a sports event will probably mean using an OB vehicle or radio car, complete with link equipment to get the programme back to the studio. Even recording a quiz in a village hall will mean taking a number of microphones and a mixer to be able to pick up and select all the different voices. In order for the audience to be able to hear properly, there should be a public address system ('PA') consisting of an amplifier and at least two loudspeakers.

As a producer, other equipment decisions may have been made for you. For example, if you are working for a radio station, you will have to make do with whatever equipment has been chosen by the studio engineer. There may only be quarter-inch tape recorders or even cassettes. There could be digital audio recording and editing facilities – and on some radio stations the whole studio complex uses computer disks to store and play out all the audio material.

Timescale
The timescale is the amount of time you have to produce the item. The deadline is all-important, because if the product is not ready for transmission when it is needed, it may be of no use later on. Also, a gap in the programming would have been left – and someone else would have had to fill that gap. Similarly, a training tape-slide presentation may be needed for a particular presentation or course, and the client will not be pleased if it is not ready on time.

Activity 6.1

VARIETY RADIO

Production brief for:	Quiz/documentary/magazine/drama*
Function:	Entertainment/information*
Subject:	Popular music/film/crime*
Audience:	National, 16–35 years, C1C2DE
Equipment:	To be supplied on quarter-inch tape or MiniDisc
Timescale:	Five weeks
Duration:	30 minutes

* Choose ONE only

---

1 Look at the brief above, given to you by Variety Radio. They want the programmes for transmission on several different ILR stations, alongside a sponsorship package of advertising – which is how they will cover their costs and make their profit. You must consider the requirements of the briefs, before deciding to accept ONE of the jobs – to produce a quiz, documentary, drama or magazine.

2 Write down how the requirements of the brief will be met. For each requirement, say how you intend to produce what is wanted, and explain the effect each requirement will have on the way you will work and how the product will sound. Explain how the budget will be affected by choices you make about content, equipment and personnel. List the equipment you decide to use and say why. All your answers are to form part of a report to be handed in later. If you are making a magazine, it must include at least one recorded item.

Production roles

A 'researcher' carries out all the main research functions in planning the content and style of a sound product. That means everything from finding out exactly what is wanted (in more detail than is given in the brief) to finding contributors, locations, staff and equipment. Multi-skilling means there are few people in the sound industries who work only as researchers. Most producers, journalists, and even presenters have to take on the role of researcher as well for some of the time.

The first research job is to get more information than is contained in the brief about what kind of programme is wanted and what the target audience wants to hear. Matching product with target audience is covered in greater depth in Chapter 3.

Planning content, equipment, logistics, and personnel come next. Good decisions can only be made on the basis of relevant information – and finding that information takes thorough research. Without it, the product cannot possibly be good enough to fulfill the requirements of the brief and the client.

The role of interviewer is important in any journalistic production, from a feature in a magazine programme to a longer documentary. As a magazine programme may well contain 'live' interviews, the presenter of the programme should have good interviewing skills too.

The title of sound recordist is usually given to someone recording sound for a television, video or film production. Their job is every bit as important as a camera operator if 'live' sound is required. Much of the information in this chapter about microphones, formats, mixing and editing skills applies to film, television and video as well.

Actors are required in drama productions of any kind, and choosing the right ones for each role is the job of the casting director. Again, multi-skilling means it is usually the producer of a sound product who will perform this role.

The scriptwriter does just what the title suggests – but usually this has to be done in consultation with the producer, who may want part or all of the script to be rewritten.

The editor may be someone who is editing the tape of a recorded production, but it is more likely to be the name given to someone working on a magazine programme who has overall control of the content. The editor knows what subjects have been covered in recent editions of the programme, and plans the content of future programmes, selecting from ideas and suggestions made by people inside and outside the team.

A music editor or 'head of music' has responsibility for the musical content of a radio station – deciding which music is put on the playlist each week, and which tracks are taken off because they are dropping down the charts or have been played too much and need to make way for others.

An effects editor is a very specialised role – probably found only in the BBC where special sound effects might need to be created for radio or television drama.

Other roles are:

- Presenter
- Producer
- Technical operator

The presenter will link the magazine programme together, as described in Chapter 3. In a quiz, it is the presenter who hosts the programme, introducing the two teams and other personalities, such as the scorer – as well as asking the questions and giving the answers where necessary. The job of presenter is always high-profile, and someone with a 'big' personality and a way with words is most likely to succed in the role.

A documentary should have a presenter, too – although the title 'reporter' is more suitable for what is really a reporting role. A tape-slide presentation may also have a presenter if a commentary is needed, and so will a breakfast or dance music show.

The producer's role

Whatever the programme, the producer is the person responsible for making sure everything happens on time and according to plan – which means deciding the production schedule, choosing personnel and making sure they keep to the requirements of the brief and the schedule. The operation of the studio should be the responsibility of the technical operator – called a studio manager ('SM') in the BBC. The SM should make sure the producer's requirements for the studio are all ready for use before recording or transmission, as well as operating the mixing desk and any other equipment. The more complicated productions will have an extra SM or two, depending on whether the producer has booked them. Naturally, more staff mean more cost – and the programme budget has to be able to afford them.

Producers must make sure that programmes keep within realistic financial limits

In the commercial world, the producer has overall responsibility for the end product. In your assignment work, where you may be working in a group, everyone should take equal responsibility for the work – because if the work is poor, it will be no good trying to explain to your assessor that it is not your fault! This means that work normally done by the producer and technical operator will probably have to be shared out, rather than left to one person. This is actually a good preparation for the realities of the radio industry, where increasingly, employees are required to be multi-skilled – that is, capable of taking on different job roles at different times. This is especially true in newer, smaller radio stations which have been set up on smaller budgets in areas which ten years ago would not have been able to support their own station.

Activity 6.2

1 For your chosen product, hold a meeting of your group and share out roles among team members. Exact responsibilities will depend on the type of product and the amount of work to be done by each person. Make sure that the work is evenly spread out, and begin an individual production log, noting down everything team members do towards the programme. Keep adding to the log, commenting upon the strengths and weaknesses of everything done.

2 Start to write a production schedule, showing how the different personnel are to be used, when and where.

Product content

For a tape-slide sequence, the soundtrack must match what is being shown on screen. Sometimes the visuals are chosen first by the scriptwriter, and the soundtrack is created to suit them. In other cases, the script will be written in such a way as to cover all the content required, and then suitable images will be chosen to add more information. They could be words or images or a mixture of both.

Fiction and non-fiction

For radio programmes, there is no need to consider anything other than the sound. The content will depend very much upon the brief, and on the research you do in gathering material to put in the programme. Fiction may be based upon reality, or it may leave reality behind. The success of Orson Welles's *War of the Worlds* in terrifying America lay in the fact that it seemed real, even though the idea of Martians landing and conquering the world was very far-fetched. Welles's script included many of the conventions of real reporting, such as the use of newsflashes to interrupt normal music programmes and reporters interviewing experts and describing events 'live' from the scene of an incident. Your own fictional programme may do just that – or it may sound more like a conventional play, set in a room or an outside location.

Radio drama can be alarmingly realistic

If you are producing non-fiction you have a responsibility not to add fictional elements just to fill up air time. A quiz with made-up answers to serious questions will annoy the contestants and the audience, unless the programme is intended to be a send-up. Likewise, a documentary must be based on fact, as must the serious features in a magazine. You automatically have the trust of the listener when you broadcast, and to pretend something is true when it is not is to betray that trust. You are also expected to check your facts, and not be sloppy in your reporting, and that means careful attention to detail. All this does not at all mean that non-fiction must be serious. Many documentaries and magazine items are light-hearted – even humorous. Depending upn your brief, you may well decide that it is right to produce a programme with a high content of amusing material.

Music or speech-based?

Radio may be music-based or speech-based, or a mixture of the two. Being one or the other is just a matter of which a programme has more of.

A music-based programme is one where the content is mainly music. It may be a documentary about a band or an era – for example, the 1970s – or it may be a music sequence for a specific time of day or featuring a specific type of music. The breakfast show on a music station will have certain items in between the music which are meant to make the show more interesting to the target audience, who will therefore be more inclined to listen the next day.

The running order

Most important for many people are the timechecks in every link. Rushing to get out of the house or on the way to work, school or college, many people need to hear constant reminders of the time to tell them whether they are running late. There may not be a clock handy in the bathroom, but if the radio is on, they will know what time it is. People are far more inclined to trust a radio timecheck than their own watch. If they hear something on the radio, it *must* be true. So if you are responsible for giving timechecks, make sure you get them right or you will panic the nation – without even mentioning a Martian!

```
07.00   News
07.03   Station ident and disc
07.07   Disc
07.11   Traffic and travel
07.12   Ads
07.14   Station ident and disc
07.18   Teaser competition and disc
07.21   Mystery voice competition (phone)
07.23   Ads
07.25   Traffic and travel
07.26   Disc
07.30   News headlines and sport
07.33   Ads and station ident
07.35   Disc
07.39   Traffic and travel
```

Running order for a breakfast show

Listeners are also creatures of habit and get used to hearing certain items at the same time each day. If an item gets changed from its regular timeslot, it can confuse and worry them. All this means that the running order for the programme should be fixed and not changed without careful thought.

The programme mix

Other music-based programmes at other times of the day may also contain regular feature items: a dance music show may have a review of new releases or a rave guide. A responsible producer might want to put in a feature about, say, the dangers of Ecstasy. It would certainly add some extra interest to the programme, and you have to remember that people at home or in the car need a reason to listen to the radio rather than to one of their old tapes or CDs. Making the programme as topical and interesting as possible through your choice of music and speech is one very good way to use the flexibility of radio to be new, refreshing, familiar and a friend, all at the same time.

Gathering and reporting the latest news is another way in which radio attracts, serves and keeps listeners. It is much more immediate than newspapers – which have to be printed – and often carries much more actual information than television news: when a story breaks, radio reporters are not tied up with trying to find pictures and editing pieces of library footage, as are their colleagues in television. A growing number of news sources are available via the Internet, but as yet the technology needed to receive the information is far less portable and easily accessible than a transistor radio.

Activity 6.3 (optional)

1 Turn your classroom into a radio newsroom for a morning or afternoon. Working in teams of four or five, prepare a three-minute news bulletin to be read at a set time. That time is your deadline for having all the news stories ready, in order of importance to your 'target audience'. You may monitor other radio stations or Teletext to get up-to-the minute news, but you should rewrite the copy in your own words to avoid copyright problems. If you decide to use stories from local or national newspapers, remember that they will be out of date already, so see if you can find a new angle to the stories or get local reaction to an important national one. A news editor should be appointed, to make final decisions about which stories are included, and in what order. He or she should begin by holding a news meeting and assigning a reporter to each story.

2 Choose one newsreader for each team to present the bulletin and read all the 'live' copy. A technical operator should 'drive' the mixing desk in the studio, playing the audio wraps and voicers in at the correct points. In order to allow different members of the team to have their voices in the bulletin, prepare some stories as voicers, and others as wraps, in the style of an Independent Radio News bulletin (see Chapter 3, pages 102-105).

3 When the deadline arrives, produce the bulletin, and record it. If there is a mistake, carry on, because in live radio, you must avoid long pauses – the show must go on! Next lesson, each group should play back their bulletin to the whole class. It is likely that the choice of stories will be different in each bulletin. The order of items will change too. Each editor should explain the reasons for all the decisions made. This news exercise is often done even better the second time round, so your tutor may want you to repeat it two or three weeks later.

The radio documentary

The radio documentary is very similar to the magazine feature in a number of ways. It is longer than a feature, and rather than being just one item in a longer magazine programme, it forms a programme in its own right. Otherwise, many of the conventions of style and structure for a feature apply (see page 122).

In a magazine programme, a listener who is not enjoying one feature may stay tuned, knowing that it will not be long before the subject changes and a new item comes along. However, a documentary must hold the listener's attention from the start. If it does not capture their interest and hold it, the listener is more likely to tune away or turn off the radio.

Because there will be people turning on or tuning in while a long documentary is running, they also need to be able to quickly work out what it is about – otherwise it might just as well be a confused jumble of sounds. So a documentary has to have clear direction and **purpose** – the purpose being what it is there for, and the direction being the way the subject matter is dealt with. Regular signposting will help: the script should often sum up what has been said and point which way the programme is going. For example:

```
'… So, if the dog owners want the controls relaxed, and the
general public want the controls to be tightened up, who is
right? Ken Tudor is one of a growing number of MPs who say
the government should think again …'
```

In this way, new listeners are given a 'way in' to the programme, without having to have heard all that has been said so far. A documentary may also begin and end with a suitable piece of music, if there is one which will really add to the programme, although it is not essential.

Radio drama

Drama content was covered in Chapter 3, but producing soap operas was not. While there are many similarities between the single play and the soap opera series, there are also important differences. The soap has ongoing characters and storylines, and the narrative structure is **serial** (or **multi-strand**) rather than closed because usually a number of storylines will be continuing at any one time. If you produce a soap opera, you not only need to write one episode, but you need to plan how the storylines might be developed in the next ones. A cliffhanger is a good way to encourage listeners to tune in next time.

Quizzes and panel games

The content of a quiz is usually broken into different rounds to provide a structure. The end of each round also gives the presenter the opportunity to give the score, as well as signposting the programme – for example:

```
'… So, with the men's team on seventeen and the women on
eighteen, we'll move on to the third and final round: spot
the celebrity voice!'
```

Often rounds consist of questions and answers, perhaps with music, sound effects or voices to identify. Improvisation often works well if the contestants are quick-witted enough. Radio 4's 'Just a Minute' has entertained audiences for many years, with its clever formula of asking the players to speak on a particular topic for sixty seconds without hesitation, deviation or repetition.

Comedy

An example of 'effects-based' comedy is the BBC series 'The Hitchhiker's Guide to the Galaxy' which included special effects created by the BBC Radiophonic Workshop. It is also possible to create musical tracks which sound out of the ordinary, using samplers, digital effects generators and processors.

The BBC Radiophonic workshop supplies radio and TV producers with creative sound effects

Target audience

The audience for any sound product must be taken into account at every stage. Every individual is different, but when you are producing for a mass medium, you have to make assumptions about what the audience are 'like', often based upon the type of demographic information shown below:

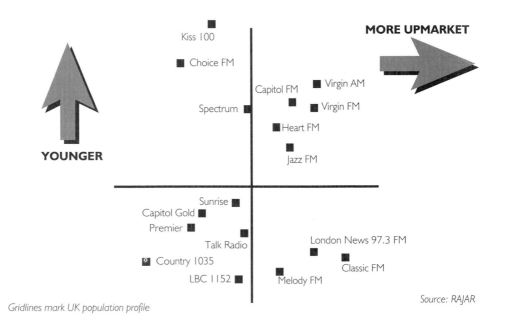

Gridlines mark UK population profile

Source: RAJAR

Scatter chart showing demographic information about commercial radio stations heard in London

Target audiences are groups of people who are expected to have the same interests. They may be classified by gender or by age. Lifestyle is another good way of classifying people into target groups, because people who like dance music are likely to go to raves. In the same way, people who follow football are likely to listen to match reports on Saturday, and people who listen to chart shows are likely to enjoy competitions with questions about pop stars. Advertisers make similar judgements about the type of people who are likely to buy their products.

Activity 6.4

1 For your chosen sound product, decide what content you should include, bearing in mind the target audience and the brief. What are the needs of the target audience, and how are they influenced by age, gender and lifestyle? Explain your decisions.

2 Each genre has its own set of conventions, so listen to some examples of your chosen genre and identify which conventions you need to follow to produce a professional-sounding product. Add all your decisions to the report begun in Activity 6.1.

3 Begin your primary and secondary research into the content, as described in Chapter 3. Start a 'research' file, containing all relevant findings, and make a list of what is in it, stating whether it comes from a primary or secondary source.

The importance of research

As we have seen in earlier chapters, information sources can be divided into primary and secondary:

Primary	Secondary
First-hand interviews with:	Books
— Eyewitnesses	Magazines
— People involved	Internet
— Inventors, rescuers	CD-ROM
experts, etc.	Videos
(including by phone)	Audiotapes
Questionnaires sent out by you	Archives

Each piece of research from each source should be carefully checked for accuracy. The importance you place upon the information should reflect how reliable you think that source is. Using the Internet may be an exciting and modern way of accessing information, but who exactly publishes the information? If it is a university research department which has a special knowledge of the subject, then the information and opinions given should be very reliable. But many people and organisations set up Web sites, and the ease of publishing on the Internet means it is all too easy to create pages of information which other Internet users – such as you – then take as fact. You need to ask yourself whether the publisher is in a position to obtain the information at first hand and whether they are qualified to form a worthwhile opinion on it. They may not have been as responsible as you would be in checking the accuracy of the information!

Most books go through a careful selection and editing process, so the danger here is less, but you should still ask yourself if the author of the book you are quoting is perhaps only giving their own point of view. There may be other views that are not represented. Books also date quickly, and the information you use should always be the most up-to-date available.

Newspapers and magazines are often biased towards a particular viewpoint – especially in the realm of politics and economics. It may be necessary to get a balancing view from a different newspaper – for example, comparing what the *Times* says with the *Guardian*.

Spelling and pronunciation

As well as the facts you use in your own sound product, you should check for accuracy in spelling. A mistake over the spelling of a name could affect your pronunciation of it when you come to read your script. Mispronouncing a word your listeners recognise is a sure way to damage your credibility – and getting somebody's name wrong when you interview them or introduce them on air is unprofessional and can cause great embarrassment.

It is often difficult to check the pronunciation of an unfamiliar word or, for example, a foreign name. The BBC Pronunciation Unit produces lists of topical pronunciations for newsreaders, and their book of placenames is a good reference point. Otherwise, dictionaries, experts on the subject and other colleagues are the normal route for checking pronunciation.

Good grammar, correct punctuation and spelling are all very important when you write your own script. But remember that your style of writing should suit the medium you are working in and the genre of sound product you are producing. More formal speech is probably best in a speech-based documentary or a tape-slide presentation to be used in education. However, a dance music sequence or a quiz may be better using the sort of language used by the target audience. That probably means using the correct slang when talking about subjects the audience will know about already.

Using quotes

The use of direct quotes is rather difficult when writing for sound. Newspapers and books can and do use long quotes from different people, and the readers can tell they are quotes because they are framed by speech marks and other clues, such as the use of 'he said', 'she announced', or 'they repeated'.

With sound only, the use of speech marks can only be hinted at by the person changing their tone of voice to make it seem as if they are quoting somebody. This is a **convention** and it is used widely. It is also a convention that the technique is not over-used, and so direct quotes are not very common on radio. Sound can win over the written word in the way you can let the listener actually hear the interviewee saying what they think.

The effect of this is that it is more usual to record people speaking directly than to quote their words in your script. However, you are still likely to want to paraphrase an interviewee when writing a link, as described in Chapter 3.

If somebody is unavailable for interview but is prepared to send you a written statement, you may consider their contribution worth including, even though you have to get an 'actor' from your class to read their words for them. You should always explain that it is a statement being read by an actor, and never ever try to pass somebody off as being someone else just because they were not available to speak into your microphone.

Legal issues

There are legal aspects to the checking of research findings and writing scripts. These include:

- Slander and libel
- Blasphemy
- Court proceedings
- Political restrictions

Slander and libel centre around defamation (see Chapter 3, page 126), i.e. the unjustified damaging of a person's reputation. It is libel, rather than slander, which concerns you once you speak into a microphone. However, you should be aware that it is possible to slander a person when talking to someone else – for example, in the course of researching a subject or fixing up an interview.

Blasphemy

This is defined by law as insulting somebody's religious belief or holding it, or their god, up to ridicule or insult. The law is old and in practice relates only to Christianity, the 'official' religion of the UK. British Muslims, for example, found Salman Rushdie's book *The Satanic Verses* insulting to their beliefs, but had no legal grounds for preventing publication. Although a blasphemous statement may not break the law, it is well worth stopping for a moment to consider the feelings of people of other religions before rushing to say something which could insult or offend them.

The 'sub judice' rule

Specific rules apply to the reporting of matters which are 'sub judice', i.e. the subject of court proceedings. There are two main reasons for this:

1 To protect the identity of certain people who may be harmed by publicity
2 To prevent a jury being influenced by what they hear on radio, or see on TV and in the print media

People who especially need to be protected from publicity are minors (persons under 16 years) and victims of sex attacks. Judges may also place reporting restrictions on certain facts which come out in court, if they consider it to be in the public interest. The actual restrictions on court reporting would fill many pages, but the basic principle is that once a court case becomes 'live' – meaning 'active' – what you can report is very limited. When in doubt, many journalists consult McNae's *Essential Law for Journalists* – you could, too, but at this stage in your career you would be forgiven for asking for advice from your tutor first.

Political restrictions

Under the Representation of the People Acts, there are political restrictions on reporting which apply during an election period. These are intended to protect the democratic process from being harmed by biased coverage by the broadcast media. The restraints apply both to local and by-elections, and to the general elections which decide who runs the country. However, many of the controls do not apply to the print media, and the newspapers will unashamedly tell their readers who they think they ought to vote for.

The rule is that in the run-up to the election (i.e. from the closing of nominations for candidates), if a radio programme deals with an election issue and allows one candidate to speak on the matter, *all the other candidates must also be allowed equal time.* When only three or four candidates are standing in an election area (or 'constituency'), getting them all onto the same programme may not be too much of a problem. But when there are many more, including 'fringe' candidates and those from single-issue parties, getting perhaps a dozen people on the programme and giving them all equal airtime can not only be difficult to arrange, but it can also make for very boring radio.

Another problem is that, if even one of them decides not to turn up, the programme could have to be cancelled at short notice unless the producer can prove that the absent politician consented to the programme continuing without him or her.

In reality, discussion programmes with all the candidates in the studio at one time tend to be very rare. You will also be aware that in spite of the restrictions candidates *are* heard on radio and television in election periods. The reason for this is that the leader of the Conservative or Labour Party may well be a candidate in his or her own constituency, but as long as they talk only about national issues and not about what is happening in their own constituency, the rule does not apply. It is only thanks to this loophole in the Act of Parliament that all that exciting election coverage gets broadcast!

However, on the day of the election itself, no candidate may be seen or heard to broadcast in the constituency in which they are standing for election. It does not matter what they talk about – they cannot even read the weather. Election issues must not be discussed on air, and so reporting is usually limited to the size of the poll, and the effects of the weather on voting.

Choosing recording locations

Recording on location involves making choices based upon research into all the possible locations. If recording indoors, you must consider acoustics. The size of the room and the amount of soft furnishings (carpets, curtains, furniture, etc.) may all deaden the sound. You should also think about how many people will be present during the recording, because human beings can have the same effect.

If recording outdoors, the acoustic may be that of a cave or a tunnel entrance. This ambient (or 'natural') sound is an excellent way to begin to create a picture in the mind of each listener, by making them create an image in their own head based upon the sound 'clues' given.

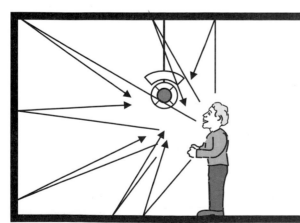

Sound is reflected back towards a microphone in a room

No sound is reflected back when talking in a field

Changing location can alter the acoustic effect quite dramatically

A proper broadcasting or recording studio is acoustically treated to prevent unwanted sound being reflected back to the microphones. The materials and expertise needed to 'deaden' a new studio can be very costly, although some cheap in-college solutions to the problem include foam packaging stuck to walls, or even egg boxes! (But beware of the fire risk when using flammable materials in such large quantities.)

In the past, new ILR stations had to undergo very strict testing to make sure that the studios had been deadened correctly as well as being soundproofed against noise or vibrations coming into the room from outside. Since 1991, the regulations have been relaxed, but some of the most expensive studios in use are actually floating on a bed of oil which prevents soundwaves being transmitted by the ground when trains or lorries rumble by. It is unlikely that any indoor location you choose will be as effectively treated as these, and reflections from the walls and unwanted background noise from outside will have to be considered when you choose your locations for recording.

Background sounds in a location can be an advantage. They can add to the listener's 'mind picture' of where the action is – or is meant to be, in the case of fiction. An interview about heavy traffic clogging up the roads, or about pollution, could be even better if we can hear the heavy traffic. The recording would be called actuality – and the background is atmosphere.

Transport and logistics

Each location you consider must be thought of in terms of its strengths and weaknesses, and how well suited it is to your recording. As well as ambient and background sound, you must also consider the cost of getting people and equipment to the location, and the cost implications – train tickets and even car parking will all have to be paid for. If the location is private property, you must get permission to gain access to it. The owner should be told right at the start what you intend to do there – and if you were really working on a broadcaster's budget, you might well be asked to pay a fee to make it worth their while.

The time it takes to get there and the distance you will have to travel will also affect how much time you will have left to do other things – if the cons outweigh the pros, you may well be better off looking for somewhere more convenient to record!

Activity 6.5

1 Check your research findings for accuracy, as described above. Add to your report your conclusions about which sources are worth using and why, as well as explaining what makes the information you decide to use worth including.

2 Research possible locations for use during any indoor or outdoor recordings you need to make. List the strengths and weaknesses of each location and then give the reasons for your final decisions about where to record.

Recording schedule

The next task is to finalise the recording schedule, as all the different recorded items need to be 'in the can' by a certain date – the final deadline.

Working back from the deadline, enough time needs to be allowed for each item, depending on how complicated the recording is going to be. If the programme is to be topical, recording may have to be done as close to transmission as possible, but there are great risks in leaving work to the last minute, especially as unforeseen problems such as illness or breakdowns may occur. A play or a quiz could probably be recorded much sooner than a topical documentary, but many subjects are relatively 'timeless' anyway. For a programme about the first moon landing, it is most unlikely you would have to wait until the last minute for late-breaking information since the key event happened years ago!

For a magazine, plan to have a number of 'standby' items in case something goes wrong. A standby need not be as complicated or ambitious as the planned item – just something acceptable to fall back on. Running a standby is better than having 'dead air' (i.e. silence), but if you have to use it, be prepared for people to complain that that part of the programme could have been better.

The recording schedule should include the following information:

- **Order of recording** – What is to be recorded and when (probably putting the most difficult bits first)
- **Crew details for each recording** – Who should be where, on what dates, and when.

Scriptwriting

This can be started straight away, but unless your product is fictional, such as a radio drama, parts of the scriptwriting will have to wait until vital research has been completed and interviews recorded.

The conventions of script layout described in Chapter 3 apply to your more advanced work in this chapter. A drama script will need to show dialogue, effects, music and directions to the actors.

A documentary script, like that for the feature, will show links in full, as well as music and effects needed – but again, there is no need to transcribe all the words spoken in the audio clips taken from your longer interviews. Just include tape in-cues and out-cues, together with the duration of each clip. There will be many more audio clips than for the feature, and it is likely that you will 'return' to some interviewees later in the programme. Each time they 'reappear', you will need to remind the audience who they are.

For example, an interviewee may be introduced in this way:

```
ME:                 George Deakin is the leader of the protest
                    group. He thinks that a residential area is no
                    place for a slaughterhouse.

I/V DEAKIN:         'People live here...
                    ...animals being killed'    DUR 19"
```

After interview clips from two other people, the listeners are unlikely to recognise Deakin from the sound of his voice alone – or even what he is saying. He needs re-introducing to the audience at this point, but to avoid being boring, it needs to be done in a different way:

```
ME:                 What has been the reaction of the residents to
                    the re-opening of the abattoir? George Deakin
                    again:

I/V DEAKIN:         'We've heard screams...
                    ...I just felt awful'       DUR 21"
```

The third time Deakin is heard, a third way must be used:

```
ME:                 Some residents have tried to sell their homes,
                    but without success. George Deakin was one:

I/V DEAKIN:         'We had no takers...
                    ...prices tumbling down'        DUR 13"
```

It is more work using short clips of audio, and more creativity is needed in writing the links, but the effect of using short items and short links where possible is to create a more varied programme with lots 'happening'. Producing a documentary with long pieces of interview means that listeners have to put up with the same person droning on and on. Variety is the best way to keep the programme interesting. That is not to say that sometimes a longer clip may not be used – perhaps if the speaker is talking in detail about something particularly moving or exciting that happened to them.

The script for a magazine programme will feature introductions for feature items (as described in Chapter 3) which you can lift off the cue sheet for each feature. In the case of live interviews carried out by the programme's presenter, he or she will need to have the key interview questions listed at the correct points. Remember that the presenter should welcome the listeners to the programme at the start, give a menu of the programme's contents, and signpost what is coming up in the programme, as well as 'teasing' the listener with a promise of what will be in the next programme.

The finishing touches are often added to the script just before the transmission of a magazine, as the last items to arrive in the studio become available – depending upon how topical the programme needs to be.

Health and safety

Everything you plan to do must place health and safety first. When recording, the hazards include carrying equipment, large or small. Even a UHER portable tape recorder can cause shoulder strain if carried for too long, because although small, it is a heavy piece of equipment. This is one reason why cassette recorders, and now DAT or MiniDisc, are a popular alternative. Whenever possible, you should swap shoulders or place the machine on a firm, safe surface where it is not going to fall or be knocked off by someone passing.

If you are involved in any other type of outside broadcast or recording, you may find you have to carry microphone stands, loudspeakers, portable transmitters or amplifiers for a public address system. Great care should be taken when lifting, as well as picking up and putting down. Heavy objects such as loudspeakers should not be placed where they might fall on people, or where the audience, participants or passers-by could knock them over. Cables should be on the floor, rather than strung in mid-air, and covered with gaffer tape to make sure people do not trip over them.

Electrical equipment

If you are using electrical equipment, you must take proper safety precautions. Remember that liquids spilt onto electrical items or objects stuck inside them can not only cause equipment failure, but also electric shock.

All leads should be carefully inspected in case the cables have been damaged or have worked loose at the plugs. Plugs should always be wired by a qualified person and given a fuse with the correct amp rating. You should never be tempted to tamper with or try to repair a mains electrical connection or piece of equipment without turning the power off and unplugging it first. If you spill liquid into a computer editing workstation, quickly save your work if it is safe to do so, then turn off the equipment at the mains.

When using an outside broadcast radio car, never raise the aerial without checking first that there are no overhead power cables or other obstructions. An engineer died once because his radio car aerial touched a power cable. After use, the aerial should be lowered. Again, one reporter ripped the roof off a radio car, trying to drive into a multi-storey car park with the aerial up.

Another hazard when editing is the use of razor blades. See Chapter 3 to check on razor blade safety.

Activity 6.6

1 Prepare a recording schedule for your product. Show how you will use the crew, time, resources and locations at each stage of the production.
2 Write the script for the production. For a non-fiction product which includes interview material still to be recorded, you will only be able to write rough cues in some places, but you should write what you can at this stage.
3 List all possible health and safety hazards that you will have to consider before beginning to record and edit the programme. Discuss with others in your group what action to take to avoid each risk, and write down the decisions taken.

Review questions

1 What is multi-skilling?
2 What is the difference between 'music-based' and 'speech-based'?
3 What are the differences between a documentary and a magazine feature?
4 Which London radio station has the oldest, most downmarket audience?
5 What are acoustics?

Element 6.2 Record and edit sound products

Recording source material

An effective sound producer records only what is needed for the finished product, and not hours and hours of unwanted material. This means being *focused* – knowing exactly what is needed from each interviewee, and having questions worked out to extract the answers that are needed. In practice, there is nearly always some unwanted material to be cut out, as well as items which need to be put together in the correct order. But this editing task is very much easier and quicker if you have done the recordings as carefully as possible, sticking to the production schedule and the prepared questions.

Making sure that the recordings are done correctly first time means choosing the correct equipment and operating it correctly. You will have to make choices under the following headings:
- Suitability for the task
- Portability
- Availability
- Ease of operation
- Cost

For this element you will need to produce two finished sound products – one should be the programme commission for Variety Radio which you prepared in Element 6.1, and the other could be a much simpler product – for example some 'vox pops'.

Recording vox pops

Vox pops are used in news bulletins, features, documentaries and magazine programmes – in fact, any sound product where a range of views from a cross-section of the public would be interesting and relevant. They could be used to start a phone-in, for example, to spark off a lively debate among the listeners.

The name 'vox pop' is short for the Latin 'vox populi' – which means 'voice of the people'. The people whose voices you record will be chosen by you – and you will have to decide very carefully who to approach. Most vox pops are done in shopping centres, because there is usually a good range of people there – especially on a Saturday, when people who are normally at work are out and about. This allows you to get a fairly representative sample of society – young, old, male, female, black, white and so on. Asking a number of different people the same question can get you a very interesting range of different answers. When edited together back at base, the different answers can make for a short but very interesting and entertaining piece of radio.

Sometimes you may want to get views about a particular subject, such as parents' opinions about the rights and wrongs of smacking children. Here you may find you waste a lot of time in the shopping centre, because many of the people you talk to may turn out not to have children – or not children of the right age. A better choice might be to record outside a school gate at 'home time' instead. Make sure you telephone the headteacher first and ask for permission – not because recording vox pops is against the law, but out of courtesy and so no one gets alarmed by what you are doing. (Remember, however, that causing an obstruction on a public pavement or being on private property without permission *is* unlawful, and you do not want to get moved on or spoken to by the police.)

A radio journalist recording vox pops for the County Sound Radio Network

Wherever you are recording vox pops, you must remember to be polite with people. It is professional to explain briefly who you are and what you are doing, and then ask whether they would be prepared to give you their views. Many people will be unhelpful or just hurry away. Some may be rude: if so, ignore them and ask somebody else. Never be rude back. This would not only be unprofessional but could cause you trouble that you could do without.

The question you ask should need as little explanation as possible – and it should be an open one (see Chapter 3). A vox pop consisting of a string of 'yes and no' answers would be very dull. Here are some good vox pop questions:

> *'What do you think of smacking children?'*
> *'What should be done about drug dealers?'*
> *'Where do you think the new motorway should be built?'*

Some people will just say:

> *'I dunno, do I?'*

but many answers will be very useable. Some interviewees will be real 'characters' who will give your vox pops that extra spark of interest – perhaps used as the last voice on the tape, to raise a smile. Some answers may prompt you to ask further questions. You can always cut them out later if the extra audio is not useable, or if you end up with too much material.

Equipment for outdoor recording

The equipment you use must always be suitable for the job. The choice of microphone depends on how each microphone type performs in picking up sound. Stereo microphones are able to detect whether a sound is coming more fom the left or more from the right, and then to feed a stereo signal into the mixer or the record machine. They can be very useful in recording drama, because voices or sounds coming from different places from left to right can sound very effective when listened to through twin loudspeakers or headphones.

For most jobs mono microphones are used. Even in drama, you can create a stereo effect anyway by giving each actor a microphone of their own and 'panning' each microphone channel to the left or right on the mixer.

Choosing your microphone

You will probably choose your mono microphone by its direction of 'pick up'. 'Omni-directional' means 'all directions'. 'Directional' or 'uni-directional 'means the microphone picks up sound mainly from one particular direction. A rifle microphone is 'highly directional', in that when pointed in a direction, it is very good at picking out sounds from that particular place. Radio producers do not often use rifle microphones; they are more often used in video, where a hand holding a microphone up close would be visible on screen.

Omni-directional microphones are used for interviewing and many location recordings, mainly because of their ability to pick up sounds from all around. If you use an omni-directional microphone, it means there will be background sounds on your recorded interview. Remember that the amount of background is under your control, because the closer you place the microphone to the source of a sound – an interviewee's mouth, for example – the louder it will sound against the background (see Chapter 3). However, beware of rattle, because the microphone will be sensitive to any knocks against its body or lead.

More directional microphones are needed where there is any element of mixing sounds. To pick up audience reaction at a live quiz show, an effects microphone will need to be directional or it will pick up output from the public address system and cause **howlround** or electronic feedback. Miking up a band or orchestra can be done very precisely, with one microphone per instrument if necessary, but make sure the microphone for the piano does not also pick up other instruments nearby. A drum kit may need more than one microphone.

The basic principle of any microphone is that it converts sound waves into electrical energy. The 'dynamic' response is the amount of accuracy in the microphone's translation of sound into electrical signal. 'Condensor' microphones are those which have variable pick-up areas that can be set to cover the required area. 'Cardioid' microphones have a heart-shaped pick-up area.

It is important to choose the correct microphone for the job. That means deciding exactly what sounds you want the microphone to pick up, and what direction they will be coming from. Using a directional microphone with a particular pattern of sensitivity will allow you to reduce unwanted sounds from a particular direction – the direction of the microphone's 'blind spot'.

Choosing a tape recorder

The choice of recording machine is important too. A tape recorder may be analogue (quarter-inch or cassette), or digital (DAT, MiniDisc or hard-disk based). Currently, digital machines are much more expensive than cassette, but

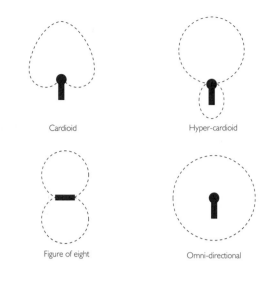

Cardioid   Hyper-cardioid

Figure of eight   Omni-directional

Microphone types

they do offer greatly improved recording quality. The difference between digital and quarter-inch reel-to-reel is not as great, but although quarter-inch tape offers better quality than cassette, any of the formats, used correctly, can give perfectly acceptable broadcast-quality recording. It is unlikely that anything other than reporting would be done on cassette – the format is chosen only because the cassette machines are usually lighter and smaller than Uhers. Sound recording of musicians in a band or orchestra, for example, is now most likely to be done in a digital format. In a studio, the recording would probably be done directly onto a hard-disk system, such as Pro-Tools.

The mixer
The mixer is the centrepiece of any sound studio. Mixers are also used on location whenever more than one individual sound source is to be put into the programme mix. A sound source may be a microphone, a CD or record player, a tape machine used for playback, a MiniDisc, or even a special effects generator.

Any source of live or recorded sound may be routed into a mixer, and the mixer is where the producer's decisions about what sound should be heard at any one time are put into effect. Depending on how a recording or live programme is to be crewed, the mixer may be operated by a technical operator (or SM), a producer, a 'self-operating' presenter, or an assistant. A reporter would usually 'drive' a simpler studio alone, to produce a wrap, feature or voice-piece. The other sound sources which feed into the mixer will be operated by the same person – or in a complicated production, by another SM or assistant.

A location recording such as a drama or a quiz may well also have a portable mixer at the heart of the technical operations. Where there is a live audience, a second mixer may be used to produce a different version of the proceedings, or that second version may be produced on the same mixer as the programme output. Any situation where a large number of different people are due to speak will need a mixer with several microphone inputs, so that each microphone can be turned off and on individually.

An audio mixer suitable for a radio studio — note the script space in the centre.

Principles of mixing sound

The principle behind any mixer is that there is one channel for each sound source. Usually each channel will be labelled with the name of the sound source connected to it. Sometimes the production will require the channels to be reorganised – for example, when more microphones are added for a quiz, or outside broadcast feeds from sports grounds need to be connected.

Each channel has a number of different controls as well as a fader. Some mixers have a channel-on switch, but it is the fader which allows you to raise or lower the volume of the sound source to the level required. When two or more different sources are being mixed, the operator must find the correct balance between the sounds. A voice over a musical track should be clearly heard over the music, so the fader for the CD player must be set low enough not to drown the voice. If the CD fader is set too low, the music may not be heard at all.

In general, each fader should be in the 'quiet' position except when the sound source needs to be mixed into the output. The meter or meters on the mixer are used to measure the levels going through the mixer (or 'desk' – as in 'mixing desk'). Remember, though, that if more than one source is playing through the desk at any one time, the mixer will only be showing the level of the loudest source. When making a recording through a mixer, you should therefore take care to set the level of each source one at a time, so it peaks at the correct level on the meter. A common peak level for music is 4, and for speech 5 (when the meter is a 'peak programme meter' or a 'PPM').

If, when the fader is pushed up as high as it will go, the level from that source is still not high enough, the gain control should be adjusted until it is. If the level is too high, the gain control should be altered once more. The gain is usually at the top end of the channel. (You should note that on most mixing desks, to fade a source *up*, the fader should be pushed *up*, and to fade *down*, the fader should be brought *down*. Many older desks in the BBC still work the other way round, because early sound engineers were afraid of accidentally pushing up faders that should be down. They thought it was better that a source should be accidentally faded out than faded in. They were right, so take care not to knock faders on by accident yourself!)

Mixing sound live

Often, you will be using a mixing a desk 'live' – that is, connected to a transmitter or PA. Here, it will not be possible to set up levels on the desk with the faders open, because your audience will hear the tapes, discs or microphones being 'lined up'. A radio programme would not sound very professional if *'testing, testing 1, 2, 3 …'* was heard each time an interviewee was lined up!

All mixers for live use have a 'PFL' or 'pre-fade listen' facility to allow levels to be set before faders are opened. The operator can then actually listen to any different source before it is put on air. For example, a presenter may wish to hear the start or end of a music track before it is broadcast, in order to plan how to 'talk in' to or 'talk out' of it. Lining up the start of a tape or a track is made possible by the PFL function on the mixer. Normally, the operator selects PFL by pushing a button on the channel to be heard. That channel then 'takes over' the headphones and the studio speakers, or both.

Other features on a standard sound mixer are:

Feature	Function
Aux output	Allows you to send a different choice of sources to a particular destination
Pan control	Moves a source to the left or right in the stereo 'image'
Talkback	An intercom system allowing you to talk to another studio or location
Ducking	Can be set to lower the level of one source for a voice to do a 'talk over' over it
Mono	Can put either leg of a stereo recording onto both legs of the output
'EQ'	Equalisation

'Equalisation' means changing the way something sounds. That is, if it sounds too 'woolly', turning up the higher frequencies will make it crisper. If a sound is too tinny, then the high frequencies can be turned down, and the middle and low frequencies turned up. A mixer may have a full range of equalisation controls on each channel, or the facility may only be available on some of the channels. Equalisation – or 'EQ' – works the same way as the graphic equalisation on the more expensive stereo hi-fi equipment or car stereos.

'Graphic equalisation' is available on studio sound processing equipment, and on some digital audio production software too. The different frequencies are displayed visually, and the amount of each different frequency range can be seen on the screen and turned up or down as required.

Activity 6.7

1 Think of a good subject for a vox pop recording. Decide where to record and what to ask. Now select suitable equipment and do the recordings, sticking to safe working practices at all times.

2 Select the most appropriate equipment for each recording task you have to do for your Variety Radio programme. Follow as closely as possible the recording schedule from Element 6.1, paying particular attention to the requirements of the brief, the target audience and the deadlines you set yourself. Note down on the schedule which equipment you choose and why. Health and safety requirements must be followed, and new hazards identified as soon as possible.

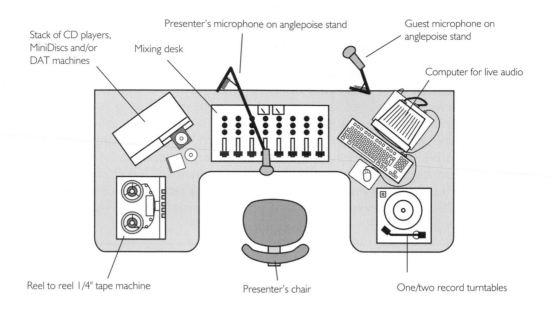

Stack of CD players, MiniDiscs and/or DAT machines

Mixing desk

Presenter's microphone on anglepoise stand

Guest microphone on anglepoise stand

Computer for live audio

Reel to reel 1/4" tape machine

Presenter's chair

One/two record turntables

A typical self-operated radio studio

Editing sound products

As you complete your recordings, you will be able to build up a rough edit list. The differences between this and your final edit list may be many or few, but from an early stage you should be making decisions about how the different pieces of recorded material are going to fit together.

Recordings on cassette will generally need to be dubbed on to reel-to-reel for ease of handling, but you can edit on a digital system instead of quarter-inch tape if you have access to one. DAT recordings need dubbing into another format in order to be edited and if you have gone to the expense of recording digitally, it would be well worth staying digital and keeping the extra quality. A recording made on to quarter-inch can be edited straight away with a razor blade, with no need for dubbing at all. MiniDisc recordings can be easily edited on the actual recording machine.

Dubbing

A 'dub' is a copy, either from one format to another, or to the same format (for example, if you need two different finished versions of the same recording). Whatever the format, it involves recording from one machine to another. During this copying process, it is very important that the levels are correct or the copy will either distort (level too high), or be too low compared with the audio on either side of it – or even become lost in the background hiss. Dubbing can be done straight from one machine to another or through a mixer. The direct method needs you to connect the two machines together with the correct leads plugged into the correct sockets.

Dubbing direct   Dubbing through studio

Dubbing through a studio mixer has two clear advantages:

- The equipment is probably already set up exactly as you need it, with no need to find or connect leads
- The levels may be easier to set and adjust, using the correct fader on the mixer. In the studio, you could also make use of the equalisation if the sound needs cleaning up a bit.

The order in which you dub the recorded material can be a rough edit in itself. You may save time later by dubbing only the pieces of audio you want to use – and in the order you will need them. When you dub there is no need to get the different items lined up against each other exactly as you will want them to be in the finished product. The joins can be tidied up later, either with a razor blade or using the controls of your digital editing system.

If your script requires two or more sounds be mixed, now is the time to do it. Once a recording has been made onto a piece of tape, the only way to add sound over or under it is to transfer it through a mixer onto another tape. An extra track cannot be added unless you are using a multi-track recording system, such as an 8-track or 16-track machine of the type used in the music recording industry. (Some of the digital audio production software does allow you to overlay different tracks as well – for example, SADiE or Pro-Tools.)

If you are simply dubbing sound onto quarter-inch, you will have to mix any background music or atmosphere from another source through a mixer at the same time as the dub. Take care to balance the levels correctly: 'take a level' off each piece of audio first, but also listen critically to the result, asking yourself if it really gives you the effect you wanted to create.

When you are ready to do the final edit on your sound products, you will need to cut the quarter-inch tape with a razor blade, removing all unwanted material, gaps, coughs, and so on, and then splice each edit point back together again with splicing tape, as explained in Chapter 3, page 143.

Activity 6.8

1 Produce a rough edit list, listing all the audio clips needed for each product, in the order in which they are to be assembled. All edit lists should show the timing and content of each item to be used. Do the rough edit as you dub the audio across, following safe working practices at all times – particularly over electrical safety.

2 Play through the material, noting down the final edits required to tidy up the tape. As you work, make sure that the edits you are planning do not sound too sudden or leave too much of a gap between one item and another. Now do the final edits on the list, carefully evaluating each one. Follow safe working practices at all times, particularly over electrical and razor blade safety (see above).

Review questions

1 What is meant by 'vox populi'?
2 Explain the difference between directional and omni-directional microphones.
3 Name TWO analogue and THREE digital recording formats.
4 When you should you use PFL?
5 How are sound sources selected on a mixer?

Element 6.3 Evaluate completed sound products

Reviewing sound products

Once a sound product is ready to be heard by the audience, it must be evaluated against the original brief. This is in order to help the producers judge how well they have done their job. It also gives them an idea of how the audience will respond, and a chance to make last-minute changes if the product does not match up to the requirements of the brief in some way. In the case of a live programme such as a magazine it is probably too late to make big changes, but there may still be time to put items in a different order, to re-work the script, or to replace an item with a standby – and at least faults that are picked up at this stage can be avoided next time.

Activity 6.9

1 Look carefully back over the brief for your Variety Radio programme and listen through all recorded material to check that each requirement has been met. Put down all the points you consider, and your conclusions, in a report on each product. How much of the original brief has been met? Check over Element 6.1 to remind you what to look for.

2 If you have been working on a live magazine programme, present it in front of a live audience. Record the whole programme, as you will need evidence for your file. Be ready to get feedback from the audience, as described below. Afterwards play back the tape and judge it against the brief. Write down your findings.

Collecting feedback about effectiveness

After it has been heard, a sound product must be judged in terms of what its target audience thought of it. Careers are made and broken on the strength of the actual work produced: top sequence programme presenters such as Chris Tarrant, Chris Evans and Simon Mayo are highly paid because the listening figures for their programmes are high. Their employers believe it is worth paying large fees in order to hold on to them. Sometimes stars are 'poached' by rival radio stations. This happens in local radio as much as on national radio networks, but it is usually only the national stars who hit the headlines.

National radio station	Audience (millions)	
BBC Radio 1	9.7	
BBC Radio 2	8.6	
BBC Radio 3	2.3	
BBC Radio 4	8.2	
BBC Radio 5 Live	4.9	
Atlantic 252	3.5	
Classic FM	4.7	
Talk Radio	2.2	
Virgin Radio (AM)	2.9	*Source: RAJAR, Q2 1997*

Remember that audience figures show how many people are listening, and the larger the audience, the more money a commercial radio station can charge for advertising. The BBC also needs to be able to show that large numbers of people listen to their services, in order to be able to justify the licence fee.

As important as the audience figures is what listeners *thought* about what they heard: whether they enjoyed it or just had it on in the background. The high cost of BBC Radio 3 is often justified on the basis that the cultural network has a very loyal group of listeners who enjoy the classical music, intellectual talks and more challenging drama which are only to be found on that station. As we have already seen, audience research can therefore be *quantitative* (how many people are listening?) as well as *qualitative* (what do people think about what they heard?).

Criteria for evaluation

Different sound products have to be judged in different ways. A tape-slide presentation should make the learning task more rewarding for a group of students: perhaps it made it easier for a lecturer to put across some difficult information, or perhaps a group of people who would otherwise have fallen asleep gave the subject more attention (and so learnt more) because the information was presented in an interesting way.

An in-store demonstration tape may be judged by its success in selling a particular product: was more of the product sold because the tape was playing and shoppers heard it – or might it just as easily have not been there at all? Certainly, from a quantitative point of view, if the tape was not effective in creating more sales, the money and effort put into making it would have been wasted. But qualitatively, even though the tape may not have succeeded in increasing sales of the product, if shoppers who heard the tape still enjoyed it, it may well have made their shopping in that store more enjoyable – and they might therefore be more likely to come back another day. The possibility of 'hidden' effects shows that sometimes extra research needs to be done in order to judge the true worth of a sound product. A producer whose work does well in audience research is more likely to keep finding paid work than someone who tries to meet the needs of target audiences, but fails every time!

Choosing your audience

Feedback from an audience is most useful when the sample audience matches the profile of the actual target audience. Your colleagues may hate the programme you have produced, but that might be because they are not very like the actual **target audience**. At the time of writing, the leisure company Saga is targeting the over-fifties with a range of proposed new radio services. People in their teens may not like the programmes, but that does not necessarily mean that they won't be a hit with the target audience!

However, most professional producers are skilled at judging how well a sound product serves a particular audience – and there are times when the judgement of a peer is very useful. You will get to know whose opinions to trust and whose to ignore when you compare feedback from your peers with feedback from the target audience. Sometimes it will be very hard for somebody outside the target audience to put themselves in the position of the type of person you are trying to serve. A talking newspaper for the blind might mean one thing to someone who can see, but something else entirely to someone who cannot. In the same way, a 'sound tour' for playing at an exhibition or on a bus ride may not make any sense at all until the listener sees what the target audience will see at the time it is played!

What you want to know from your target audience is:

- How many listened
- How much audience appeal did it have?
- Was the language used right for the audience or did they feel 'talked down to' or unable to understand what you were saying?
- Was any of the language offensive? Slang or swearing can really turn an audience off if they do not think it is appropriate for the time of day. For that reason, swearing is very unusual on radio. Slang can also put up a barrier between the broadcaster and the listeners, if the listeners feel that the person talking is not really 'their kind of person'. The smallest things can cause listeners to turn off, or tune to another station.

In short, you must decide how *effective* the production was. You have to decide how to get the kind of feedback you want – and how to make the information you collect as accurate as possible. If you ask a question that the audience do not understand, the answer they give is likely to be wrong or misleading. The problem with a questionnaire is just that: if you do not get the questions right, the information you collect may be useless. The strength of using a questionnaire, though, is that you can get a large number of responses that can be compared with each other.

Other methods

Although questionnaires can help you to get reactions from a large number of people, other methods may be better for getting them to use their own words to describe how they felt about what they heard.

Doing interviews with members of the audience is one way of asking different people open questions which encourage them to talk, rather than just choosing from 'yes' and 'no' on a sheet of paper. The questions must be planned before beginning the interviews, although asking extra questions on the spur of the moment will help you to get even more **qualitative** data about their thoughts.

Another method is to do the interviews as if they were a sound product and turn them into vox pops. Radio stations often do this, and play the (good) comments on air in the form of station promos or as testimonials from successful advertisers. Positive comments broadcast on a station can add to the general impression of a 'quality product, enjoyed and admired by all'.

Statistical analysis

Presenting a truthful account of the feedback to your sound products is a vital part of the evaluation process. To be able to write about your findings, you also need to do a statistical analysis. That means working out some method of counting all the positive responses to a questionnaire, and also showing the negative responses.

Doing an analysis of qualitative data is less straightforward: you are likely to get as many different reactions as the people you ask. Counting them may not be very useful, but just quoting them in your written report may add interesting detail. However, it is important that if reactions to your programme were mixed you reflect this honestly in your report.

Activity 6.10

1 Play your sound products to a sample of the target audience – or as close to the target audience as you can find. Collect feedback from them, using a quantitative method AND a qualitative method which you have planned beforehand.
2 Write down all your findings and add them to the reports on the two sound products.

Reviewing the effectiveness of the production processes

In order to become more successful, everyone involved in producing sound products must regularly review their own performance. Most companies have a system in place for appraising the performance of their employees – which usually means the employee sitting down at regular intervals with the line manager to go through their work.

It is a very good idea to review your own work – if only to make sure that bad news at an appraisal does not come as a surprise! Usually, if you know your work is not up to standard, you can take steps to correct it before things get serious.

The log is a record of everything done at each production stage and is a useful tool for spotting what went wrong and what to put right next time. Reviewing your own work should also be done in the light of feedback from peers and the target audience: if the feedback was positive, any room for improvement will be a chance to shine even more next time. If the feedback was poor, the review will need to be even more searching, to find out where the problems lay.

A very important factor will be how you used your time. If you wasted time at the beginning you probably found you had to cut corners later on as a result. Another problem may have been resources. Not having the right equipment may have affected quality. Not booking the equipment in time may have caused delays too.

Activity 6.11

1 Use the technical checklist below to assess the quality of the two sound products you have made. Carefully listen through both of the tapes, deciding at each point whether you can hear any of the faults described. Are there any other faults not mentioned in the checklist? Add all your findings to the reports you began in Activity 6.9.

Technical feature	Possible fault
Level of foreground	Too quiet? Lost in hiss?
Level of background	Too loud? Drowns foreground?
Levels overall	Distortion? Interviewer and interviewee not balanced? Up and down with no real reason?
Microphone technique	Microphone rattle?
Mixing	Music drowns voice? Some sounds lost in mix?
Dubbing	Levels correct?
Editing	Long gaps left in? Words, music or Fx cut in suddenly? Words cut off? Splices done correctly – no ragged ends? Leader put on correctly – at both ends? Tape labelled correctly – matching cue sheet?

2 Carry out a review of your own individual performance while working on the two products – when did you work effectively, and when could your performance have been improved? Say why, and give reasons. Do not be afraid to write about the good things that happened, too! Add your findings to the reports.

Review questions

1   Explain how audience figures can affect pay.
2   What is the difference between qualitative and quantitative data?
3   Which kind of question is most effective when collecting qualitative data?
4   Explain why it is important to review and evaluate work.
5   Which possible faults in a sound product can ruin it?

Assignment 6
Plan and produce sound products

This assignment provides evidence for:

Elements: 6.1   Prepare and plan sound products to a given brief
          6.2   Record and edit sound products
          6.3   Evaluate completed sound products

and the following key skills:

Communication:	2.1, 2.2, 2.4
Information Technology:	2.1, 2.2, 2.3
Application of Numbers:	2.1, 2.2, 2.3

1 Put together a new 'sound product' file, containing all your notes, logs and production paperwork from the activities in Elements 6.1, 6.2, and 6.3, each under the appropriate element heading.
2 Include your two tapes: the Variety Radio commission and the vox pop. Make sure both are properly labelled and have cue sheets attached.
3 Add to the sound product file all the reports and evaluations you have done on the different activities.
4 Make a careful cross-check to make sure all the work produced is there, and submit the file to your tutor, with your name and group clearly marked.

7 Preparing and producing a graphical product

What is covered in this chapter

- Preparing and planning a graphical product
- The production of a graphical product
- Ways to promote a finished graphical product
- Testing other people's reaction to the graphical product

Your 'graphical product' file will need to contain:
- A selection of newspapers, magazines, fanzines, comics, brochures and newsletters
- Your written answers to the activities and questions in this chapter
- Your completed assignments

Introduction

This chapter follows on from the work you did in Chapter 2 on producing a graphical product. It also draws on what you learned about target audiences and following a brief in Chapter 1.

Element 7.1 Prepare a graphical product to an agreed brief

There are thousands of examples of graphical products all around us in the form of newspapers, magazines, newsletters, fanzines, brochures and comics. No doubt you will have some that you prefer to read, such as a football or music magazine, a particular comic or even a local paper.

It is highly likely that the design of each of these graphical products started out as a **brief**. When a company is asked to design a graphical product they are given a brief by the business/company/organisation/group of people requiring the publication. Everyone working on the project must be totally clear what is in the brief.

The brief can be broken down into a checklist of points:

- **Background** – Information about the people wishing to produce the product
- **Purpose** – What is the product trying to do (inform? entertain? advertise? etc.)
- **Description** – How do those requiring the product imagine it to look?
- **Target audience** – Who is the product aimed at?
- **Budget** – How much can be spent on the design and production?
- **Timescale** – How much time do you have to produce the product?

The target audience

Every graphical product has been carefully produced with its **target audience** in mind. In fact, it is really the audience that decides the look and the feel of the product. People who read the *Daily Telegraph* are receiving items of news information in a very particular style, and one that is different from the *Sun* or *Independent*. The *Top of the Pops* magazine knows that its readers are likely to be young adults, whereas *Homes and Gardens* can expect to have a more adult reader.

Whatever the type of graphical product, the aim is always to communicate with an audience. Information will be mainly in the form of writing, but visual images including photographs, tables, charts, sketches and cartoons are also used. Pages are set out so they are eye-catching and easy to read or follow. When planning the pages of a graphical product it is important to think about what they will look like as well as what they say.

One picture is worth a thousand words

Many people are involved in the production of a graphical product, whether it is a national magazine or a local newsletter. It is important for everyone to work together as a team and communicate with one another, so that everyone is fully informed about what is going on. More information about the people involved in the production of a graphical product will be found in Element 7.2.

The success of a graphical product can be gauged by how well it sells. If people like the content, design, layout, price, etc., they will continue to buy it and even recommend it to others. You will shortly have the chance to produce your own graphical product and to **evaluate** your results. This means that you will have to ask your readers what they think of it and improve or change your ideas accordingly. Further information about appraising graphical products will be found in Element 7.3.

The production brief for a graphical product

A brief may be needed during various different stages in the production of a graphical product. Once a decision has been taken to set up the product (magazine, newsletter, newspaper, fanzine or comic) then the initial brief is written. This will explain to all those involved just what is required. It will probably contain information under the following headings:

Objectives

The objectives are what the product is trying to achieve. One of the objectives might be to make a stated profit or to capture a particular target audience. Another might be to develop an environment-friendly policy, or to extend into the European market within five years.

Function

The function of the product follows on from its objectives. Is it to inform its readers? To entertain? To educate? Both? Everyone working on a brief should be clear about what the function of the product is supposed to be.

Subject

The subject of a graphical product is probably easier to understand than the function because the subject is exactly what the product is *about*. It could be about news, sport, politics, humour, fashion, motor bikes – any number of subjects. Unlike a function, it can deal with more than one.

Appeal

What makes a magazine or comic appeal to you? It may be the subject matter, the writing style, the humour, the pictures or the fact that it is very informative. Whatever the reason, you can be sure that someone has worked hard to find the best way to appeal to a wide audience – particularly to those readers who normally read a rival product. A great deal of market research has to be carried out in order to discover what does appeal to target audiences. It is part of the job of the initial brief to identify how this to be achieved.

Budget

In order to set a budget for a new graphical product, all costs must be taken into account. These can range from a few pounds for a newsletter to thousands of pounds for the launch of a new comic. The costs will include practical things like stationery, equipment such as computers and printers, staff salaries and even rent for office space. Promotion also costs money, but advertising can bring in money too if the product is big enough to carry advertisements.

Timescale

Setting up the product will take time and effort, but a specific timescale will have to be agreed. Once the product is in production, time is all-important. Everyone must stick to the deadline they have been given, otherwise publication could be delayed and readers could be lost. If a child wants a particular comic and it misses its publication date, he or she will probably buy an alternative rather than go back the next day to see if the usual one is there. Timescales and deadlines very much depend upon the type of product. A monthly newsletter produced by the local karate club will have weeks in which to organise the contents, whereas a daily news reporter may only have minutes!

Other types of briefs

During the publication process other briefs may be written in order to explain specific tasks to editors or writers. A magazine journalist may have a brief which outlines a feature they must write. It may suggest people who need to be interviewed, and will certainly give details of the number of words to be written (and therefore how much space is available in the magazine) and the number of pictures or illustrations allowed. It may also specify the style or tone of the writing, particularly if the author is a freelance journalist who doesn't normally work for the magazine.

Activity 7.1

In groups, think of four different target audiences (e.g. new students at your school or college; people who like skateboarding, families who own dogs, etc). Think up an idea for a graphical product which you could produce for each of them. For each idea you should write down:
- The target audience
- The type of product (magazine, newsletter, fanzine, etc.)
- The function and aims of the product
- The subject
- How it will appeal to the target audience
- Where and how often it will be distributed
- The price (remember, it could be free)

Designing the product

Once market research about a graphical product has been carried out, the production team will be able to come up with some ideas about the layout design and content, based on the preferences of the target audience.

Layout

The **layout design** refers to the way the content is arranged on the pages. This often starts with ideas being jotted down on paper but, as you will see later, a desktop publishing package can make the process of laying out the design of pages much easier.

Any page of any graphical product is based on a grid which defines the height, width and position of the margins, columns and headings. Usually, a series of rough thumbnail sketches is done first to try out different page layouts. These are small, quick drawings to show the possible layout of a page. Examples of thumbnail grids are shown in Chapter 2, page 92.

Case Study: researching a college newsletter

Bridgewater College has just appointed Hollie Green as editor of a new college newsletter aimed at informing students about events in college and the local area. As the college has over 1,000 full-time students, communication is not always easy.

The newsletter must not only inform the students but also encourage them to communicate with each other.

Hollie's first task as editor is to find out the following:

- Who will be the audience?
- What sort of content is required?
- In what style will the content be written?
- How frequently will it be produced?
- What is the best way of distributing it?

In order to find the answers, Hollie will have to carry out some sort of survey or market research. She needs to know which type of students are likely to want to read the newsletter and what they would like to see in it.

Hollie knows that she must work within the guidelines she has been given by the college principal, but at the same time she must provide her readers with the sort of information they want to read.

She produced the following questionnaire in order to find the answers.

```
                    BRIDGEWATER COLLEGE
               STUDENT NEWSLETTER QUESTIONNAIRE

As editor of a new college newsletter, I would like to hear your
views on its style, content, etc. to ensure I provide you with
the sort of information you need. I would be very grateful if
you would answer the following brief questions and return this
questionnaire to me as soon as possible.

Many thanks,
Hollie Green

Please state the name of your course
......................................

Age:      16-18 ☐   19-21 ☐   22-24 ☐   25-28 ☐   28+ ☐

1. Are you likely to read a College newsletter regularly?

          YES ☐    NO ☐     (if no, please state reason.)

          ...............................................

2. Would you use a newsletter to pass information on to others?

          YES ☐    NO ☐     (if no, please state reason.)

          ...............................................

3. What general style of writing would you prefer?

          Lighthearted ☐   Serious ☐    Both ☐

                                        (Continued opposite)
```

Case Study (Contd.)

```
4. Which of the following items would you like to see appear in
   the newsletter?

        College events ☐    Local events ☐
        Classified ads ☐
        Reviews of films/videos/music/theatre ☐
        Articles by students ☐
        Articles by lecturers ☐
        Dateline ☐
        Exam information ☐
        Other (please give details)

        ..............................................

5. How frequent should the newsletter be?

        Weekly ☐          Fortnightly ☐       Monthly ☐

6. Where would you like the newsletter to be available?

        Reception ☐    Canteen ☐        Library ☐
        All three ☐
```

The questionnaire generated 1,000 responses. Some results are shown below:

Results of the questionnaire

1. The respondents are attending a variety of courses. The students' ages break down as follows:

   16–18: **125**   19–21: **350**   22–24: **175**   25–28: **170**   28+: **180**

2. 465 students said that they would use the newsletter to communicate to other students.

3. 598 preferred a mixture of styles, lighthearted and serious.

4. Below is a breakdown of the number of people who said they wanted to see each type of item in the newsletter:

College/local events	520
Classified ads	520
Films/video/music/theatre reviews	710
Articles by students	180
Dateline	845

5. 620 would like the newsletter to be fortnightly.

6. 590 would collect it from all three of the locations mentioned.

Activity 7.2

Read the Case Study on pages 228–229. Imagine you are a member of Hollie's team working on the college newsletter. Your job is to present the results of the questionnaire shown opposite in a clear way so that Hollie and her team can plan the newsletter to suit the needs of the students. You may wish to use graphs or pie charts in order to show some of the results clearly and simply. For example, the various age groups of the students could be presented in the form of a bar chart.

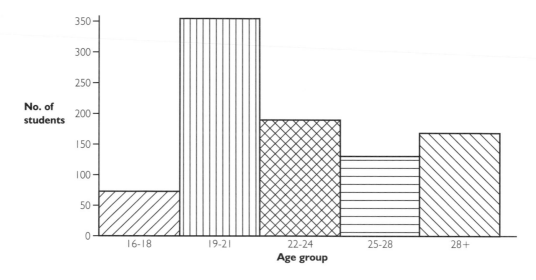

A bar chart showing student age groups

Using stylesheets

Once it has been decided which page layouts to use, all the details can be stored as grids or templates on a computer desktop publishing package.

Font type and size can also be decided in advance and stored on the computer as a 'stylesheet' so that they can be easily selected when importing or typing copy into the grid. These methods ensure the product keeps to an agreed style or design.

Finalising design

You need to look at as many different types of newsletter as you can find in order to get ideas or inspiration about the layout design. Try to decide what you think works and does not work.

Ask yourself the following questions:

- Are the items of news well spread out and clearly identified?
- Does each item have a headline?
- Are sub-headings used? Is this effective?
- How do the fonts differ in text and heading (type, size, weight)?
- How many different fonts can you identify?
- What improvements would you make to the layout design?
- Are photographs or artwork used?
- Are these used effectively? Do they improve the newsletter?
- Are graphical effects used to improve the overall design? How?

Content

The **content** refers to all the articles, information, stories, charts, tables, photographs, artwork, etc., included in the product – in other words, everything it will contain. You will need to decide which items will appear in each issue and which will appear less regularly. For example, classified ads may have a regular spot whereas articles written by students may only appear when suitable material is sent in.

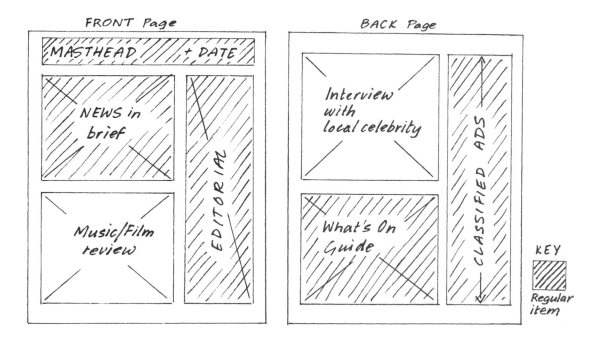

Possible layout of a college newsletter

Once the text has been agreed, it can be 'imported' or moved into the correct position on the page. Artwork can also be put in place if it has been scanned and stored in a digital format (see page 232).

Activity 7.3

Using thumbnail sketches, design a possible layout of two A4 pages for Hollie's college newsletter. It may be helpful for you to work with a partner at this stage. When you are satisfied with your thumbnail sketches, produce your layout design as a grid, preferably using a DTP package, and show it to other members of your group.

The advantages of DTP

Wordprocessors are computers that have been programmed for storing, correcting and printing out text that has been typed in on a keyboard. The more sophisticated the computer, the more complex functions the wordprocessor will perform. However, for the production of a graphics product, **desktop publishing (DTP)** has a number of advantages.

Desktop publishing systems are production tools that enable graphical products to be produced quickly and easily. They are not electronic designers – you will still need to be creative! The DTP package is used to develop and produce a graphical product, rather than design it. The advantages are:

- It is flexible, so that many different variations of the same page can be tested
- Alterations and corrections can be made easily and cheaply
- You can check your idea will work before spending money on production
- A particular style can be stored and repeated in future productions.

A scanner is an electronic device used to transfer an image onto a computer. The image can then be imported onto your page, altered in size, shape, etc., and printed out. Scanners are also able to identify the density of colours in an image and convert them into separate films.

Cut and paste

As an alternative to DTP, 'cut and paste' is a quick and simple way to arrange a page. The required text and pictures are physically cut up and placed on the page where they can be moved around and re-arranged until the desired effect is reached, when they are carefully stuck down in place.

Cut and paste does not have the professional finish possible with other techniques but it is cheap and easy to do.

DTP (right) has many advantages over traditional methods (left)

Printing

There are many methods of printing graphics products. We will look at some of the ones you are likely to use for your own graphical products, and also at some of the most commonly used techniques used for printing commercial products.

Most DTP systems are linked to laser printers. Lasers vary in size but mostly print out one A4 page at a time. The quality is good enough for letters, newsletters, or even an in-house magazine. Some laser printers can handle large volumes of paper, or different sizes of paper such as A3. Some can even print in colour, but these are still very expensive.

Photocopying

If you want to produce more than one or two copies of an in-house document, the best way is probably to print off one copy on a laser printer and then photocopy as many other copies as you need. Most colleges have photocopying facilities, and you may be able to use these. Alternatively, there are many high-street photocopying shops which will do the job for you, although probably at a higher price than the college photocopier.

Some photocopiers can copy in colour, but this is very expensive compared with black-only copying.

Offset litho

One of the most commonly used commercial printing methods is **offset litho**. This method is based upon the principle that oil and water do not mix. When oil-based ink and water are applied to a roller, the image picks up the ink while the blank space picks up water.

The image to be printed is photographed onto a thin aluminium plate which is wrapped around a cylinder. This then comes into contact with three sets of rollers. The first one dampens and the second applies ink. The ink is accepted by the image and repelled by the blank spaces. The third cylinder is a 'blanket' cylinder made from rubber which picks up the image. The image can then be transferred from the blanket to the paper.

The diagram on page 234 shows in a very simple form how litho printing works.

Other printing methods

Other methods of printing graphical products include:
- **Gravure** An expensive process used for high-quality magazines, books, some cigarette packets, photographic calendars, etc.
- **Letterpress** A slow process but useful for books with lots of text, business cards and letterheads
- **Screen printing** A relatively cheap process that can be used on many surfaces such as drinks cans, bottles, CDs and posters
- **Flexigraph** An economic process that does not produce a high-quality end product; used for chocolate bar wrappers.

Activity 7.4

Study examples of graphical products produced by both professionals and amateurs. How do the printing techniques differ? How is this reflected in their price? Make notes on your findings.

Activity 7.5

The college newsletter team must now produce their first issue using a combination of simple DTP techniques and 'cut and paste'. An offset litho machine is available for printing.

a As a class or group, discuss and make notes on the possible problems that may arise using these techniques and how they can be overcome.

b What are the advantages of these techniques? In what way would production change if a scanner were also to be used? Make your own notes for your file.

Offset litho printing

Offset lithography works on the principle that oil and water do not mix. The printing plate holds ink because the image area is treated so that it is receptive to oil-based ink but not to water. There are five basic stages:

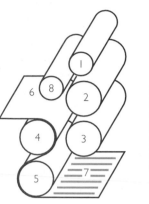

1. Ink roller
2. Plate cylinder
3. Blanket cylinder
4. Impression cylinder
5. Sheet transfer cylinder
6. Unprinted sheet
7. Printed sheet
8. Damping roller

1 Platemaking

Using a photographic process, a printer exposes the reversed image from the film separation (a negative) onto a flat plate with a light-sensitive coating.

2 Wetting

The plate is mounted on a rotating cylinder. When the press starts, the plate comes into contact with water rollers first. The last water roller wets the entire printing plate, except where it has been treated to resist water.

3 Inking

The ink roller applies oil-based ink to the plate. When the last ink roller contacts the wet printing plate, it smoothly distributes ink across the water-resistant image area.

4 Offsetting

The final roller is a rubber blanket, which is pressed against the printing plate and carries away a reversed inked image.

5 Printing

In the last step, the paper passes between the blanket and an impression cylinder. The inked blanket cylinder with its reversed image presses against the paper, printing the positive image.

Activity 7.6

Working either individually, with a partner or in a group, produce a sample A4 page of Hollie's college newsletter. It does not need to contain real articles or information because the idea is to compare the techniques used in designing and printing the pages. You can type or 'flow in' any piece of text. Photographs and pictures will also be needed – again, use any pictures for this exercise. They can be photocopied, scanned, hand drawn, or produced using a graphics package.

If you are working in a group, try to use a variety of different techniques in order to make comparisons and come to conclusions about which techniques are most effective and for what purpose. Write up your findings.

Costs and budgeting

Anyone producing a graphical product must ensure that they do not spend more than their allocated budget. This means production must be costed very carefully. If the budget is not all spent, the producer will be able to reinvest money in the next product.

In order to calculate the cost of producing a graphical product, the following factors need to be taken into account:

- **Paper sizes** are labelled with letters and numbers. The sizes used most frequently are known as 'A' sizes. For example, A4 is the size mainly used for official letters. It is also likely to be the size of paper (lined or plain) that you use when keeping work in a folder. A5 is half the size of A4 and A3 is twice the size of A4. The diagram on page 236 illustrates how the various 'A' sizes relate to each other.

- **Paper weight** refers to the paper's thickness. Paper is weighed in grams per square metre (gsm). As a guide, most paper used in colleges will weigh 80gsm. Paper is sold by its weight, so if expensive paper is used during production then the publication will cost the reader more money. You only have to look at the price of a glossy, full-colour magazine and compare it with a daily newspaper to realise this.

- **Paper type** refers to the paper's texture and colour. The surface of paper may be glossy or matt, rough or smooth. This surface texture will affect its end use. Matt paper, for example is more absorbent than glossy paper. A huge range of coloured papers, surface finishes and textures are available.

Activity 7.7

1 Using the diagram on page 236, investigate and make notes on different sizes of paper and suggest ways in which they might be used (for example, A3 and A2 are useful sizes for design work).
2 Find out and make note of which size, weight and finish of paper is usually used for a tabloid newspaper, a glossy magazine, a school letter to parents and a school or local newsletter

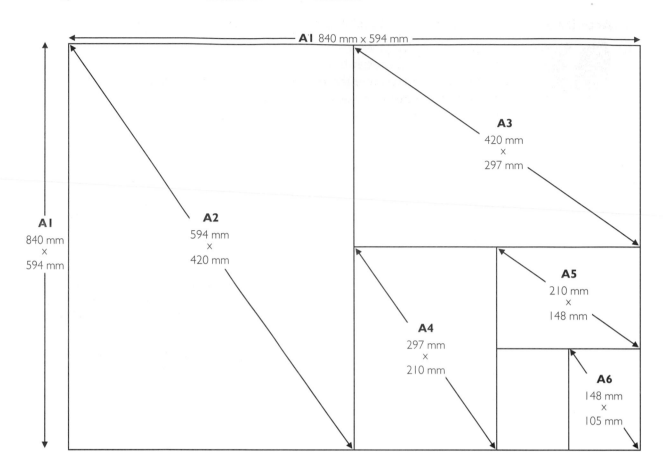

Standard paper 'A' sizes

- **Number of pages** Magazines and newspapers are made up of multiples of four pages. This means that if you want to add one more page you actually have to add four more pages. The more pages used, the more paper is needed and therefore the greater the cost.

- **Number of colours** Graphical products can be printed in one or two colours only, or they can be printed in **full colour**. The more colours you use, the more expensive the product will be. This is because each colour plate has to be printed separately and also because colour products usually need to be printed on better quality paper.

- **Collating and binding** If several pages are used for a graphical product they will need to be **collated** (i.e. sorted into the right order) and **bound** together. At its simplest this can involve stapling pages together. Larger products can be comb or wiro-bound, heat bound, glued or sewn.

- If the production becomes too large to be printed in-house (for example, in a college), it can be contracted out to a printing firm. This is known as **contract printing** and is often done by large newspaper companies.

- As a publication grows, **sponsorship** can be used to provide some financial support. Companies and businesses can pay to have an advertising slot within the publication.

- **Personnel costs** Staff need to be paid, too! The more people required to do the work, the greater the budget for salaries.

Activity 7.8

Make contact with a local firm of printers and find out what their charges are. You should each contact someone different in order to make comparisons. Each person should find out the cost of printing 1,000 copies of an A3, one-colour newsletter using matt finish 80gsm paper. Present the group's results in the form of a table.

Review questions

1 What are 'thumbnail sketches' and how can they be used when planning and preparing a page layout design?

2 What printing techniques can be used for producing a graphical product? Write a paragraph to describe each of the techniques available.

3 What costs would an editor need to take into account before producing a magazine? List all the possibilities.

Element 7.2 Produce a graphical product

The importance of teamwork

The assignment for this element requires you to work as part of a 'team' to produce your own college newsletter. The nature of the newsletter and its target audience will have to be identifed by the whole team. It is essential that the target audience is kept in mind throughout the planning of the newsletter, so you need to be very clear about how you will identify your readers.

The greater the number of people in a team, the more negotiation is required. Discussions can be lengthy and will often lead to compromises rather than everyone getting their own way. Think carefully about how best you can work, as well as who works best with you.

Keeping a production log

You will also be expected to keep a **production log** showing the progress of the newsletter and your input into its production. The book can be regarded as a diary in which you record each step of the newsletter's production, but it will be of much greater value to you if you make detailed notes and back them up with diagrams and sketches where appropriate. This can then be used as a reference for any subsequent work that you do.

Stages in planning a newsletter

In order to produce a newsletter (or any graphical product) you need to work through the following stages as a team:

1 Nature of newsletter

Working as a team, you need to decide upon the type of newsletter you aim to produce. Some examples might be a newsletter for:

- Teachers
- Students (generally)
- Parents
- Prospective students
- The local community
- The previous year's students

You should also decide at this stage how often the newsletter would be produced – weekly, termly, annually, etc.

2 The target audience

The nature of your newsletter will largely determine your target audience, but do not expect to succeed if they are not interested in your idea! You will need to carry out some market research to find out their requirements.

3 Aim

Once the target audience has been identified, the aim of the newsletter should be clear. If you are unsure, ask yourself:

- What is the purpose of the newsletter?
- What are you trying to provide for your readers?

4 Style

Once the aim and audience have been established, a style can be decided on. You need to think about:

- **Writing style** – Remember your readers!
- **Font and font size** – You will need to decide on a typeface both for the name of your newsletter, and for the main text, headings, sub-headings, etc.
- **Format** – Will the pages be mainly text or pictures?
- **Printing techniques** – What will be available for you to use?

5 Content

As a team you will need to agree on the sort of articles, items of information, facts, pictures, artwork, graphics, tables/charts, etc., you want to include.

6 Layout

As a team you will need to agree on an overall layout grid and individual styles for each item to be included in the newsletter. Each person could take responsibility for the design of a particular page or feature – although you need to make sure that it all fits the required length.

7 Costing

Where possible, you should produce a costing sheet showing all items used and their approximate cost. This could lead to an estimated price for the newsletter based on the production of a sample run, (e.g. 10 copies).

8 Competition

Working in competition with other teams in the group could lead to greater motivation and a higher standard of end-product!

The term 'graphical product' describes a wide range of different publications

Production roles

We are now going to look in some detail at the different roles or jobs involved in producing a graphical product. These fall broadly into four groups:

- Writers
- Editors
- Designers/artists
- Printers

Writers

You have already learned that all graphical products aim to communicate to their audience. They do so using a variety of different writing styles such as light-hearted, technical, factual, humorous, etc. It is the writer's job to communicate the information clearly and in keeping with the style of the product. A writer should have a good understanding of the English language.

Writers who contribute to most graphical products are generally referred to as journalists. A newspaper, for example, will employ journalists or news reporters to provide the main items of news. Other journalists will contribute to specialist areas such as sport, politics, finance, features and women's pages. Like most graphical products, newspapers may use freelance journalists. These are self-employed writers who sell their articles and often specialise in a particular subject.

Although a national daily newspaper might employ anything from 30 to 60 reporters, a local evening paper may only have 6 to 12. A magazine may employ just a small number of people and rely heavily on freelance writers to write articles. They may also give the freelance journalists a contract for a set period of time to ensure they produce, say, one article a week.

A newsletter, being a relatively small product, might be written, edited and produced all by the same person.

Editors

The **editor** of a newspaper, magazine, newsletter, etc., is the person responsible for overseeing what goes into the product, how the product is presented and for ensuring everything is done on time. Legally, an editor is responsible for the product being published and so is presumed to have seen everything in it. If anyone decides to sue the newspaper or magazine, it is the editor who risks going to jail! How the law can affect journalists will be discussed later.

Editors tend to work in different ways. They may be 'writing editors' which means they began their career as a journalist or writer and worked their way up. These tend to be more concerned with content than presentation and usually write their own 'leader', i.e. leading article or column. Other editors might be production people who are more concerned with pictures, headlines and layout. An editor will have a deputy who can take over in his or her absence.

The main role of a newspaper is to inform the public about very recent news. It is the job of the news editor to organise the news gathering and news writing of the day. The sports editor will do the same for all sports items. A newspaper or magazine will have a features editor who is responsible for deciding which features and articles will go in each issue. Other editors include the political editor, financial editor and foreign editor. Each of these roles will involve checking the finished work before it is passed to the sub-editors.

A sub-editor's job is to read through text that someone else has written and to check it. It has to be checked to make sure it is accurate in what it says and that it is legally safe. The 'sub' also corrects errors of grammar and spelling – how the text is 'subbed' is discussed on page 249. The text may have to be cut and or reworded so that it fits the allocated space. Computer commands may have to be typed in so that the text is set in the correct type size and with correct page and column information. The sub-editor may also write the headline. This job is a very important one and needs to be carried out with care.

Designers/artists

A graphic designer is the person responsible for the design of a graphical product. If it is a large publication such as a newspaper, more than one graphic designer will be required to cover the different aspects of the design, such as the layout and initial grids, the typography (typeface and size, spacing, etc.), illustrative work, artwork and visual identity.

Like writers, photographers can either be employed by a company producing a graphical product, or they can work on a freelance basis. Pictures are a very important part of any graphic communication. If you think about magazines, many are full of colour photographs which help to bring the text to life. Newspapers use photographs to illustrate a story and to make it real – the photographer needs to take a picture which will achieve just the right effect. A photographer who works for a newspaper is often referred to as a 'press photographer'.

Printers

The printers' job is to print and bind the graphical product. Printing can either be done by the newspaper/magazine company itself, or it can be contracted out to a specialist printer. A variety of different methods of printing are used (see Element 7.1, page 232) and it is up to the newspaper/magazine company to inform the printer of its specific requirements, so that the most appropriate and cost-effective method is chosen.

The production process

The production process for all graphical products (newspapers, magazines, fanzines, comics or newsletters) is similar, but different products involve time, money and people to a differing degree. In describing these processes we will look at examples from a variety of different products.

At the heart of any national daily newspaper you will find the newsroom. This is where the reporters sit at their desks with computer terminals, telephones and fax machines. Very often the newsroom is arranged so that the newsdesk is at its centre. As the time for 'going to press' approaches, the newsroom becomes full of noise and activity. Last-minute alterations are made to stories as further details are phoned through by other reporters, ensuring that when the paper is published it has all the up-to-date information.

The newsroom is the heart of a national daily newspaper

Planning content

Planning for production obviously takes different forms for different graphical products. However, there are likely to be certain aspects that have already been planned for and are now fixed. For example, to make it easier for the reading audience, a particular feature or column will be placed on the same page each time.

Daily newspapers require frequent **planning meetings** – perhaps two a day, to discuss morning and afternoon issues. An early planning meeting will be needed to discuss items of news and features for the morning issue. Editors representing the different departments will attend, and suitable stories will be debated. A **story list** will be drawn up showing the morning's stories and possible follow-ups. However, news items that will interest the readers may change if more exciting stories occur during the morning, and stories are often changed just before going to press.

These planning meetings are needed to decide on the main news items for the day. However, part of the paper will already be 'in hand' because certain pages containing television programmes or longer features are usually set up the day before.

Each department within the paper will hold its own planning meeting. For example, the features department can plan further ahead, as they produce longer articles rather than items of news. They might meet on a Monday afternoon and plan what will go in the following week's editions. The features editor will discuss with editors from the theatre, film, television, gardening, women's pages, etc., any ideas they have for features. Usually they are free to decide what they will write and how it will be presented. However, occasionally a newsworthy item may arise which the editor wants covered immediately.

A Sunday newspaper or weekly magazine has fewer meetings, but they are likely to take longer and involve planning further ahead. A monthly magazine could be working on an issue four months ahead of time, so the planning has to be done very carefully. At these lengthy meetings, someone must take notes and write up the minutes so that all decisions are accurately recorded.

To return to a daily newspaper, further planning will be required on the main news pages, so a **production conference** is held. Here, the chief editors have to 'sell' their story ideas to the editor and convince him or her that they are worthy of being main news items. A decision must also be taken about the choice of front page 'splash' story.

Planning illustrations

The importance of photographs has already been discussed, and it is during the production process that pictures are found and photograph lists compiled. Just as with story lists, the pictures may be replaced with more appropriate ones or new pictures found to suit new stories at the last minute. Sometimes photographs are obtained from syndication agencies who keep stocks of images and offer them on loan. A newspaper or magazine may also have its own photograph 'archive', famous people and politicians being particularly useful ones to have. A picture editor (or chief photographer) will decide whether or not a photograph will print well and enhance the page.

An art editor is in charge of the art desk for a newspaper or magazine, comic or fanzine. Their job is to organise an illustrations list, stating any graphics needed such as line drawings, maps or cartoons. If the 'in-house' artists cannot do the work it will be commissioned from artists outside the company.

Planning layout

During the planning of a graphical product, page plans are needed in order to plan what will go on each page. As has been mentioned, certain features may have a regular position in each issue, such as the editor's letter, the problem page, and so on. However, the rest of the content must also fit into a pre-arranged plan, and it is the editor's responsibility an overall idea of what it should contain. A magazine will use 'flatplans' to organise its pages. These are usually set out as follows:

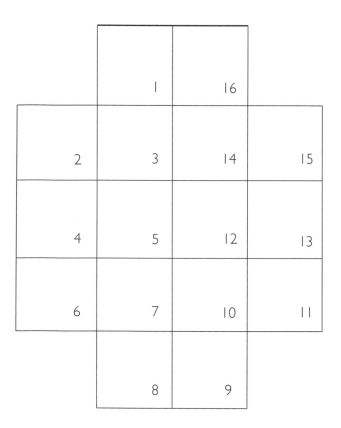

A magazine flatplan

Regular items can be filled in straight away while the most suitable position for new features can be discussed and decided. The number of words in the text and the number of pictures or illustrations will also be agreed. There is, of course, only a certain amount of space available so it is important for writers to know the number of words allowed and keep to it.

The publication process for any graphical product begins at the initial ideas stage and runs right through the production processes outlined above, until the printed end product is handed out or sold to its readers. A diagram showing the planning and production process of a national newspaper is shown on page 244.

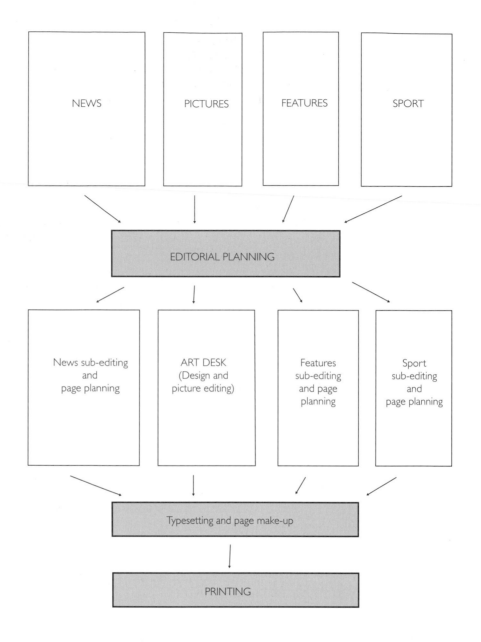

Planning and production sequence in a national or large provincial newspaper

Writing the product content

The type of story, feature, article or information that goes into a graphical product will very much depend on the product itself. A fanzine may include interviews with famous people; a school newsletter will inform parents about events; a comic may contain several cartoon stories; a women's magazine may include a fictional romantic story. Usually a graphical product will contain a variety of different items, but they will all be in keeping with the style of that product.

News stories make up the main content of a newspaper. 'News' can be described as a 'current item of interest to the general public'. It has to be current because no-one wants to read yesterday's news. It also has to interest people and that usually means it is about people. A news headline stating 'Dog bites man' does not really grab the reader's attention, but if the headline were 'Man bites dog' then it might make a more interesting read!

Stories suitable for a newspaper can be found anywhere and everywhere. A reporter will have contacts in his or her area such as a headteacher, the local MP or a police officer who can provide details about a story if necessary. Reporters will also talk to people in the community: taxi drivers, shopkeepers, postmen/ women, pub landlords, etc. – in fact, anybody who might have a story to tell.

All local newspapers, magazines and newsletters will have an events diary to remind readers about interesting events such as fêtes, concerts or jumble sales. This will automatically provide them with a story, feature or item of information for their next publication.

Newspapers and some magazines also receive press releases from businesses and other organisations. These give the details of events or other pieces of information which a journalist can then use to write up as an item of news.

A news item may be useful for a magazine to follow up as a feature or article. For example, a newspaper might carry the following item:

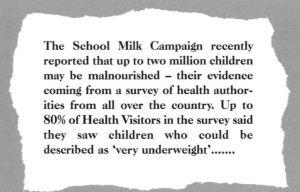

The magazine or features department might then carry out research into the subject, find out more details about the survey, ask a dietician for some healthy recipes for children and produce an article entitled:

Looking for stories and ideas

Journalists who write for magazines may come up with their own ideas for an article just by going about their daily business. They have to learn to think and question and ask about all sorts of things that could become an article of interest to the reader. A lighthearted piece could be written following a particularly traumatic visit to the dentist; or a gift of a salmon caught by a friend could develop into an article about the popularity of fishing as a hobby – and so on.

Fictional stories for comics or magazines require creative writing skills as well as a good imagination. An idea for a story could be sparked off by an everyday event which the writer then develops into something interesting and amusing.

Newsletters tend to have an easier time looking for stories because by their very nature they are usually passing on items of information. That is not to say they cannot be written in an interesting or even humorous way.

As we have already seen, stories and articles can be brought to life with photographs and illustrations. Cartoons are a good example of graphic illustrations working together with text. Recent advances in technology have meant that both photographs and graphics have improved significantly in quality. Computer graphics packages, such as CorelDraw have revolutionised the work of the graphic designer during the last few years, as they allow much more flexibility in the creation of graphics.

Legal considerations relating to content

It is extremely important for anyone writing for any type of publication to know and understand the law. The law is there to protect their own rights as well as to protect the rights of the people who may be written about.

There are many laws which govern what can and cannot be written and these are clearly explained in *McNae's Essential Law for Journalists* by Tom Welsh and Walter Grenwood (1995). Some of the most important areas have already been covered in previous chapters of this book. To recap, the main areas that writers need to be aware of are:

- **Infringement of copyright** If you use material which was written by someone else in an article of your own and do not acknowledge the original author, you are guilty of an infringement of copyright. Even worse, if you pretend you wrote it then you are guilty of plagiarism. In the eyes of the law this is stealing, and you have committed a crime.
- **Libel** This is an area of the law which prevents writers from writing something untrue that might harm others. You can be found guilty of libel if you publish something about someone else which may harm that person's reputation in the eyes of anyone who might read it. The person does not even have to be named, as long as they can be recognised. In a libel case, a person's 'reputation' can mean either their character or their business or professional reputation. Other types of libel include **obscene libel** which deals with offensive material and **blasphemous libel** which deals with the use of blasphemy in written material.
- **Sedition** This aspect of the law prevents writers from writing anything that is against the monarchy or against Parliament. Anything that might endanger the security of the state – for example, a story revealing a state secret – would be taken very seriously in the eyes of the law.
- **Other offensive material** This covers statements that might cause offence to particular groups of people, for example, anything that is racist, sexist or might offend the disabled, elderly, or any other section of society.

Activity 7.9

1 Look through the plans you made as a group for your own student newsletter. Decide upon one topic, subject, issue, story, item of news, etc. Taking on the role of a writer, write an article for the student newspaper. Aim to write about 250 words and, if possible, include a photograph or picture.

2 Taking on the role of graphic designer, use DTP to lay out your story (with graphics). Include a headline, sub-headings and quotes if possible. Look at the examples of newspaper pages to give you some ideas for the layout.

Computer skills

Anyone involved in producing a graphical product should make use of computer technology and fully develop their computer skills. Computers provide greater speed and flexibility, particularly in the area of design and layout.

Computer technology allows text and design to be changed quickly and easily

The text of a graphical product usually needs to be available on disk as well as printed or 'hard' copy. Once on disk, it can be imported into a page in the appropriate place, as has been mentioned in Element 7.1.

In order to produce text for a story, article, etc., it is helpful to have a good understanding of **keyboard techniques**. This means knowing all the shortcuts that are possible, such as using command keys rather than going into a main menu to activate a particular command.

The **font** and **type size** will be chosen by the graphic designers to fit the particular style of the product. **Font** or **typeface** refers to the style of lettering used. There are literally thousands of typefaces available and each one creates its own visual effect. Different fonts may be chosen for headlines, captions, main text, etc., and they can be divided into serif and sans serif:

Serif type   *Sans serif type*

The following examples show different fonts and how they can be made bold or italic.

This sentence is printed in italic type.

Caslon Old Face Italic

This sentence is printed in bold type.

Caslon Old Face Heavy

This sentence is printed in italic type.

Gill Sans Italic

This sentence is printed in bold type.

Gill Sans Bold

You will need to experiment with different fonts in order to decide what style you are after.

The type size may also be altered to suit the style of the product and the particular piece you are working on. The size of the text is measured in 'points'.

There are approximately 72 points to 2.5 cm. The point size refers to the height of the 'block' in which the letter sits and this may vary for each type of font. Helvetica 12 point (12pt) is in fact slightly larger than 12pt Times Roman.

Many word processors and DTP packages have a 'spell check' command which can help to reduce the amount of editing that has to be done. When the text has been typed, the spell check will go through and highlight any words which do not match with its dictionary. This may mean that it highlights people's names which are in fact spelled correctly, but otherwise it is a very quick way of checking the accuracy of the text. A single word can also be checked if you are unsure of the spelling. Type in what you think the spelling should be and the spell check will show the correct version.

Activity 7.10

1 Look at a variety of cartoons in comics, magazines and newspapers. Consider the style of writing, type of language and illustrations used.
2 Design your own cartoon to fit either an A3 or A4 spread. You must decide exactly who you will be aiming at and whether it will be fun or have a serious message. How will you illustrate it?
3 Design the layout of your cartoon page using DTP.

Proof-reading skills

Today much of the work of the proof-reader is done by the sub-editor. Proof-readers used to check for mistakes in the setting of 'galley proofs'. This was in the days when typesetting was done by hand using hot metal letters. Now we are able to edit or correct text while it is on the screen and even **justify** the writing so it lines up straight at both edges.

An editor, sub-editor or proof-reader will use symbols on a printed copy of the text in order to show the corrections and changes that need to be made. Examples of the symbols are shown on page 250. However, it is becoming more common these days for 'subbing' to be carried out on-screen so any corrections are made immediately by one person.

Checking the text

However, accurate spelling is as important as ever, and text must still be checked thoroughly. Spell checks are useful, but you should also read everything through, because a spellchecker will not pick up every mistake.

Equally important, the grammar must be checked for accuracy. Writers should understand grammar and the correct way to structure sentences. Unfortunately grammatical mistakes cannot be corrected by a computer, so whoever is checking the copy needs to be able to spot them! There are many books on the subject of grammar which can help writers, but a few simple points to remember are:

- Keep the sentences simple and avoid starting them with 'and' or 'but'
- Do not over-use the shortened forms of words such as 'can't', 'don't', 'won't'
- Avoid using too many adjectives and adverbs such as 'really good' or 'completely untrue'
- Avoid splitting infinitives – for example, the correct form is 'to examine carefully' – *not* 'to carefully examine'

Punctuation needs to be checked carefully too. If readers have to go back and read sentences twice to make sense of them, the punctuation is not doing its job. If a sentence contains a lot of commas then it is probably best to divide it into smaller sentences. Once again, there are many books on the subject of punctuation, but a few key points are:

- Sentences always begin with a capital letter and end with a full stop.
- A comma is used for a pause in a sentence.
- When quoting what someone has said, use a comma followed by quotation marks, put a full stop at the end and close the quotation marks.

Checking the visual aspects

The importance of typeface and style have already been discussed, but they are only two aspects of typography. Typography is about the appearance of words: it can be used to attract attention, to look decorative and to suggest a particular time or place. You can see from the examples of fonts shown opposite that each type of lettering has its own style and that style can add visual appeal to a text.

Another way in which you can improve the visual appeal of a graphical product is to look at the spacing. Using DTP packages, the spacing between letters can be altered. Standard letter spacing, like the text you are reading, is close but the letters do not actually touch. Titles or sub-titles usually have a looser spacing. The space between individual letters can be adjusted using 'kerning', and the more sophisticated DTP systems will do this automatically. Some typefaces need looser or tighter spacing for easy reading.

Marks for proof correction

Instruction	Textual mark	Margin mark
Leave unchanged	‒ ‒ ‒ ‒ under characters to remain	⟨✓⟩
Insert material indicated in margin	⋏	New matter followed by ⋏
Delete	/ through character or ⊢⎯⊣ through words to be deleted	
Transpose characters or words	⎍⌐ between characters or words, numbered when necessary	⎍⌐
Set in or change to italic	⎯⎯ under characters to be set or changed	⎣ ⎪ ⎦
Set in or change to capital letters	≡ under characters to be set or changed	≡
Set in or change to small capital letters	= under characters to be set or changed	=
Set in or change to bold type	∿ under characters to be set or changed	∿
Change capitals to lower case	Encircle character(s) to be changed	≢
Change italic to upright type	Encircle character(s) to be changed	⎣⊤⎦
Insert space between characters	/ between characters affected	Y
Reduce space between characters	/ between characters affected	⊤

The space between words can also be changed. If there is not enough space, words will merge together, but too much and the reader can be distracted by the patterns of space created between the words (known as **rivers**). As a guide, the ideal space between each word should be just under a half the width of a lower-case 'o'.

Text is usually lined up to the left hand-margin ('ranged left') although it can be 'right-aligned' or centred as appropriate. Often the text seen in newspaper and magazine columns is 'justified' which means that it is automatically lined up to both edges of the column. This produces a neat shape to the text but can cause problems if the column is narrow. If, say, only two words fit onto the line a large space can be created when they are justified.

Text is usually lined up to the left hand-margin although it can be 'right-aligned' or centred as appropriate. Often the text seen in newspaper and magazine columns is **justified** which means that it is automatically lined up to both edges of the column. This produces a neat shape to the text but can cause problems if the column is narrow. If, say, only two words fit onto the line a large space can be created when they are justified.

Ranged left

Text is usually lined up to the left hand-margin although it can be 'right-aligned' or centred as appropriate. Often the text seen in newspaper and magazine columns is **justified** which means that it is automatically lined up to both edges of the column. This produces a neat shape to the text but can cause problems if the column is narrow. If, say, only two words fit onto the line a large space can be created when they are justified.

Centred

Text is usually lined up to the left hand-margin although it can be 'right-aligned' or centred as appropriate. Often the text seen in newspaper and magazine columns is **justified** which means that it is automatically lined up to both edges of the column. This produces a neat shape to the text but can cause problems if the column is narrow. If, say, only two words fit onto the line a large space can be created when they are justified.

Justified

As well as the space between words, line spacing can alter the visual character of text. A general guide to remember is that the line spacing should be greater than word spacing, and that the longer the lines are, the more space is needed between them.

Too little line spacing can result in letters touching and too much makes the text difficult to connect together visually.

The space between lines is known as 'leading' and is measured in point sizes. Just as kerning can be automatic or manually adjusted, so too can leading. Usually the point size for leading is 20% more than the point size for the lettering.

Paragraphs can be spaced either by indenting them or by leaving an extra line space between each one. At the beginning of the first paragraph a 'drop cap' (capital letter) may be used, as in this example:

Text is usually lined up to the left hand-margin although it can be 'right-aligned' or centred as appropriate. Often the text seen in newspaper and magazine columns is **justified** which means that it is automatically lined up to both edges of the column. This produces a neat shape to the text but can cause problems if the column is narrow.

Activity 7.11

1 Imagine you are working as a sub-editor and read through the passage below. Mark any corrections using the proof-correction marks shown on page 250.

> Friday 13th will find many poeple able to 'stand above' others, Confident in the knowledge that they have carried out. numerous bizarre rituals everyday since the last unlucky Friday.
>
> The word 'superstition' comes from the latin 'super' meaning above and 'stare' meaning to stand. Therefore, to 'stand above' refers to those who have avoided falling foul of any unpleasantries sent by fate.
>
> The 'bizarre rituals' refer to those all too familiar daily activities.
>
> avoiding walking under a ladder, desperately looking for a second magpie, **throwing** split salt over the left shoulder or not putting up and umbrella indoors.
>
> Not every one regards themselves as being supersstitious, of course; but some of these actions have become almost second nature and their original meaning long since forgotton, like saying 'Bless you' after a sneeze.

2 Now plan the design and layout of the passage to provide the maximum visual appeal for the reader. If you do not have the time to produce a final layout using DTP, write down instructions which show your intentions, i.e. font, point size, leading, etc.

Review questions

1 Choose two production roles involved in producing a graphical product. Describe these roles as if explaining them to someone else.
2 Why is detailed planning so important in the production process?
3 Suggest ways in which a journalist can find ideas for stories and features.

Element 7.3 Appraise a graphical product

This element looks at:
- How graphical products are promoted
- How graphical products are analysed

Promoting a graphical product

An exciting, new magazine for teenagers is in the shops today! But did you know? No matter how good a product is, if readers do not know about it before it is launched, it is doomed to fail. Even a free product may need promotion.

Promoting a product means informing the public about it, but this has to be done in a very carefully planned way. Planning a promotion must start as soon as the product idea has begun – in fact, it may well be discussed alongside the idea. Promotion does not apply only to new products. Consider all the advertisements there are on the television: the majority are for well-known products that are trying to increase their sales figures.

When you are planning a promotion, you need to gather as much information as possible. Knowledge about who buys or reads the product (or potential buyers and readers) and who the competitors are will help to build ideas for an approach to the promotion. Different products appeal to different groups of people, and they appeal in differing degrees – so the more information you have about your market, the more likely you are to succeed.

The marketing mix

Promotion is just one part of what is called the marketing mix for a product. The ingredients of the mix can be remembered by the 'Four P's':

- Product
- Price
- Place
- Promotion

Product

As we saw in Element 7.1, before you develop a new product, it is vital to spend time finding out what your target audience likes and dislikes so that you can make a product which will appeal to them. If the product is wrong it doesn't matter how good the promotion is: it will not sell. It is also vital that the people responsible for promoting a product know as much as possible about it, including its target audience. This will enable them to emphasise the product's good points (for example, high quality photographs) and play down the less good points (high cost compared to other photography magazines).

Price

The price of the product depends on its target audience and on the quality of the product. This is often a difficult balancing act: if the product is very expensive to produce, the price is likely to be higher, but it must not be so high that the target audience cannot afford to buy it.

Place

Where the product will be sold has a strong influence over the way it is promoted. If the outlet is a large supermarket chain, television might be the best way to reach all the potential customers of that store. On the other hand, if the retail outlet is a small local newsagents then posters in the shop window would be more appropriate.

Promotion

There are many different ways a product can be promoted. Again, a balancing act is needed to find the one that will promote the product most effectively within the budget available.

The importance of market research

We have seen that market research is vital in *developing* products. But it is also very important for people who are *promoting* products to find out information from the target audience. The people creating advertisements or sales promotions must try to get inside the head of the potential buyer or target audience. They need to know what information they will welcome and what form of persuasion they will respond to. Various market research techniques can be used, some of which are considered here.

Every publication should be produced with a well defined target audience in mind.

- **Usage and attitude studies** find out how many people use or purchase the product. This figure can be compared with groups of the population, so an advertiser can see how large the potential audience is and will know where to target the advertising.
- **Concept tests** find out how people will react to an advertising idea (or concept) so that advertisers have a better idea of the potential success of an advert. The advert is shown to a representative sample of people and their reaction is analysed.
- **Advertising pre-tests** are similar except that the advert is at a more finished stage at the time of testing.
- **Tests of finished adverts** are carried out on advertisements that are new.
- **Product tests** are used by market researchers to compare two or more products and get potential audiences to say what they think of them.
- **Observed behaviour** involves watching what people actually buy rather than what they *say* they will buy.
- **Consumer audits** are a quick and easy way to see how many products are purchased. Electronic scanners are used by retailers for stock control purposes but the information can prove very useful for advertisers.

Methods of promotion for graphical products

Advertising

This is a common method of promotion which includes advertising on television, radio and cinema commercials, on posters and hoardings, on the side of buses and vehicles, in printed media such as magazines or through the post by direct mail or 'fliers'.

Small businesses or people working on their own may choose to do their own advertising whereas larger firms may have their own marketing department or be able to afford to hire an advertising agency. Effective advertising should be able to:

- **Inform** you about the quality of a product
- **Persuade** you to buy the product
- **Convince** you of the product's quality

When there is little difference between products, advertising is vital as people need convincing that one product is better than another.

Once sufficient research has been carried out by the advertisers they should be able to see which type of advertisement is most suited to the promotion of their product. This can range from very expensive and technically advanced television advertising to printed leaflets pushed through letterboxes by hand.

As has already been mentioned, consideration must be given to the cost of the advertising, as a budget will have been set. Also the timescale involved must be taken into account. The promotion planning must begin with the initial idea for a new product, but if that product is an A4 newsletter which only takes two weeks to produce, the advertising must be ready in advance.

Legal issues affecting promotion

Just as the content of a graphical product must keep within the law, so too must the advertising. There are legal restrictions about what adverts can be used and where. For example, the Independent Television Commission (ITC) carefully regulates the number and content of commercials which appear on ITV and Channel 4.

As we saw in Chapter 1, advertising is not only governed by laws but also by 'codes of practice' set up by the advertisers themselves. These are described as 'self-imposed' rules and are contained in the British Code of Advertising Practice (BCAP) and British Code of Sales Promotion Practice (BCSPP).

The two bodies responsible for ensuring that the rules are followed are the Advertising Standards Authority (ASA) and the Committee of Advertising Practice. Whether the rules are law or self-imposed, their aim is the same – to ensure that all advertising is honest and fair.

Advertising must not make false or misleading claims about a product. To describe or show a magazine in an advert as being colour, glossy and full of photographs when in reality it is black and white and full of text, will anger many people. It is also misleading and inaccurate. Any advertising that does this will probably ensure the product has a very short life.

Public Relations (PR)

This is often thought of as being an extension of advertising, or even the same thing. In fact, PR is another form of promotion which may be regarded as a business communication tool. It uses different methods of communication to help companies and organisations market their products.

The channels of communication used by PR are similar to those of advertising. For example, PR may use editorial space in the media, brochures and pamphlets, visual designs such as logos and even face-to-face contact at conferences. The 'electronic media' (radio, television, cable) are probably the most commonly used communication channels for PR activity.

However, the difference between PR and advertising is that people in PR deal directly with journalists. They try to persuade them to write stories, articles or make broadcasts based on the information they provide. This information will be about the product or company being promoted.

Like advertising, PR has to be carefully planned and usually works on a long-term basis to influence people and persuade them to change their opinions. Using PR does not mean that a company will not use advertising to promote its product as well. Usually when the two work together they are part of a much larger marketing plan. PR is however expensive and is unlikely to be used by small, low-budget businesses.

PR is similar to advertising in that it must also take account of the target audience and consider other potential customers. The service may be provided by an agency, or large companies can carry out their own PR.

Sales promotion

This can be an effective way to increase sales, although usually only on a short-term basis. It is only over the last hundred years or so that the media have come to be so dominant in this area, in the form of the press, television and radio.

The aim of sales promotion is directly to promote sales. Typical methods include free gifts, money-off coupons or 'two-for-the-price-of-one' offers. Traditionally, sales promotion was considered to be a part of advertising. More recently it has come to be seen as an activity in its own right.

Planning a sales promotion

The stages of planning a sales promotion are similar to those used in planning a PR or advertising campaign. They include:

- Finding out about the product
- Finding out about the target audience
- Deciding on a suitable date for the promotion
- Deciding the best location for the promotion
- Studying the competition.

Sales promotions may be put into two categories:

Immediate	Delayed
Money-off with purchase	Mail-in offers
Free extra product	Competitions
Two-for-the-price-of-one	Money-off coupons
	Prize draws

Activity 7.12

1 Discuss all the methods of promotion that you have read about and decide which would be most suitable for promoting your student newspaper.
2 Justify your choice by explaining how you think it could promote your product effectively. Describe its advantages over the other methods.
3 Now make a rough plan to show how you could use that method to promote your student newspaper. Consider the following factors:

- Target audience
- Methods of distribution of product
- Timescale for promotion
- Technical skills needed to carry out promotion
- Cost considerations
- Constraints that may hinder the promotion

4 Write a report to show your planned method of promotion.

Analysing a graphical product

All products need to be appraised or analysed throughout the production process, and again when they have been completed. In this way the producer learns what works and what doesn't work. If something is not working, changes can be made to the product or to the type of promotion being used. If something is working well, other similar products can be developed.

A good analysis of a graphical product will look at:

- All the costs of production (money, people, equipment, advertising, etc.)
- Feedback from the target audience (e.g. about value for money, appeal, quality, etc.)
- Feasibility (is the effort of making it justified by the rewards in terms of size of readership or income generated?)

Analysis of cost

Measuring cost

Companies need to analyse the total cost of producing their products. Factors affecting the cost of a graphical product are likely to include:

- **Paper quality** This was mentioned in Element 7.1. Clearly, if better-quality paper is used such as a thick, glossy paper, the product price will increase
- The **printing method** chosen for the product affects the cost – some are much more expensive than others. Gravure is a costly method of printing so it is used to print glossy magazines which have a relatively high price. If **colour** is required this will also increase the cost.
- If a product is produced on a daily basis like a newspaper, it is likely to be cheaper to produce and buy than a monthly magazine. So the **frequency of the issue** is a further cost consideration.
- New graphical products, i.e. products that are at the launch stage, rely heavily on **promotion and advertising**. Readers need to be made aware of them and persuaded to buy. However, as we have already seen, even the most successful products continue to be promoted in order to attract readers away from rival products. Advertising of this kind can be expensive – particularly a television advert – so its cost must be allowed for in the sale price.

Measuring success

As well as analysing costs, the company must have ways of measuring how successful products are. Two important ways in which companies measure the success of graphical products are:

- **Size of the readership** This is the traditional measure of the success or otherwise of a graphical product. If the product is sold, more readers mean more money. Even if the product is given away free, the company can still benefit from an increased readership because the unit cost of producing one copy of the product go down as more copies are produced. Also, the bigger the readership, the easier it is likely to be to sell advertising space.
- **Advertising revenue** Companies need to take into account how much money they can make by selling advertising space. This can be a major source of income (or revenue) for the company producing a graphical product. In the case of a free product, it can be the only source of income. This can help to reduce production costs and increase profits.

Getting feedback

From the target audience

When analysing a graphical product the producer will want feedback on how it appealed to the consumer. The appeal of a product is made up of many different factors, including the look of the product, its style, its content, its values, its price and its overall quality.

- A reader's first reaction to a product is likely to have much to do with its **look**. The impact it has visually can be important, although this varies from product to product. A financial magazine will be more concerned about informing its readers, whereas a child's comic will want to be more eye-catching.
- The **style** of a product is another factor to be considered, and this is connected to many of the aspects mentioned above. The style may be determined by the quality of the writing, as well as the visual side, choice of font, layout, graphics, etc.
- **The content** of a publication can appeal in different ways. If it is supposed to inform the reader then the subjects covered and how they are delivered will be very important. If it is to entertain, then its success at this will form an essential part of its appeal.
- **The values or beliefs** that are portrayed in a graphical product can have an appeal for its audience. In the case of a newspaper it might be the political beliefs that appeal, or a magazine may attract readers by promoting environmentally-friendly values.
- Consciously or unconsciously, readers will also ask themselves whether a product seems to be good **value for money**– in other words, is it worth the cover price? If the reader feels it provides good value for money it will have greater appeal than a similar, more expensive product.

Taking all the aspects above into account can lead to an analysis of a product in terms of its **quality**. The quality of a product is a difficult thing to measure. A quality newspaper for one person could be regarded as rubbish by someone else. When analysing a graphical product that *you* make, it is worth finding out what readers feel about various aspects and perhaps asking them to give an overall grade for quality at the end.

Feedback from your peers

When appraising your own work it is also necessary to get feedback from your peers – i.e. your friends and people from your own age group. They can provide you with a different perspective or way of looking at the work you have done. Sometimes when you are close to your work, it is difficult to spot mistakes or think of improvements, and yet they may be obvious to someone else.

Conducting a survey

The most common way to find out what an audience thinks of a product is to carry out a **survey**. A questionnaire is an effective way to gain information from a survey but it does require careful preparation and planning. If you want to brush up your questionnaire-writing technique, turn to Chapter 1, page 37.

When conducting a survey it is often useful to divide the target audience into a variety of groups to see if different groups give different responses. Age is an obvious category into which readers can be placed. This can be done in a very broad way such as:

Category	Age range
Children	Under 12
Teenagers	13 – 19
Young adults	20 – 29
Adults	30+
Older people	65+

However, it is unusual for a graphical product to have such a wide-ranging audience. The target audience of a comic might be children under the age of five but a women's magazine might have a target audience of women aged 18–29. Remember that some people can be sensitive about giving away their age, so using age groups is a diplomatic way to get around this.

The target audience can also be classified by their gender. This can be very important, depending upon the product being appraised. For example, a motorbike magazine might want to find out how many of their readers are women. They could do this by getting the audience to tick a male/female box on the questionnaire.

Social class or 'socio-economic status' is often used during surveys in order to 'pigeonhole' people into categories according to their occupation, income and education. Although categorising people in this way is controversial, it is common for market researchers in the UK to use the following broad 'socio-economic grading system':

Grade	Occupation/status
A	Higher managerial, administrative or professional
B	Intermediate, managerial, administrative or professional
C1	Supervisory, clerical, junior administrative or professional
C2	Skilled manual workers
D	Semi-skilled and unskilled manual workers
E	State pensioners, widows, casual and lowest-grade workers

Rather than use these categories, most questionnaires ask respondents to give their occupation and tick a box denoting their broad 'income group'.

As Britain is made up of many different cultures, religions and beliefs, it may be useful to know someone's race when carrying out a survey. However, it is important to be very careful when deciding whether or not this information would be relevant. Once again, it can be a sensitive area.

The type of newspaper a person likes to read is said to show their 'reading preference' and this is another way in which market researchers can categorise people. There are many very different types of newspaper on the market, so someone who reads the *Financial Times* regularly may well have a different outlook on life from someone who reads the *Sun*. This information can be useful in helping to form a clearer picture of your audience.

Activity 7.13

Study a variety of graphical products, such as newsletters, magazines, comics, fanzines and newspapers. Decide who the reading audience might be by considering each of the following categories in turn:

– Age
– Gender
– Social class
– Race
– Reading preference

State your reasons for choosing each category.

Feasibility

Once a company has analysed the costs of producing a graphical product and the feedback from consumers, it will be able to decide whether it is feasible to produce it. As always, there is a balancing act to be done. It may be that the product is very well liked by consumers, but the costs are far too high so the company makes no profit. Or it may be that the costs are acceptable, and the consumers like the quality, but the price is too high. In this case, the company may decide to reduce the price. If a balance cannot be achieved, then the product is not feasible.

Review questions

1　Explain what is meant by the 'Four P's' in the marketing mix.
2　Describe the differences between advertising and PR.
3　Why is it important to analyse or appraise a graphical product? Explain how this could be done.

Assignment 7.1
Planning a college newsletter

This assignment provides evidence for **Element 7.1 Prepare a graphical product to an agreed brief** and the following key skills:

Communication: 2.1, 2.2
Information Technology: 2.1
Application of Numbers: 2.1, 2.2, 2.3

For this assignment you need to form teams of 4, 8, 12 or 16 (i.e. multiples of 4). Your brief is to plan an issue of your school or college newsletter. Within the team you must each be responsible for one A4 page. To improve the layout, two of you may wish to work together on an A3 page.

Your tutor has the final say if a decision cannot be reached or if ideas/expectations are unrealistic. Effectively, he/she will be acting as editor.

Each student should keep a **production log** and record the progress of the newsletter and their own personal input into the project.

Now work through the following steps:

1 Working as a team, decide upon the type of newsletter you aim to produce (e.g. should it be aimed at tutors? Parents? Prospective students? etc.) and how often it will be produced – weekly, termly, annually, etc.
2 Carry out some market research to identify your target audience (based on the type of product you have decided on in **1** above) and find out their requirements.
3 As a group, share the results of the market research and write down the aims of the newsletter (i.e. what is its purpose? What are you trying to provide?).
4 As a group, decide on the style and content of your newsletter.
5 Design the layout grids and the individual features of your newsletter. You could allocate different parts of this job to different team members, as long as the team is happy with the final results.
6 As a group, produce a costing sheet for the newsletter.

Assignment 7.2
Produce a college newsletter

This assignment provides evidence for **Element 7.2: Produce a graphical product** and the following key skills:

Communication: 2.1, 2.2, 2.3, 2.4

1 Using the plans you made in Assignment 7.1, you are now going to prduce your own student newsletter.
2 Roles will need to be allocated to everyone in the group and some roles may have to be doubled up. If you worked in a very small group on Assignment 7.1 you may need to combine with another group for this Assignment. The example below shows how the roles could be divided for a group of 12 students:

Writers	3 students
Editor	1 student, but also works as a writer
Sub-editors	2 students
Graphic designers	3 students
News editor	1 student, but also works as a writer
Features editor	1 student, but also works as a writer
Sport editor	1 student, but also works as a writer

In addition, there are optional roles of photographer and printer.

3 Follow the plans you made originally (they may need revising in the light of new information you have learned) and work through the production of your graphical product through to its publication. Keep notes in your production log of your contributions to the newspaper.

4 Write an evaluation of how the final product compares with the aims set out in your original plan.

5 You may wish to consider promoting your publication by organising a press launch. This is where members of the media (press, radio, television) are invited along to find out about a new product and in return they publicise the product through their media.

Assignment 7.3
Evaluate a college newsletter

This assignment provides evidence for **Element 7.3: Appraise a graphical product** and the following key skills:

Communication: 2.2, 2.4
Information Technology: 2.1, 2.2, 2.3
Application of Numbers: 2.1, 2.2, 2.3

1 Design a questionnaire for a small group (10) of your friends. The aim of the questionnaire is to test their reaction to your newsletter. Remember that this is for a group of your friends and it is supposed to help you to appraise or evaluate your newsletter. It might help to use a computer for designing the layout of the questionnaire. Carry out the survey and then analyse the results. Computer packages may help you to analyse and present your results more effectively – for example, using graphs, pie charts, etc.

2 Design a questionnaire and carry out a survey aimed at the target audience for your student newsletter. This should be a much larger group of people (25+). Analyse the results.

3 Evaluate your student newsletter in the light of the results of both surveys. Produce a detailed report suggesting ways in which it could be improved in the future. Outline any mistakes you feel may have been made and explain any problems you faced in its production.

4 Finally, write a report evaluating the methods/processes used when promoting your product. If you were able to carry out a press launch, evaluate its success and suggest ways it could be improved next time.

8 Photography

What is covered in this chapter

- Planning for a photographic assignment
- Choosing equipment
- Taking a photograph
- Processing the film
- Developing the print
- Presenting and reviewing a photograph

Your 'photography' file should contain the following items:
- A comprehensive plan for a photographic project, including requirement, equipment and location lists
- A contact sheet of a black and white film
- Five images, selected and cropped
- The images in presentation format
- A presentation report

Introduction

A photographer has to make many decisions which affect the look of the finished photograph. This chapter will guide you through the processes involved in planning photography, taking and developing pictures and presenting the finished product to a critical audience. Colour and black and white photography will be discussed in the planning and picture-taking stages. Emphasis will be placed on black and white photography in the processing and developing stages.

Element 8.1 Planning for a photographic assignment

Photography – the capturing of a single moment of time on a single frame of film – has many applications in the modern world. Some of the most common are fashion, news, advertising, commercial and artistic. A single photograph may fit more than one application. For example, a picture taken at a fashion show for a fashion publication may become a news photograph if something remarkable or newsworthy happens to the model or the designer that day.

The key factors to consider when looking at a picture are:

- Use of light
- Colour
- Use of film
- Subject matter
- Composition

Each time a picture is taken, the photographer has to make decisions in all these areas. Some are made for technical reasons, others are for purely creative reasons. All have an impact on the picture produced.

In this chapter you will learn about the technical and creative decisions that a photographer has to make, and how those decisions affect the picture.

Activity 8.1

1 In small groups look through a newspaper and a magazine. Study the photographs and discuss the differences in:
   - The type of photographs
   - Where they appear in the publication
2 Are the photographs in colour or black and white? Which has more impact?
3 Are photographs posed or natural? Why?

The photographic brief

A photographer is often given a **brief** by a client who will have a specific need or purpose in mind. The brief will include some or all of the following information:

- Budget
- Timescale
- The purpose for which the photograph(s) will be used
- The target audience

Budget

A photographer may be given a specific budget, or they may agree a price with the client. A price is a fixed amount of money to be paid for the job. It is based on the number of days' work involved, the difficulty of the assignment and the distance the photographer has to travel. A fashion shoot for a week in Morocco will cost a lot more than half a day in Birmingham for a London photographer.

A **budget** is an amount of money that the client has available to pay for the commission. Often the photographer may be unsure of the exact costs involved. If a budget is stated, the photographer must inform the client if the cost is likely to exceed it. The photographer must also try to complete the commission for the amount of money stated or less. A budget is more usual if the photographs are part of an ongoing or large project.

Timescale

When commissioning a photographer, the client will normally give a deadline for delivery of the pictures. The photographer will often be consulted about the delivery date, especially if s/he is heavily in demand or the pictures are complicated to take.

A photographer is often one link in a chain of people that includes graphic designers, printers, copywriters, multimedia designers and so on, all working on the same project. This means that the photographer has to know the deadlines of the other people in the chain. If there is a delay or problem, this will affect other people and may hold up publication.

Timescales are not, generally, flexible. However, if there are factors beyond the control of the photographer, such as bad weather on a location, most clients will understand and try to extend the deadline.

Purpose and use

Photographers not only need to know *what* to photograph, but also *how*. In order to use their technical and creative judgement, they need to know the purpose and use of the pictures. For example, a stately home may be photographed in several ways: if the photographs are for an architectural magazine, the photographer may wish to concentrate on the distinctive features of the building, but if they are for a magazine for wealthy landowners, it may be more appropriate to show the building in relation to the gardens and surrounding landscape.

The 'purpose' is the aim behind the photographs and the 'use' is how that purpose will be achieved. For instance, a purpose might be to sell, promote, record or illustrate, whereas a use might be print, posters, multimedia or packaging.

The same subject can be photographed in many different ways depending on the brief

The purpose and use can often be summed up in a few words. For example: 'Photographs to advertise clothing for professional women aged twenty-five to forty. To be published in a national colour glossy magazine.'

Target audience

The client who commissions the photographs will nearly always have a specific target audience in mind. The **target audience** is the group of people that will eventually see the photographs. Again, the client can usually indicate the nature of the audience in a few words – for example, 'business shareholders' or 'night clubbers under 24'. This information will influence the colour, grain and style of the photographs taken.

As we saw earlier, the photographer is usually part of a chain of people. To make sure the pictures are right for the target audience, the photographer will often ask for help from the designer or printer in charge of the finished design.

Activity 8.2

1 Write a photographic brief for a health campaign on teenage pregnancy. Include full details of timescale, the purpose and use of the photographs, the target audience and how the pictures will be distributed. Make sure that the photographer has all the information they need to take the pictures that you want.
2 Think about the requirements of the brief and try to decide on a reasonable budget for the photography. Write a summary to justify the amount of money in the budget.

Choosing materials and equipment

Photographers today can choose from a huge range of photographic equipment and different types of camera. At some stage every photographer has to decide on the equipment that they need to buy. They will use this to take most of the pictures throughout their career. If they are lucky enough to have a large studio and stock of equipment, they will have to decide which materials, camera, tripod, lighting equipment and tools they need for a specific job.

Choosing film

Choosing which type of film to use is one of the most important decisions on any photographic assignment. Sometimes this is specified in the brief. A newspaper, for instance, may require a black and white film, whereas a magazine might prefer colour. Other times you can decide for yourself. It is not as simple as just colour or black and white. You will also have to decide whether to use slide or print film, and what colour balance, format, speed and grain size the film should be.

1 Print film and slide

Film comes in two types, slide film and print film. Print film captures the image as a negative. For instance, white becomes black and orange becomes green. This kind of film is known as 'negative film'. Slide film captures the image in the original colours. It is known as 'reversal film', because it is the reverse of the more common print film.

2 Colour balance

The colour balance of the film tells you whether the film has been designed to be used in artificial light or daylight. Daylight is slightly blue and artificial and tungsten light is slightly orange. You can see the differences when photographing white. Tungsten-balanced film has been compensated to accept that pure white under artificial light – which would normally be orange – is white.

If you have already loaded a daylight-balanced film and would like to take a picture in artificial light, it is possible to use a correcting **filter**. Colour balance problems only apply to slide film in 35 mm format; colour negative films are universally balanced.

3 Format

The most common format is 35 mm. Other formats are medium (5 x 4) and large (6 x 7). Medium and large format cameras are very expensive, and make use of more costly film. As 35 mm film is much cheaper, this is the format you should use for the activities in this chapter. Digital cameras are now available which store pictures in memory or on floppy disk, until it can be downloaded to a computer. Whilst this is a good way of experimenting cheaply, the size of the digital pixels is much larger than the grain of conventional film and the difference can be seen in the quality of the end result.

4 Film speed

Film speed indicates how sensitive the film is to light and is expressed in ASA. The higher the ASA number, the more sensitive the film. For instance 500 ASA – fast film – may be used at night. Slow film such as 64 ASA is best used on a very bright day or in a well-lit studio.

Again, the purpose and use of the pictures, the location and the character of light are all factors which have a bearing on your choice of film speed. Photojournalists prefer to use a fast film because it will do well under low light conditions. Studio photographers prefer a slower film because the chemical grain is much smaller than fast film and so the quality is higher.

5 Film grain

This depends on the size of the chemical crystals or grain on the film. The faster the film speed, the coarser the grain. This is an effect that some photographers deliberately use for artistic reasons. There are several ways of achieving 'grain-iness' (the correct term is **high granularity**). The first method is to choose a fast film speed with large crystals and the second is to **push** the film during the processing stage, i.e. extend the development time.

Equipment

Choosing a camera

The choice of camera depends on the format of film, the size and range of lenses available and to some extent on your personal preference. As we saw earlier, there are several different formats of film available, each requiring a different camera. For most people, 35 mm cameras are the most readily available and affordable.

When choosing a camera body, you need to look at the type of viewfinder and functions that it has. There are several types of viewfinders, the two most common being the **reflex** viewfinder and the **parallax** viewer. The reflex allows you to look through the lens of the camera, using a set of mirrors. You can set the focus, aperture and zoom using your eye to judge the result. A camera body with this type of viewer and a single lens is known as a 'single lens reflex' or 'SLR'.

Parallax viewers are more usually associated with snapshot cameras. They allow you to frame the picture, but not change any of the lens settings by eye. In fact, most snapshot cameras only have a pre-set lens.

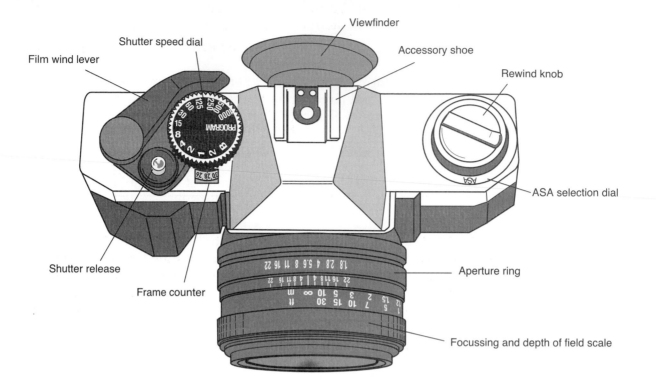

A typical SLR camera and lens

SLR cameras can have a number of different functions and features, including the following:

- Adjustable shutter speed
- ASA setting
- Frame counter
- Flash mounting
- Self-timer
- Built-in light meter

All these functions have important uses in taking a picture that will be discussed later.

The lens

Photographers often carry a range of different lenses. This gives them a choice of distortion, **angles of view** and **perspective effects**. Lenses are referred to by their **focal length**, e.g. 24 mm, and by the 'family' to which they belong, e.g. wide angle, telephoto, etc. The angle of view is dependent on the focal length of the lens. A short focal length gives a wide angle of view and a long focal length gives a narrow angle of view. There are literally hundreds of lenses and accessories for lenses – far too many to cover in this chapter – but the table below shows the most common types.

Focal length	Function
50 mm	This lens is considered as the normal lens. It has an angle of view of 46 degrees, comparable to the human eye. It has little perspective distortion.
35 mm	This lens has angle of view of 62 degrees and little perspective distortion. This allows the photographer to get closer to the subject without losing anything from the frame.
35–70 mm zoom	This is a good lens for a variety of uses. The focal length incorporates the range covered by other lenses. It is often a good choice for a photographer who can afford only one lens. The only problem is that it is not so good in low light conditions.

Activity 8.3

Arrange two objects in front of a camera. One should be further away from you than the other. If you have a range of lenses, try each lens on the camera. Work out what the effect of different focal lengths is on the relative distance of the objects (the perspective) and the framing. If you do not have a range of lenses, try this exercise with a zoom lens using four different settings for the zoom.

The tripod

Some photographers have several tripods – short, tall and 'special'. For general use, it is sufficient to have a single good-quality aluminium tripod with sturdy locking devices on the telescopic legs.

It is a good idea to use a tripod whenever possible, especially in low light conditions when exposures are likely to be longer. On these occasions a cable release should also be used. A tripod will reduce the amount of camera movement when taking a picture, and this will give clearer pictures.

A tripod can often be bought in two parts, the head and the legs. The tripod head must be able to **pan and tilt**, so that the photographer can point the camera in the required direction. In order to make sure the camera is level on uneven ground, some tripods have adjustable heads with a built-in spirit level. These are very expensive, but many photographers feel the investment is worthwhile. A good tripod, well looked after, can last a lifetime.

Activity 8.4

Using a camera and a tripod, try to frame the following pictures:
- A portrait-orientation picture, with the short sides of the frame at the top and bottom, on a sloping floor
- A forty-five degree angle on a flat floor
- A picture looking straight down on top of an object

Lighting

There are several approaches to lighting depending on the location and type of photograph being taken. If it is outdoors during the day there may be no need for artificial light, but there may be a need for reflectors or screens. Reflectors are usually white, gold or silver. Their function is to bounce light around and direct it where it is needed. They can be used to soften shadows or give a warm colour to a person's face.

If you are working in a studio or low-light conditions you may find you need flash or tungsten light. Flash is a very powerful light source triggered automatically by the camera at the instant the shutter is opened. The most basic type of flash sits on top of the camera and can be angled to bounce light around the room. A more sophisticated arrangement can involve several flashes, mounted on lighting stands, all connected to the camera.

For certain situations, tungsten lighting can often offer a better solution. Professional tungsten lights range from 650 watts up to several kilowatts. In a studio it is possible to use floodlights for general lighting and smaller spotlights to provide highlights. Tungsten lights, unlike flash, are on all the time. Sometimes this makes it easier to set up a shot or take photographs and video pictures.

Filters and **scrims** are also used with artificial light. A filter, or 'gel', is a piece of coloured plastic that colours the light entering the lens. There are hundreds of colours available, but the most useful are corrective colours. For example, daylight blue will correct tungsten light to a daylight colour temperature. Scrims are pieces of material like tracing paper which are fitted in front of a light to cut down or soften the light.

Activity 8.5

1 Arrange two light sources of equal intensity so that they shine on to a blank white wall. Cover one light with a piece of scrim or tracing paper. Be careful not to touch the light bulb with your hands or the paper. What effect does the scrim have?
2 Put another piece of scrim in front of the lamp. What effect does this have?
3 Ask someone to stand in front of the lights and repeat this activity from the start. Is their face more clearly defined with or without the scrim?

Tools and accessories

Apart from the items listed above, photographers often carry a variety of tools and accessories, including lens cleaning tissue, a blower brush for cleaning inside the camera, possibly a hand-held **light meter**, clothes pegs, grey cards and lens filters. Most of these are self-explanatory and later in the chapter it will be clear how they are used. As modern SLRs have built-in light meters, a separate external light-meter is not strictly necessary. However, many professional photographers also use a hand-held light meter to ensure more accurate readings.

Photographers are also expected to supply backdrop materials both for studio and in some cases for location work. In a studio they may have a permanent arrangement called an 'infinity cove'. This is a piece of white or black material that reaches from the floor to either the ceiling or a high frame. The way that it drapes, in a concave curve, creates a backdrop with no corners. This means that it can be lit with no shadows and gives the effect of an infinite space behind the subject. On location, it is sometimes useful to have a small, portable, infinity cove for photographing small objects.

Some photographers also carry a white and/or black sheet with them as a universal background. Sometimes the client might arrange a more complex background with the photographer. It is also possible to use graduated coloured backgrounds that go from blue to white, red to white, green to white, and so on.

Processing materials

Film processing is covered more fully on pages 279-283. All that you need should be available in a properly equipped darkroom. The main materials that you need are chemicals and papers. The chemicals are black and white developer and fixer. The paper is light-sensitive silver-based printing paper.

Researching the brief

Before taking the photograph it is important to prepare thoroughly. You must make sure that the correct equipment is chosen and available. Check, also, that the location is suitable and the subjects – whether people or objects – are available to be photographed.

The location

If possible, you should visit the location before designing the photograph and make notes on the power supplies and other facilities that you will need. If you are photographing a model, you may need an area in which they can change or apply make-up. You should already have an idea about how you want to take the picture. Visiting the location helps you to take the picture in the way you want. You may also find that visiting the location will spark new ideas.

At the location you should also check the lighting conditions. Is it daylight, fluorescent or tungsten light? Mixed light sources are covered later in the chapter, but a single light source is much to be preferred. Take a light meter, if possible, when scouting a location, to measure the relative strengths of the light.

The studio

If the photographs are to be shot in a studio, most of the information you need can probably be obtained over the telephone. Most studios will also be happy for you to visit, but you will need to telephone in advance to arrange a convenient time. Points to check include:

- Availability of backdrop material and infinity coves of the right size
- The dimensions of the floor
- The type of light source (daylight or tungsten)
- Access (can you fit the object that you are photographing through the doors?)
- Other facilities, such as changing rooms, refreshments and toilets

The subject

If you are photographing objects rather than people you will have more freedom to be experimental. Objects do not mind being positioned or altered and they have eternal patience. People often do not like being told what to do, what to wear and waiting around while the camera is adjusted.

Professional models or actors are more used to 'art direction' than most human subjects. They are more used to the discomfort and boredom, but it often depends on the personality of the person. If you find that there are two or three models that you can easily work with, try to use them as often as possible.

Correct choice of camera angle is essential to a successful shot

General planning issues

If you are sure that the right people will be in the right place at the right time then most of the planning is done. Sometimes you are unable to complete all the photographs needed within the time span arranged. If this happens, you should always have a 'fall-back' plan. Some problems can be predicted as you get closer to the time of the shoot. Always check the weather report in advance, as there is no point in taking photos outside if it is raining and overcast.

If the photograph you plan to take is technically difficult, it may be worth trying a 'dummy run'. This will allow you to set up much more easily on the day and will help you to discover any pitfalls in advance. During a mock-up it is wise to take notes, especially if you are using complicated equipment.

Health and safety

Part of the purpose of any research process is to identify health and safety hazards. Your research should highlight potential problems, such as electrical cabling, excessive heat from lighting and dangerous chemicals. If you know the dangers, you can take steps to reduce them. You should also make other members of the team aware of the dangers, so that everyone can act with care.

Review questions

1 Give two reasons for setting a timescale with a client.
2 What is meant by the 'purpose' of a photograph?
3 What is meant by 'daylight balance'?
4 In what circumstances might you use scrim?
5 In what circumstances might you use a gold or silver reflector?
6 How will the target audience influence a photograph?
7 What is meant by film speed?
8 Why do some photographers use a separate light meter ?
9 How are different types of lenses measured?
10 What does 'SLR' mean and how does it work?

Element 8.2 Create photographs for a given brief

There are two distinct stages to creating a photographic image:
- Taking the picture
- Developing the image

Many people choose to specialise in one of these two areas as they are equally complex. It is useful for a photographer to understand the developing and printing process as many effects can be created in the darkroom. A developer and printer should also understand the photographic process so that they can interpret the pictures and crop them as needed.

Portrait showing the use of three-point lighting (see page 274)

Taking the picture

In order to take a successful photograph, you need to consider a number of different factors. These include the use of light and colour, framing and composition, exposure levels, background, focus and correct use of lenses. The right decision for these points are not the only keys to making a good image. Care of the film and cleaning of equipment also contribute to the quality of the final result.

Light and colour

Light adds mood and texture to a flat picture. By carefully drawing attention to certain shapes or lines within the picture, a photographer can give a picture a three-dimensional feel. The shapes made by the light itself are also important – for example, vertical bars of light can give the feeling that the subject is imprisoned.

Colour can also add to the mood. Blue light can be used to indicate night time; oranges and yellows add warmth; white symbolises purity; black creates a sense of drama. Different cultures attach other meanings to colours: in Islamic countries, for example, green is a holy colour, while in Japan white is associated with death. When deciding colour, it is important to consider the target audience.

The quality and availability of natural light is a vital factor. A sunny day could be ideal if you are trying to photograph bottles of suntan lotion. News photographers often have little choice about lighting conditions. The pictures that they take have to use either natural light or flash. This is the only way that they can be reasonably sure of getting a good exposure.

Single and three-point lighting

Whichever light source you use, there are two basic lighting arrangements. The first is single-source lighting, where the light comes from a single point and is usually greatly dispersed and very bright. A single source gives good coverage of light to all of the picture. If you correctly frame the picture, the shadows will pick out the forms.

The second is known as three-point lighting. Three-point lighting has a key light, hair light and a fill light. The key light is stronger than the rest and is used to emphasise the main features of the picture. These can be the logo of the product or the best side of a model's face. The fill light is a less powerful light used to soften the shadows created by the key light. The **hair light** is used to separate the foreground from the background. It is called a hair light because it is traditionally used to light a person's hair from behind. However, any object can be illuminated in this way.

It is not necessary to use three lights all the time – often a reflector can replace the fill light or the hair light. Sometimes a hair light is not necessary at all, as the background may reflect light into the hair from behind.

Varying the amounts of light from the three different sources can create different effects. A strong hair light can lend a very dramatic edge to a picture and a very soft fill light can make it seem sinister.

Always avoid mixed light sources. A picture taken on tungsten-balanced film, with tungsten light as the main source, will be ruined if there is daylight or fluorescent light on the subject. Daylight creates a blue shadow and fluorescent light creates a green shadow. Similarly, tungsten and fluorescent light can ruin daylight-balanced film, since tungsten gives an orange shadow.

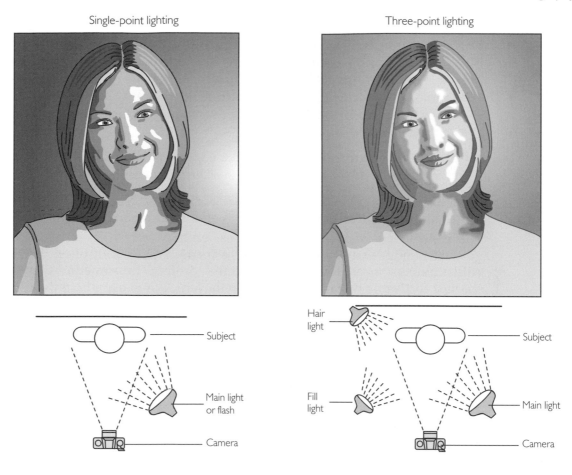

Single-point lighting

Three-point lighting

Subject

Main light
or flash

Camera

Hair
light

Fill
light

Subject

Main light

Camera

Activity 8.6

1 Arrange five objects on a table-top. Using three light sources only, light the objects so that they clearly define all the objects.
2 Adjust the lighting so that one object is the obvious subject of the composition.

Subject matter and composition

A photojournalist or commercial photographer may not have very much choice of subject matter, but they often have quite a free choice in how to compose the shot. Composition is the art of placing all the elements in the frame to make the picture look as pleasing as possible to the eye. A photographer considers the relative positions of the elements within the picture to each other and to the outer edge of the picture. This is called 'framing'.

Framing a picture means deciding what is left in and what is discarded, where the centre of attention should be and how close the camera is to the subject matter. If you are taking a picture in which you can change the camera angle, try walking around the subject whilst looking through the viewfinder. You may find that there is a better angle to shoot from.

Consider, also, the relative focus on each element in the picture. Camera lenses only have a small focusable area, known as **depth of field**, and the closer the subject matter, the smaller the area becomes. The aperture of the lens will also affect the depth of field (see **Focus and lenses**, page 276).

Activity 8.7

1 Using a camera and a tripod, frame a picture of a still life in your viewfinder. You will not be taking the picture, so lighting is not necessary. However, if you want to experiment, this might be a good opportunity. The still life that you choose could be a fruit bowl or a desktop. There should be no more than four or five objects. Arrange them, paying attention to the edge of frame and focus, until you are happy with the composition.

2 Get someone else to look at your composition in the viewfinder and swap ideas and criticisms. Try the exercise again with different subject matter.

Focus and lenses

The camera lens has several functions, each of which is controlled by a graduated ring. The primary function is **focus**. This is controlled by the ring with numbers measured in either metres or feet, or sometimes both. The shortest **focusable distance** depends on the lens, but is usually in the region of 0.4 to 1 metre. The furthest focusable distance is usually infinity.

The next function is the **aperture**, which contributes towards exposure control. The aperture ring is marked in numbers ranging from 1.4, 2.8 or 3.5 to 22. These numbers are called 'f-stop' numbers and correspond to the numbers given by a light meter. High numbers correspond to high light levels and low numbers correspond to lower light levels. The aperture setting affects the depth of field of the lens. The higher the number, the smaller the aperture. A small aperture has an optical effect and acts like another lens which extends the area in focus, the depth of field. The depth of field will affect how you balance the shutter speed with the aperture size and keep the necessary subject matter in focus.

The last function is only available on zoom lenses, where the focal length is variable. This function, known as 'zoom', alters the angle of view of the lens and, consequently, the perceived size of the image in the frame. If you have a choice of angles of view, you have more choice when composing your picture. Something as simple as taking a picture, then zooming out and taking it again can give you two strikingly different photographs. The numbers marked on this ring are the key focal lengths, such as 35, 50 and 70.

The distance between objects in the foreground and the background becomes more compressed as focal length increases. This optical effect, also known as perspective distortion, is sometimes useful if you want to photograph two people next to each other when in fact they are some distance apart.

Exposure

A simplistic way of thinking about exposure is that this is how light or dark a picture is. However, it is slightly more complex than this. Getting the correct exposure means achieving the right balance between available light, the shutter speed, the speed of the film and the aperture setting.

The difficulty arises because of the choice available. The selection of the film often depends on the preference of the photographer. A slower speed gives much better quality but needs more light. A higher speed is easier to light, but has a lower-quality image. Most photographers usually use a film between 64 ASA and 400 ASA. Generally a film within the range 100 ASA to 200 ASA has the correct flexibility for most needs.

The available light depends on whether or not you decide to use artificial light. If you are photographing a news event or something that happens quickly, such as motor racing, you cannot spend time arranging lights. A simple flash or plain daylight will set the limit of available light.

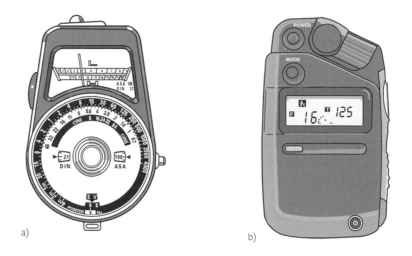

a)   b)

(a) An analogue and (b) a digital light meter

Taking exposure readings

When you have programmed your light meter with the speed of film that you are using you must take some readings. If you are using a **TTL light meter**, i.e. one built-in to the camera which measures the light entering the lens, you should point the camera at the subject and read from the meter. Move the camera slightly and take another reading. If you are getting significantly varying readings from different parts of the subject, you may have 'hot-spots' or patches of extreme light. Try to work out which light is causing the problem and put some scrim on it.

If you are using a hand-held light meter, you can build up a better idea of how to expose the picture. Hand-held light meters allow you to take both reflected light readings and incident or direct light readings.

Taking a reflected light reading is similar to a TTL light reading – you simply point the photo-electric cell of the meter towards the subject from the camera lens. This will measure the light entering the camera.

The direct light reading is a little more complex. A light meter is supplied with a white coloured piece of plastic, either dome or saucer-shaped, called an 'inver-cone'. When it is fitted to the photo-electric cell on the light meter, you can measure the light falling in a certain area. Hold the light meter as close to the place you want to measure as possible. Point the inver-cone towards the camera lens and take a reading. In a particular set-up you may have several different values for light, as you may want to make some parts darker than others.

While you are taking readings, you should be constantly adjusting the balance between shutter speed and aperture until you reach the best balance. If you have a short shutter speed, you will get a crisp, clear picture. This is because the camera will have little chance to move whilst the shutter is open.

Any movement by the camera will blur the image. Overall, the shorter the shutter speed, the better the image, but there are circumstances in which you may have no choice about shutter speed. If you are photographing an event involving fast-moving action, such as car racing or show-jumping, you will need a fast shutter speed. Conversely, if you are taking a night-time picture of a street with trailing car lights, you will need a long exposure.

If you have taken meter readings but still find it hard to decide on the correct exposure, a sensible precaution is to 'bracket the stops'. Take the picture once, then take it again, twice, using the aperture settings on either side of the one that you first used. This method means that you can be reasonably sure that you will get the picture that you want.

You should attempt to keep the shutter speed as fast as possible, but you also need to have the correct depth of field. This may mean that you need a small aperture, which also means that there is less light reaching the film.

Experience and experimentation will usually give you the results that you want.

Activity 8.8

Use a light meter, TTL or hand-held, to decide a correct shutter speed and aperture setting for the following scenarios:

a A class portrait, outside in daylight, using 100 ASA film

b A leaf falling in daylight, using 400 ASA film

c A person standing four feet in front of a painting, with both in focus. To be taken inside, using 100 ASA film and the available light

d A person two feet in front of a painting, with only the person in focus, to be taken inside, using 100 ASA film

Other considerations

There are several tasks that need to be done before you can take a picture. The first is cleaning the camera. Any dirt inside the camera body or on the lens will leave a shadow on the film. A camera cleaning kit should include a soft brush or a blower brush (one with a squeezable bulb on the end) and lens tissues. You should clean inside the camera every time that you load a new film. This will remove tiny flakes of film base that shed from the film strip as it passes through the camera. Also, remove the lens and carefully clean the mirror and inside the camera body. Handle this area with extreme care, it is very easy to damage the mirror or dislodge the mechanism. Clean both ends of the lens with the tissue and replace it as quickly as possible to stop dust landing on the cleaned surfaces. Your camera should have a lens cap; make sure that you use it whenever you are not using the camera. You should clean the front of the lens during photography or when using a camera that already has a roll of film loaded. Lastly, you should clean the eyepiece to help you focus accurately.

Make sure that you properly anchor the tripod. Smaller tripods are often very lightweight and it helps if you can make them heavier. A good trick is to hang a sandbag or bag of stones from the centre of the tripod. This will cut down any movement.

Film storage

Finally, make sure that you look after your film properly. Film is best kept in a refrigerator and taken out a couple of hours before it is used. Do not expose it to heat or direct light – even the back of a car on a sunny day will ruin it. Whenever you have finished a roll of film, place it in a plastic film container. Mark the container with something that tells you which roll of film is inside (a number will do) and that it is exposed. This should stop your hard work accidentally going to waste.

Activity 8.9

1 Imagine that you run your own photographic studio. Your local Borough Council has asked you to take some photographs for the Economic Development Unit. The pictures are for a brochure to encourage large companies to come into the area and set up factories.

   The Council want you to take pictures of ten local businesses, showing how successful they are. They also want the pictures to show how good location has played a part in the growth of the companies.

   You decide to take two approaches. The first is to take pictures of the buildings of the businesses both from the inside and out. The second is to take pictures of the Managing Directors of the companies, to be placed alongside 'testimonial'-style text.

   a Which equipment should you use for each approach?

   b Think about the approach that you have taken. Briefly discuss the difference between the two approaches, both in terms of impact on the audience and in terms of creativity.

   – In your opinion, which is more appropriate? Why?
   – How would you convince the client that your favoured approach is correct?
   – Sketch two pictures from each approach. Show on your sketches how you would use light, colour and content. Think about all aspects of each composition. How would you convey success and authority?

2 Although you originally planned to take the pictures in the summer, you now find that you are unable to take the pictures until late October. Can you suggest which photographs this will affect, and how you might get round the problem?

   Can you think of another approach? Use all the information given to come up with an idea that the Borough Council would be happy with. In your answer explain, with sketches, how your idea will work and why it will appeal to:

   – The Borough Council
   – The target audience

Developing and printing the image

Most of the activities described in this section take place in a darkroom. The material covered includes basic steps of black and white film processing and printing, but not colour work, which is much more complicated. The equipment required in this section should be available in your school or college darkroom, but you may have to pay for consumable materials, such as chemicals and paper.

The darkroom

The darkroom should be separated into two distinct areas, dry and wet. This division will help you to find the objects that you need in the dark and keeps everything safe and organized. If it is not possible to have separate wet and dry benches, you should divide the areas with a partition. This will stop splashes from the wet area landing on any of the 'dry' equipment.

The dry area is for electrical equipment, such as safelights and enlarger. Besides this, you should have a ruler, scissors, notepad, pen, tape and an exposure timer. Another useful, but not essential, object is a rotary trimmer. If you have access to one of these, it will save time when you are trimming your final print. It is a good idea to have somewhere to store the photographic paper off the bench top, but within easy reach.

The wet area is the processing area. You will need:

- A sink with running water
- Measuring jugs
- A thermometer
- A film processing tank
- Three developing trays
- A timer
- Plastic tongs
- Storage for the chemicals
- Somewhere to dry the film and prints

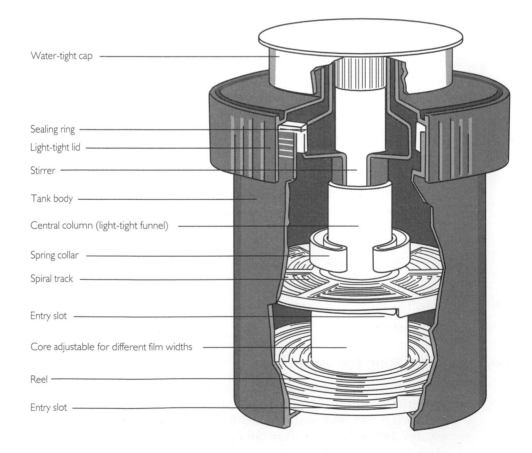

A processing tank and spiral

You must remember that you will be working with dangerous chemicals, so you may want to wear rubber gloves. Another useful precaution is to colour-code the trays and tongs, so that the chemicals do not contaminate each other. (Remember that the colour coding must be clear in safelight). Similarly, you must wash your measuring jugs or cylinders after you have put chemicals in them. If you do not, you may end up neutralising one chemical with another. Do not measure chemicals in anything that may be used for food production.

Always remember to wash your hands after you have been working in the darkroom, even if you have not been handling the chemicals. There should be no eating or drinking in the darkroom.

Processing black and white film

There are several stages to the processing operation:
- Loading the film
- Preparing the chemicals
- Developing the film
- Rinsing
- Fixing
- Washing and drying

All these stages except the first can be completed in normal light. Loading the film into the processing tank, however, must take place in total darkness.

Loading the film

The film processing tank should contain a spiral-shaped spool on which to load the film. These come in two basic types: centre-loading stainless steel and the self-loading plastic spiral. The self-loading type are the easiest to use. In darkness, remove the film from the canister (a bottle opener is useful here) and trim the end of the film between the sprocket holes. Next, place the trimmed end into the retaining lugs at the start of the spiral – you should feel it catch when it is properly positioned. Wind the film onto the spiral by turning the sides alternately back and forth. If the film sticks, pull it out a bit and try winding again. Do not try to force it, as you may damage the film permanently.

The centre loading spiral is a little more tricky. Remove the film from the canister and trim as previously mentioned. Gently arch the film between the finger and thumb and slide the end of the film into the clip in the centre of the spiral. Wind the film onto the spiral, being careful not to damage the edges. When you have finished winding either spiral, you should cut off the centre spool of the film canister. Drop the spiral into the processing tank and assemble according to the manufacturer's instructions.

This entire stage, right up to tightening the lid on the processing tank, should take place in complete darkness. A sensible precaution is to practise a few times in daylight, using an old roll of film. When you have mastered the technique, try again in the dark with the old roll. Lay out all the tools and pieces that you need before you switch the lights out.

If anything goes wrong and you need to take a break, have a light-proof bag (a dark bag) at the ready. You can seal it up, at whatever state you are in, before opening the door or turning on the lights.

Mixing chemicals

The next stage is to mix the chemicals. The main chemicals that you will need are the developer and fixer. You may also wish to use a stop-bath, although a thorough wash with tap water between developing and fixing the film has much the same effect.

Loading the film

Step 1: Remove film from cassette

If the end of the film is visible, gently pull the film out until the full width is reached. Cut the film with scissors between a pair of perforations. (This step can be done in the light). In the dark, open the cassette by pushing the cap off with your thumbs or use a cassette opener. If the tongue has been wound inside, open the cassette and cut the film by feel.

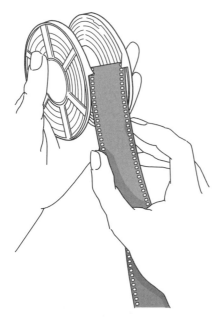

Step 2: Feed film onto spool

Hold the reel so that the entry slots face towards you. Slip the end of the film into the slots and carefully push it or pull the end into the reel until you feel resistance, taking care that the film does not get creased.

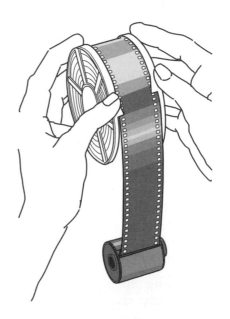

Step 3: Wind on

Rotate each half of the reel alternately back and forth and the film will feed automatically into the tracks on the reel. If it jams, don't use force; you may tear the film. Remove the film from the reel and start again.

There are several different types of developer available and each has slightly different effects and limitations. Before experimenting with the more specialist developers, it is best to use a universal developer. This is suitable for all black and white films and can be used for prints as well. Whichever developer you use, you should always follow the manufacturer's instructions on how to mix, store and use the chemicals. When you have made up all the solutions that you are going to need, you warm them to the temperature shown in the instructions. Do this by placing them in a warm water bath, allowing the temperature to increase and level out. Measure the temperature of the chemicals with a clean thermometer.

Stand the processing tank in the water bath for a few moments before you add the developer. This will help the developer to maintain a constant temperature in the tank. Remove the top lid from the tank and pour the correct quantity of developer into the tank. Try to pour the solution quickly but smoothly, as air bubbles will cause the chemicals to react unevenly with the film.

Developing the film

Start the timer, then replace the lid. Tap the tank firmly on the bench to dislodge any air bubbles. Shake the tank gently or turn it over whilst the film is developing. Check the recommended development time in the manufacturer's instructions and start to pour the developer away ten seconds before the end of this time. The chemicals will continue to react until a stop-bath is added. Add the stop solution the moment the tank is empty and shake gently for a minute. Pour the stop solution down the sink and add the fixer; start timing again.

Again, tap the tank firmly on the bench to dislodge any bubbles, then agitate. Agitating should continue for the first 30 seconds. Then you should agitate the tank every half minute after that. When you have reached the end of the manufacturers' recommended fixing time, you should pour the fixer into a storage container. Fixer can be used several times before it becomes exhausted.

Washing the film

Remove the top of the tank so that you can see the spiral. Stand the tank in the sink and turn on the water. If there is a hose fitted, put the end down the centre of the spiral. Wash the film thoroughly for 30 minutes, turning the spiral over a few times.

Finally, fill the tank with fresh water and turn the tap off. Add wetting agent to the water in the tank, following the manufacturer's instructions.

Remove the spiral and shake it gently to remove as much water as possible. If you have one, attach a film clip to the end of the film. If you do not have a film clip, handle the film carefully so as not to damage the emulsion.

Gently pull the film out of the spiral. Pull on the very end, or the film clip, only. Wipe the blades of a film squeegee to clean them, then, in one move, wipe the squeegee down the film to remove any surface water. Hang the film to dry in a warm, dry, dust-free area.

When processing film, it is extremely important to be consistent. If you start timing when you begin to pour the chemicals into the processing tank, then you should always start timing from this point. You should adjust the timing from the same starting point. Always make comprehensive notes on timings, solution concentrations and temperatures.

Over time, you can build up a very good system for deciding the correct quantities for all these elements.

Activity 8.10

In daylight, use an old piece of film to practise loading the spiral. When you have mastered this process in daylight, try loading the spiral in the dark.

Examining the exposures

A processed film will have 12, 24 or 36 exposed frames. Printing a photographic image is expensive and time-consuming. Rather than printing every frame as a separate image, it makes good sense to select a few frames – perhaps five or six. If you bracketed the stops when taking the pictures (see **Exposure,** page 276), the chances are that you have three times as many frames as you need. Some of these frames may have been experimental and may not have turned out as well as you hoped. Whatever your reasons for using or not using some pictures, you need a method of choosing the images. You can do this either by examining the negatives or by printing a contact sheet.

Examining the negatives is difficult as the blacks and whites are reversed and the untrained eye has difficulty interpreting all the data. The safest way is to look at a positive of the image on a contact sheet (see page 287).

Printing a contact sheet

In order to print a contact sheet, you lay the film, cut into strips, on top of a piece of printing paper. A piece of glass is used to flatten the strips against the paper. Light is shone on it for the correct amount of time, then the paper is developed. This gives a positive print of all the frames, at the same size as the film frame itself.

- **Preparation** Before doing anything else, you must prepare the chemicals and the work surface. You will need three chemicals for processing black and white prints. These are developer, stop-bath and fixer. You must be able to wash the print in running water.

  Make up the chemicals, following the manufacturer's instructions. Make just enough to fill the tray to a depth of 2 cm. Lay the trays out in the order in which they will be used, i.e. developer – stop-bath – fixer – water. Check that your enlarger and safelight both work. It is also worth checking that your safelight conforms with the recommendations of the manufacturer of the print paper.

- **Choosing the printing paper** There are several makes and types of printing paper available. The two basic types are fibre-based and resin-coated. Resin-coated papers are more modern and less demanding and the stop-bath can be plain water. Fibre-based papers require longer fixing times and an acid stop-bath.

  Whatever the paper base, there are six basic paper grades to choose from, numbered from 0 to 5. Zero is the lowest contrast and 5 is the highest. Grade 2 or 3 will do for most pictures. Multigrade papers are also available. These are used in combination with filters and allow several grades of contrast to be achieved from the same paper stock.

  Always make sure that the main light is off and the door to the darkroom is closed before handling printing paper. The safelight can be on.

- **Preparing the film** The next step is to cut the negative so that it fits over the paper. You will be using an 8 x 10 inch piece of paper for your contact sheet, and all of the frames must fit in this area. Trim the ends of the film, but do not throw them away, then cut the film into strips of six frames each.

A photographic enlarger

1 **Ventilation for lamphouse**

2 **Bulb** This must be an enlarger bulb of the correct wattage for the size of lamphouse.

3 **Lamphouse**

4 **Enlarger column** Enlargers with heavy heads may have twin or flat columns for extra rigidity.

5 **Head linkage to column** Many linkages have a locking wheel for rotating the head through 90° to project on to a wall.

6 **Head transport** This device may simply free the head so that it can be raised to make the image on the paper bigger, or it may move the head by friction or by rack and pinion drive.

7 **Condenser** Condensers focus the light on to the negative.

8 **Negative carrier**

9 **Lens focusing wheel** This device works the lens focusing system, altering the distance between the lens and the negative to produce a sharp image.

10 **Lens** A lens which prints 35 mm negatives will also print 126, 110, and portions of larger negatives.

11 **F stops** As on a camera, these stops control the amount of light by varying the aperture of the lens.

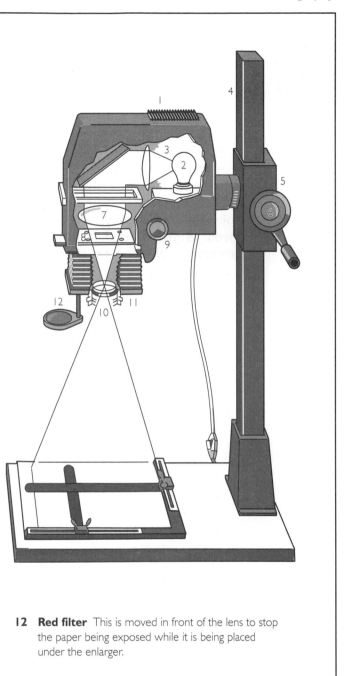

12 **Red filter** This is moved in front of the lens to stop the paper being exposed while it is being placed under the enlarger.

- **Testing the exposure** In safelight, place a small strip of printing paper, not much larger than the clear trimming that you took from the film, under the enlarger. Place the clear trimming on top, then carefully put a piece of glass on top of them both. Turn the aperture on the enlarger lens to f11. Cover the printing paper with a piece of black card, leaving about a fifth uncovered. Switch on the enlarger and start timing. After five seconds move the card to reveal a further fifth. Repeat until you have exposed the whole strip and you have exposed the final fifth for five seconds. Turn off the enlarger.

- **Developing the test strip** In safelight, drop the test strip into the developer tray, face up. Make sure that it is totally submerged and start the timer. When the image begins to appear, turn the strip over with tongs. Keep moving the tray gently. When the recommended time is reached, remove the strip from the developer, using a pair of tongs, and drop it into the stop-bath. Move the tray gently for about 30 seconds. After this, remove the strip and put it into the fixer tray, face up. Keep the fixer moving for the first 20 to 30 seconds, then occasionally rock the tray until the recommended time is over. Wash the paper in running water for five minutes.

  When you examine the strip, you should see a series of grey bands. The lightest one is the least amount of time of exposure (five seconds). The first band that gives a full black tone, not dark grey, will give you the correct exposure time; 5, 10, 15, 20, or 25 seconds. If the entire strip is black, repeat the test with a three-second exposure interval.

- **Printing the contact sheet** In safelight, lay the strips of film that you have already cut on top of a piece of printing paper that measures 8 inches by 10 inches (20 cm x 25 cm). Place a sheet of glass on top to hold the film flat against the paper. Make sure that both the film and the glass are clean, as a piece of dust can easily be mistaken for an imperfection. Switch on the enlarger for the time given by the test strip, then switch off.

  Remove the glass and film, taking care not to damage either. Develop the paper in the same way that you developed the test strip, but this time tilting the developer tray so that most of the liquid runs down to one end. Drop the paper into the shallow end, face up, then put the tray down. A wave of developer will cover the face of the paper. Start timing from this point.

Choosing and enlarging the image

In this section you will examine the contact sheet and choose the images that you want to enlarge, according to their technical and creative merits.

When choosing one or two images from up to 36 different frames, you need to consider carefully. To begin with, it is best to look at the whole of the sheet in bright light. If you have tried different exposure techniques there may be several versions of the same image.

The first decision is which of the set-ups you want to use. You may have chosen several approaches to your brief. At this point you must narrow down the choice. This is often trickier than it seems, as your photograph may be cropped in its final form.

It is sometimes useful to view the images through a mask made to the correct height and width. A simple mask can be made from two L-shaped pieces of card that you can slide towards each other to vary the height and width. An even more basic method is to draw your cropping lines onto the picture, using a special wax pencil called a **chinagraph**. Chinagraph lines can always be wiped off the paper. Always view the image through a magnifier to check that it looks good in close-up.

You should examine each version of the chosen set-ups using a magnifier. The most important factor to look for is correct exposure. If a frame is under-exposed there will be no detail in the dark areas of the picture. If it is over-exposed there will be no detail in the brighter areas. A correct exposure will have good detail in both light and dark areas.

Finally, check for clarity of focus and for unwanted blurring. For each of your choices make a note of the frame number on the edge of the film.

A contact sheet showing cropping instructions and magnifier (right)

Enlarging the image

The enlarging techniques outlined in this section take practice. An experienced printer will often know, without testing, the correct amount of exposure time. It takes many years to reach this standard, but in the short term you should aim to achieve repeatable, consistent, results.

The first step is to load your negative into the enlarger. The enlarger will have a **negative carrier,** a frame to hold the film in place. The negative and the negative carrier must be cleaned thoroughly before use. The carrier can be cleaned with a blower brush or compressed air jet. The film should be cleaned with a soft brush. Load the negative into the carrier and the carrier into the enlarger.

Adjust the masks on the enlarger easel to the correct setting or size of print that you need. Switch off all lights and switch on the enlarger. Centralize the printing area of the easel under the enlarger. Set the aperture of the lens to the widest value possible, as this will give you a bright image that will be easier to adjust.

Focussing the image takes some practice, and to begin with you may need a second opinion. First, adjust the height of the enlarger head so that the image fits the desired print area. Then adjust the focus until it is as sharp as possible. Get as close as you can to the image, without casting a shadow, to check the detail and sharpness. Close the aperture to about f11 and check the focus again.

When the focus has been set on the enlarger, it is crucial that there are no violent movements that may jog the settings.

Activity 8.11

a Place a piece of normal paper on the enlarger easel and load a negative into the enlarger. Turn on the enlarger.

b Turn out the lights in the darkroom and switch on the safelight. Focus the image to the best of your ability.

c Now switch off the safelight and look at the image in darkness. Is it still in focus? Can you see the image more clearly in the dark?

Making a test strip

In enlargement, the test strip is more important than it was with the contact sheet, as it will give the exposure time for the final image.

In safelight, cut a strip of print paper. Make sure that the red filter is in front of the enlarger lens, and switch it on. Position the paper so it has both light and dark tones falling on it. Switch off the enlarger and remove the red filter from in front of the lens. Have a piece of black card ready. Switch on the enlarger and start the timer. After five seconds, cover one fifth of the test strip with the card. After another ten seconds cover a further fifth. Keep covering in fifths at 10-second intervals until you cover the entire strip. Switch off the enlarger and develop the strip as before.

Examination of the strip will give you the best time for exposing your picture. If you are unsure, but think that the correct exposure is between two of the bands, make another test strip. This time cover the strip at smaller intervals, starting after the first time that you think may be correct and ending with the second time.

A test strip is used to gauge correct exposure time

Making the final print

In safelight, place a piece of print paper in the easel frame. Place your hand underneath the enlarger lens to block the light and switch it on. After a few moments remove your hand and start timing. Switch the enlarger off when you have reached the time that you decided from the test strip. Develop the print in the same way as you developed the contact sheet.

Activity 8.12

Consider the following case.

Smartprints is a specialist photographic developing and printing company with a staff of two. The firm are asked to develop and print photographs for a local wedding photographer. They decline – even though this represents a regular, weekly income. However, in the same week they agree to develop and print photographs for a design company. The design company specialises in brochures for classic car enthusiasts, especially motor racing of the 1940s and 1950s.

1 Why would Smartprints turn down regular work from a photographer?
2 From the information given, can you deduce:

    a The nature of the specialist printing that Smartprints does
    b Why Smartprints are not able to print wedding photos

3 Think about the work that the design company has offered Smartprints.

    a Why do the photographs have to be hand-printed?
    b What problems will Smartprints have with original negatives?
    c Why do new prints need to be made?
    d Smartprints print the same image five times. Why?

Review questions

1 What is 'three-point lighting'?
2 Why would a photographer 'bracket the stops'?
3 Why is it necessary to print a contact sheet?
4 What is a 'negative carrier'?
5 What is the function of a test strip?
6 What is a' chinagraph'?
7 Why is it important to clean the camera?
8 When and how should a camera be cleaned?
9 What is the function of a wetting agent?

Element 8.3 Review a photographic assignment

The conclusion to any brief is the publication or presentation of the photograph. Following this, there will be criticism of the picture. This process should be collected and remarked on. Whilst no-one wants to receive bad criticism, all comments will help the photographer to understand how to reach the target audience more effectively.

Presenting a photograph

Usually, the presentation format for a photograph is decided by the client. The design of the image will be geared towards this presentation format. Mostly, the photograph will go into print or an exhibition. Occasionally there will be another use for the image.

Print

Print is the easiest and cheapest method of high-quality and high-quantity reproduction. Photography is often used in print products, from postcards to magazines. Black and white and colour photography are both used.

When choosing a photograph for reproduction you need to consider the following points:

- In order to reproduce well, an original photograph should have a full tonal range from white to black that gives it good contrast.
- Good original prints show detail in their lightest and darkest areas.
- Low-contrast photos will reproduce flat and lifeless.
- Photos with too much contrast lack shadow and highlight detail.
- Images made on fast films with large grains may lose sharpness when enlarged.

Prior to printing, photographic images are scanned into a computer and then manipulated on screen for placement on the page. Scanners can be used on both the film and the developed print.

The photograph has different jobs in print products. In factual book and magazine products it can be used to explain and reinforce the information given in the text. This book shows examples of this use of the photograph. Advertising print often uses the photograph in a central, attention-grabbing role, where it is designed to convey the entire message or draw the eye to the logo of the company.

Other forms of print products often use a combination of these approaches. For example, a brochure for a holiday destination will use photographs both to reinforce the text and as enticing images to convey glamour, atmosphere and local colour.

Exhibition

Often original photographic prints are shown in exhibitions. These can consist of a display in a corridor or a stand at a corporate show. Again, the photograph here is being used to reinforce the other information available. This information may be displayed alongside the photograph, or may be given verbally by salespeople or through promotional literature. The display must be designed to show all these elements effectively. Photography will be combined with text and graphics to build up a display with impact from a distance and information closer up.

Some photographic exhibitions are purely artistic. Here photographs are displayed without any other information other than a title and the photographer's name. The photograph has no particular purpose here. It is designed to be self-explanatory and aesthetically pleasing. If there are several photographs in the display there will often be a theme connecting them. The artist and photographer will position the pictures in a way that uses the available space and shows the pictures at their best.

Activity 8.13

Look through three different types of magazine and brochure. Pick out photographs and identify their function in the brochure. Does the layout of the page influence the perceived function of the picture?

Other media

With the growth in technology and new media, the photograph has many new applications. The photographic print is still the preferred format for pictures that are to be scanned into a computer, although this may change in the future when digital cameras improve in quality and decrease in price.

Amongst the most important and exciting of these new applications are interactive multimedia compact discs and the Internet. The CD-ROM is also becoming a useful method of storing photographic images without deterioration. A disc is small and can hold several high-quality pictures.

Another medium to consider is the portfolio. Many people take photographs with the purpose of using them to sell their talents. A portfolio is a carefully selected cross-section of a person's work. If that cross-section is not large enough, or the person is beginning their life as a professional photographer, they may construct their own assignments. The results will show that the person can take different types of photographs, even if they have not had official commissions. It also shows a level of enthusiasm to a potential employer or client.

Reviewing a photograph

As with any creative work, the finished work needs to be assessed both by yourself and by a sample of your target audience.

Self-assessment

You will need to consider two aspects of your photograph, the technical quality and the aesthetic quality.

The technical quality of the photograph refers to the quality of the print, the clarity of focus, the framing of the photograph and the exposure level. To give a rigorous assessment of all these factors, you should get close to the picture. If the focus, exposure or print quality are deliberately meant to be unusual in any way, you should be able to justify your intention.

Here is a checklist you could use:

- **Focus** Check that important parts of the image are in sharp focus, especially if you plan to enlarge it.
- **Grain** Be sure that enlargement by the printer will not make the film grain structure so big that the image looks fuzzy.
- **Contrast** Study contrast (i.e. the number of distinguishable tones) to be sure you start with strong blacks, clean whites and a full tonal range.
- **Detail** Inspect shadow areas and highlights for clarity of features.
- **Flaws** Verify that the photograph is flat and has no scratches, dirt, or blemishes.
- **Photo paper** Make sure that the photograph is on smooth,semi-gloss paper.

The aesthetic quality is best evaluated by standing back from the picture. You should consider the overall shape of the images, the composition, the lighting of the subject and the quality of the print.

You have already considered the quality of the print technically, but you should also consider whether you made the right choices when printing the image and whether those choices show the picture in the best way for its purpose.

Audience assessment

If the audience does not understand or appreciate the image that you are presenting, then you have not fulfilled the brief. To judge your performance on the brief you must collect audience opinion. Ideally this would be from the intended target audience or from your peer group.

Using interview techniques, a questionnaire or a formal presentation, collect responses to your picture. Ask the audience to consider the same aspects as you did in your self-assessment.

Evaluating effectiveness

In order to evaluate the overall effectiveness of the photograph, combine the results of your self-assessment and the audience assessment.

Return to the original brief and consider whether or not you managed to fulfil the requirements. Was the photograph successful in its purpose and use? Did you manage to keep to the agreed timescale and budget?

Finally, you should decide if you have reached the intended audience and if the client need has been satisfied.

Review questions

1   Name five types of print media that might feature photographs.
2   Why is it important to have a well-balanced contrast in a photograph that will be reproduced in print?
3   What are the key technical points that you need to look for when enlarging a picture?
4   Think of three uses for a colour photograph measuring 3m x 3m.
5   Why are photographs scanned into computers?
6   What are you looking for when evaluating the aesthetic quality of a photograph?
7   What are you looking for when evaluating the technical quality of a photograph?
8   What other applications are there besides print and exhibition?

Assignment 8.1
Planning a series of photographs

This assignment provides evidence for **Element 8.1: Plan for a photographic assignment** and the following key skills:

Communication:	2.1, 2.2, 2.3, 2.4
Application of Numbers:	2.2

In this assignment you are going to plan a series of photographs for a school or college publication. Divide yourselves either into groups or pairs.

1 The series will be six black and white photographs for a school or college newspaper article entitled 'Art show'. The article has been written about the students graduating from the Art Department. The style should reflect the style of the art works. Your expense budget is £120.

2 Sketch your design for the pictures. Show composition, emphasis, light and dark and location. Also think about whether you need to use models. How will you carry out each picture? Can you get round any problems?

3 Write a list of the items that you will need to be in the pictures, the props, and the locations that you will be using. State whether you will need to work in a studio.

4 Write a list of the equipment that you will need. Include all camera equipment, lighting and film. Suggest the type of film and the quantity you think you will need.

5 Alongside each list, work out how much each item will cost, including hire costs of any equipment, props or people that you do not already have in your own kit or group. Add it up to work out your overall budget. Is it reasonable? If not, how can you economise?

6 Work out how much of your budget you have left for processing and developing. Can it be done for this cost ?

7 State how you propose to ensure that all the people involved will be safe in all the locations that you will be using. What precautions must you take in the studio and elsewhere? Have you considered public safety as well?

8 In Activity 8.1 you were asked to study and compare the characteristics of photographs in different media contexts. Write a summary of your findings, including a comparison of the technical and creative differences between the photographs that you have studied. Relate this study to your own assignment plan and how you developed it.

Assignment 8.2
Creating a series of photographs

This assignment provides evidence for **Element 8.2: Create photographs for a given brief**, and for the following key skills:

Communication: 2.2, 2.3

Using the plan and sketches that you designed in Assignment 8.1, you are now going to create the photographic images.

1 Use the equipment that you have selected to take the photographs. You must try to photograph the images so that they are as close to the sketches as possible. Remember your decisions on light and composition.

2 Process the film and make a contact sheet of the images.

3 Select at least five of the images from the contact sheet for enlarging. Write down your reasons for choosing them.

4 Enlarge and print the images that you have selected. Crop the images in the intended way. Write down your reasons for cropping the image in the way that you have.

Assignment 8.3
Presenting and assessing a series of photographs

This assignment provides evidence for **Element 8.3: Review a photographic assignment** and the following key skills:

Communication:	2.1, 2.2, 2.3
Information Technology:	2.1, 2.2, 2.3
Application of Numbers:	2.1, 2.2, 2.3

In this assignment you will be required to present and assess the images in the manner agreed in the brief.

1 Present the images that you have selected in a mock-up of the school or college newsletter. You may prefer to photocopy the image into the correct space on the page. This will give you more control over the scaling of the images.

2 Referring back to the original brief, evaluate the image in terms of technical and aesthetic quality. Write a report of your assessment.

3 Present the mock-up of the newsletter to the target audience. Collect feedback on the impact and success of the images in terms of their original purpose and use. Use a questionnaire, interviews or formal presentation to collect the audience responses. Write these responses into your report. Your results might be analysed and presented more effectively using a computer package designed to help you create pie charts, graphs, etc.

4 Evaluate the effectiveness of the images. Use your self-assessment and the audience assessment to write a report on the effectiveness of the images in meeting the requirements of the brief. You should consider not only their aesthetic effectiveness but also their technical effectiveness in terms of the budget, timescale and client need.

Glossary

Acoustics	How sound is altered by location, causing, for example, echo.
Analysis	Breaking down and examining something. In Media Studies, research findings are often broken down and examined for details that will allow people to understand important points.
Angle	A way of approaching or treating a subject. For example, romance is treated seriously in major romantic movies but situation comedies usually present romance in a funny way. Both take a different 'angle' on the subject.
Angle of view	Angle formed by the three main points of a photographic set-up. One point is the right side of the subject in view; another is the left side of the subject and the third is the camera. The angle of the triangle at the camera corner is the angle of view.
Aperture	An adjustable hole in a camera that regulates the amount of light admitted through the lens.
Appraise	To consider a product's value and quality. This needs to be done while it is being developed as well as on completion.
Audience	People at whom a media product is aimed. Usually used to describe all the people using a particular product. There are different ideas about how and why audiences use media products.
Audio	Relating to sound.
Brief	Written information or instructions that have to be followed by everyone involved in the planning and designing of a media product.
Broadsheet	Large-format newspaper usually containing more text than other papers. Broadsheets sell fewer copies than most tabloids but can make money from carrying a large amount of advertising. *The Times* is a broadsheet.
Budget	The amount of money available to spend on all areas of production.
Bulletin	A short news broadcast.
Catch, Catchline	Technical term for a story in a bulletin or a magazine.
Chinagraph pencil	Soft pencil for marking edit points on a tape or crop marks on a contact sheet.
Classification	Group into which media products can be arranged.
Codes	Features used by media products to convey meaning to audiences. Products tend to follow certain rules which are understood by audiences. For example, the use of boxed pictures with word balloons in telling a comic story is a code.
Collate	Any graphical product needs to be arranged in the correct order. This process is known as collation, after which the product is bound together.
Commission	A freelance writer may be **commissioned** to write a particular article. This means they are being requested to write and will be paid for the work.

Communicate	To convey meaning. Graphical products are one of many methods of communicating.
Competitor	A rival product or producer. For example, a newspaper or magazine may find itself competing with a very similar product and will try to achieve higher sales than its rival.
Constraints	Limitations. Very often a product is limited by factors such as time, money (budget) or staff.
Consumer profile	Information about the audience for a media product. Gathering this information helps producers match media products to audience requirements.
Contemporary	Of the present day. In Chapter 2 you are required to produce 'contemporary' print products.
Content issues	Term used to describe problems linked to decisions about the content of media products.
Convention	An accepted way of doing something – for example, ending a commercial break with a jingle to identify the station.
Copy	Original writing for use in news, programming or print media, for example, news copy, advertising copy, etc.
Cue	Signal to begin or end something. Also, a written piece of copy to be read before an item on audio or video.
Darkroom	A light-proof room used for developing photographic films and prints.
Debate	Discussion in which both sides put different arguments. Often used to describe problems in Media Studies in which two or more different arguments are presented.
Depth of field	The area between the nearest distance in focus and the furthest distance in focus.
Dissemination	Conveying information and media work to an audience, i.e. from the producer to the consumer.
Downloading	Transferring data from one computer to another.
Dub	To copy audio material from one source (e.g. tape) to another.
Duration	How long an item lasts.
Economics	Study of financial relationships or patterns within an industry, market or society.
Editing	Task of deciding on and refining contents of a media product.
EDL	Edit Decision List, now used by some computer applications for audio and video editing.
Electronic publishing	Production, dissemination and consumption of material by electronic means. Examples include Teletext, the Internet and interactive encyclopedias on CD-ROM.
Elements	Parts of a story which make up a narrative. Three important elements are **conflict**, **development** and **resolution**.
Employment pattern	Identifiable trends in the way people are taken on and employed within an industry. For example, many shops take on more staff in December because Christmas brings an increase in business.
Enlarger	Item of photographic equipment enabling image to be projected onto printing paper. It can be adjusted for the size of the projected image and for focus.

Ethical	Relating to issues of right and wrong. For example, the issue of press intrusion and invasion of privacy raises **ethical questions**. Many long-running discussions – for example, on the effects of violence on television – concern ethical issues.
Evaluate	Make a judgement about the value of something, assessing its strengths and weaknesses.
Expenditure	Sources of expense. Often used to describe the outlay of money from the media producers to other places – for example, money spent on research or promotion.
Fanzine	Independently produced magazine for a small group of readers with a common interest or loyalty. There are thousands of such magazines produced in the UK every year. Some are well established with a regular readership; others appear only once and then vanish.
Feedback	High-pitched sound caused by output being fed back into the input. Also, information on an audience's response to an audio product.
Fiction/non-fiction	Fiction is material which is 'made up'. Non-fiction is material which is based on fact.
Filter	A piece of glass or plastic that fits over the lens of a camera and colours the light entering the lens. Corrective filters are used to compensate for unwanted light colours.
Focal length	Distance between lens and film on a camera.
Focusable distance	Distance between camera and the subject.
Font	Type of lettering or typeface used in a print product. Most wordprocessing packages offer a choice of fonts.
Freesheet	Type of news publication given away free. Usually paid for by the large amount of advertising sold in its pages.
Genre	Type of media product with distinctive style, subject matter or purpose. For example, soap opera is a genre which uses similar narrative structures in both radio and television.
Hardware	Generic term for equipment used to make media products. Examples include computers, cameras and tape recorders.
Health and safety	Term used to cover any issue that may affect the physical or mental well-being of people in a workplace. Workplaces in this country are covered by the Health and Safety at Work Act. All practical activities in GNVQ Media include criteria relating to health and safety.
High granularity	Fuzziness caused by large chemical crystals in photographic film.
House style	A standard style adopted by an organisation in order to maintain consistency across different publications.
Howlround	Feedback caused by microphone picking up loudspeaker output.
Hypodermic model	Model of audience behaviour, suggesting that media simply feed information into audiences like a hypodermic needle pumping drugs into a body, and that audiences change as a result.
Image-based product	Print product featuring mainly images.
In-cue	How an audio item begins.
Income	Money coming into the media, for example, from sales of products.
Influence	To make a difference to something. For example, advertisements influence the things we buy.

Interactive	Responding directly to the user. Good examples are computer-based media such as games, which offer a choice of different actions.
Internet	Worldwide computer information network.
Jargon	Particular words or expressions used within a specific occupation, profession or group. Examples include medical jargon, legal jargon, computer jargon, etc.
Jingle	A short, catchy burst of music, often used to advertise a product.
Lifestyle magazine	Magazine based around the lifestyle of its readers.
Light meter	Instrument for measuring the intensity of light.
Local paper	Newspaper aimed at people living and working in a particular area. May take the form of a tabloid or a broadsheet. Local papers are grouped together because whatever their size and style, all feature local news.
Logistics	Organisation needed to get everything and everyone in the right place at the right time.
Magazine	Publication or broadcast programme made up of a variety of different items.
Market	Overall term describing all the people who buy or consume a media product.
Market research	Investigation into what the market (i.e. potential target audience) want, need or think about a product. Methods include questionnaire, survey and personal interview.
Media industries	Collective name for different areas of the media – radio, newspapers, etc.
Medium	Means of communication, e.g. print.
Microphone rattle	Noise caused when microphone lead is disturbed.
Mix	To combine audio from different sources (e.g. tape, disc, microphone).
Narrative	The way a story is told within a media product. Narrative can be broken into two important parts: **plot** – the basic action of the story; and **characters** – the people involved in the story.
Narrative structure	The way a narrative is sequenced or structured.
Objectives	Aims that a media product is trying to achieve.
Out-cue	How an audio or video item ends.
Pan and tilt	Side-to-side and up-and-down movement of a tripod head.
Parallax viewer	A lens set in parallel to a camera lens that allows the photographer to frame the picture.
Peak times	Times of day when large numbers of people are watching or listening to radio or TV.
Perspective distortion	Apparent compression and warping of space between objects caused by certain camera lenses.
Phone-in	Radio programme involving listeners calling-in on the telephone.
Pressure group	Organised body with a particular interest or views to promote.
Production	Act or process of producing something. Also often used to describe finished work – for example, comics, television programmes, etc. are 'media productions'.
Production methods	Techniques used in the making of a media product.
Production schedule	Detailed plan for carrying out a production.

Profile	Simplified overall picture of something or someone. For example, audience profiles include details of age, sex, income, etc.
Proposal	Document outlining a planned media product, often written in order to secure backing or approval from a sponsor.
Purpose	The reason for something being produced. Purposes are usually mixed. The media make products to make money but also to serve other purposes such as informing, entertaining, etc.
Push-processing	Over-developing the film in order to compensate for earlier under-exposure. The picture will then be correctly exposed.
Qualitative	Based on feelings and subjective perception. Qualitative research is often concerned with what things mean to an audience, for example, how much they are likely to change their attitude after watching a film about a particular subject.
Quantitative	Based on statistics and numerical information.
Reflex	A system of mirrors that allows a photographer to look directly through the camera lens.
Regulatory bodies	Organisations responsible for regulating or controlling the media.
Representations	Images of people, places or things generated by the media. All representations are the result of editorial decisions.
Research	Examining or studying a subject for a particular purpose. The media often 'research' the needs of audiences for the purpose of providing them with products they are likely to buy, watch, etc.
Resources	Materials and equipment used in making something. Examples include money, time, people, paper and production equipment.
Responsibilities	General term used to describe all of the things that the media industry must do. For example, the news media have a responsibility to report in a fair and unbiased manner.
Retailer	Outlet that sells a product, e.g. a newsagent, supermarket or bookshop.
Safelight	A dim red/orange light that will not expose black and white printing papers. Used in a darkroom so that the printer can see what to do without ruining the picture.
Schedule	Timetable for completing a piece of work. Most media work is completed according to a production schedule.
Scrim	Piece of material designed to reduce the quantity of light admitted through a camera lens without changing its colour.
Self-timer	Function on some camera bodies allowing a delay between pressing the button and exposing the film. Useful for self-portraits or family pictures where the photographer is in shot.
Sequence	Order in which the events of a story appear within a narrative. Three important aspects are **scenes**, **chronology** and **flashback**.
Serial	Built up of regular episodes, each moving a story forward and adding more information.
Shutter speed	The length of time that a film is exposed. Usually measured in fractions of a second.
Sources	People or places from which information is gathered for use in media products. Sources are divided into **primary** and **secondary**.
Sources of revenue	Activities or places from which money is earned.

Splice	To edit pieces of audiotape together with splicing tape.
Splicing block	Convenient holder for tape being spliced together.
Stereotypes	Simplistic representations which are immediately recognisable to audiences but are also potentially inaccurate and misleading.
Structure	How a media product is constructed and organised.
Style	The way a media product is presented, for example, upbeat, downbeat, serious, humorous, etc.
Subscription	Arrangement by which a customer takes out a regular order for a product, for example, a magazine.
Syndication agency	Firm supplying items of news, features or topics to newspapers who belong to the 'syndication'.
Tabloid	Small-format newspaper. Tabloids are usually A3 in size, use large pictures and headlines and aim for a large or 'popular' market. The *Sun* is a tabloid.
Target audience	Audience at which a particular media product is aimed.
Text-based product	Print product featuring all or mainly printed words, for example, a horror novel.
Treatment	Outline or description designed to convey the message, storyline, location and characters of a media product to potential producers, investors or clients.
TTL light meter	'Through the lens' light meter – i.e. one built into the body of the camera.
Tungsten	Artifical light. Bulbs contain a metal filament that glows orange. The metal is usually tungsten and the light it emits is therefore known as tungsten orange.
Uses and gratifications model	Model of audience behaviour based on the view that audiences affect the media, as well as vice versa, and that audiences use media products for their own ends.
Visual appeal	The attractiveness or otherwise of a graphical or printed product.
Voicer	A spoken report on radio.
Vox pops	Short recorded interviews with members of the public.
Working practices	The way that people are organised to work within an industry, and the skills that they use. The term is also used to describe the way people behave at work.
Wrap	A short package of audio items.

Index